Software Engineering for Students

A Programming Approach

Fourth Edition

DOUGLAS BELL

 ADDISON-WESLEY

Harlow, England • London • New York • Boston • San Francisco • Toronto
Sydney • Tokyo • Singapore • Hong Kong • Seoul • Taipei • New Delhi
Cape Town • Madrid • Mexico City • Amsterdam • Munich • Paris • Milan

Pearson Education Limited
Edinburgh Gate
Harlow
Essex CM20 2JE
England

and Associated Companies throughout the world

Visit us on the World Wide Web at:
www.pearsoned.co.uk

First published under the Prentice Hall imprint 1987
Second edition 1992
Third edition 2000
Fourth edition 2005

ISBN 0 321 26127 5

British Library Cataloguing-in-Publication Data
A catalogue record for this book is available from the British Library

Library of Congress Cataloging-in-Publication Data
Bell, Doug, 1944-
    Software engineering for student/Douglas Bell. -- 4th ed.
        p. cm.
    Rev. ed. of: Software engineering. 2000.
    ISBN 0-321-26127-5
    1. Software engineering. 2. Computer programming. I. Bell, Doug, 1944-
Software engineering. II. Title.
QA76.758.B45 2005
005.1--dc22

                                                        2004062346

10 9 8 7 6 5 4 3 2 1
09 08 07 06 05

Typeset in 9.75/12pt Galliard by 71
Printed in Great Britain by Henry Ling Ltd, at the Dorset Press, Dorchester, Dorset

The publisher's policy is to use paper manufactured from sustainable forests.

Software Engineering
for Students

Contents

Detailed contents

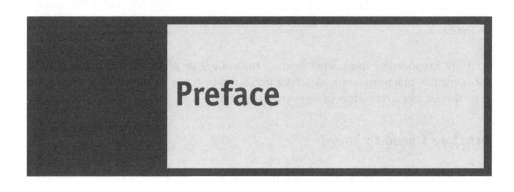

Preface

What is software engineering?

Software engineering is about the creation of large pieces of software that consist of thousands of lines of code and involve many person months of human effort.

One of the attractions of software engineering is that there is no one single best method for doing it, but instead a whole variety of different approaches. Consequently the software engineer needs a knowledge of many different techniques and tools. This diversity is one of the delights of software engineering, and this book celebrates this by presenting the range of current techniques and tools.

We shall see that some software engineering methods are well-defined while others are ill-defined. And the processes of software development are always under debate.

Challenge and creativity

Software engineering is about imagination and creativity – the process of creating something apparently tangible from nothing. Software engineering methods have not yet been completely analyzed and systematized. Thus there is still great scope for using imagination and creativity. The exercise of skill and flair is one of the joys of software engineering.

Who is this book for?

Ideally you, the reader, will have savored the joy of devising an elegant solution to a programming problem. You will also have experienced the intense frustration of trying to find an elusive bug – and the satisfaction of subsequently tracking it down and eliminating it.

This book is for people who have experienced the pleasures of writing programs and who want to see how things change in the scale up to large programs and software systems.

This book provides an introduction to software engineering for students in undergraduate programs in Computer Science, Computer Studies, Information Technology,

Software Engineering and related fields at the college or university level. The book is also aimed at practising software developers in industry and commerce who wish to keep abreast of current ideas in software engineering.

What do I need to know?

The prerequisites for understanding this book are:

■ some familiarity with a modern programming language

■ some experience with developing a moderately sized program of a few hundred lines.

What is covered in this book?

This book explains the different principles, techniques and tools that are used in software development. These are the mainstream methods that are currently used throughout the industrialized world.

This book doesn't present easy answers about the value of these techniques. Indeed, it asks the reader to make an assessment of the techniques. This is what the software engineer has to do – now and in the future – choose the appropriate techniques for the project in hand from the multiplicity of techniques that are on offer.

Notations

UML (Unified Modeling Language) is used as appropriate within the text as a graphical design notation. Some other graphical notations – flowcharts, structure charts and data flow diagrams are also used.

Java is used as an illustrative programming language and sometimes also pseudo code (program design language).

So many chapters

Yes, but each chapter deals with a separate topic. This is to enable each chapter to focus exclusively and thoroughly on a single idea.

How to read this book

Because the chapters are independent, you do not need to read them in any particular sequence – you can dip into the book at random. But you might choose to read Chapters 1 and 2 first because they set the scene. You might choose to spend one week on each chapter.

The organization of this book

The chapters are grouped into sections on:

- preliminaries
- design
- programming languages
- verification
- process models
- project management
- review.

Several of these sections present a variety of alternative techniques, for example, a variety of design approaches.

Case studies

A number of case studies are used throughout the book to illustrate the use of the various techniques. They constitute a range of typical software systems and are presented in Appendix A. Many chapters use one of the case studies. The case studies are also used as part of the exercises at the end of each chapter.

You could also use the case studies as projects carried out in parallel to the study of this book.

Self-test questions

These are placed throughout the text so that you can check your understanding of topics. They promote active learning. The answers are at the end of each chapter.

Software tools

With the notable exception of four chapters on languages, we do not have a separate chapter on software tools. Instead we ask the reader in the exercises to suggest suitable tools for use with each technique.

Is this all I need to know?

This book is about the theories behind software engineering and gives an explanation of current techniques. But many people would argue you really need to experience the reality of software development to fully appreciate the ideas. Probably, therefore, you are engaged on a project of some size while you study this book. Good luck with your practical project. (The case studies in Appendix A may serve as projects.)

Website

Visit the website associated with the book to see additional material and any updates at www.pearsoned.co.uk/bell.

Acknowledgments

Special thanks to my closest collaborator on this book, Alice Bell, particularly for writing Chapter 25. Many thanks to current and past colleagues, including (in alphabetical order) Babak Akhgar, Chris Bates, Andy Bissett, Pete Collingwood, Gordon Doole, Chuck Elliot, Jan Graba, Chris Hall, Babak Khazaei, Mehdi Mir, Ian Morrey, Mehmet Ozcan, Mike Parr, John Pugh, Chris Roast, Dharmendra Shadija, Jawed Siddiqi. All misconceptions are, of course, the author's.

PART

A

PRELIMINARIES

1 Software – problems and prospects

This chapter:

- reviews the goals of software engineering
- describes the difficulties of constructing large-scale software
- analyses the problems that software engineers face.

1.1 ● Introduction

Software Engineering is about methods, tools and techniques used for developing software. This particular chapter is concerned with the reasons for having a field of study called software engineering, and with the problems that are encountered in developing software. This book as a whole explains a variety of techniques that attempt to solve the problems and meet the goals of software engineering.

Software surrounds us everywhere in the industrialized nations – in domestic appliances, communications systems, transportation systems and in businesses. Software comes in different shapes and sizes – from the program in a mobile phone to the software to design a new automobile. In categorizing software, we can distinguish two major types:

- *system software* is the software that acts as tools to help construct or support applications software. Examples are operating systems, databases, networking software, compilers.

- *applications software* is software that helps perform some directly useful or enjoyable task. Examples are games, the software for automatic teller machines (ATMs), the control software in an airplane, e-mail software, word processors, spreadsheets.

Within the category of applications software, it can be useful to identify the following categories of software:

- games
- information systems – systems that store and access large amounts of data, for example, an airline seat reservation system

- real-time systems – in which the computer must respond quickly, for example, the control software for a power station
- embedded systems – in which the computer plays a smallish role within a larger system, for example, the software in a telephone exchange or a mobile phone. Embedded systems are usually also real-time systems
- office software – word processors, spreadsheets, e-mail
- scientific software – carrying out calculations, modeling, prediction, for example, weather forecasting.

Software can either be off-the-shelf (e.g. Microsoft Word) or tailor-made for a particular application (e.g. software for the Apollo moon shots). The latter is sometimes called bespoke software.

All these types of software – except perhaps information systems – fall within the remit of software engineering. Information systems have a different history and, generally, different techniques are used for their development. Often the nature of the data (information) is used to dictate the structure of the software, so that analysis of the data is a prime step, leading to the design of the database for the application. This approach to software development is outside the scope of this book.

Constructing software is a challenging task, essentially because software is complex. The perceived problems in software development and the goals that software development seeks to achieve are:

- meeting users' needs
- low cost of production
- high performance
- portability
- low cost of maintenance
- high reliability
- delivery on time.

Each goal is also considered to be a problem because software engineering has generally been rather unsuccessful at reaching them. We will now look at each of these goals in turn. Later we will look at how the goals relate one to another.

In the remainder of this book we shall see that the development of particular types of software requires the use of special techniques, but many development techniques have general applicability.

1.2 ● Meeting users' needs

It seems an obvious remark to make that a piece of software must do what its users want of it. Thus, logically, the first step in developing some software is to find out what the client, customer or user needs. This step is often called requirements analysis or requirements engineering. It also seems obvious that it should be carried out with some care.

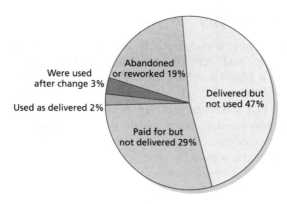

Figure 1.1 Effectiveness of typical large software projects

There is evidence, however, that this is not always the case. As evidence, one study of the effectiveness of large-scale software projects, Figure 1.1, found that less than 2% were used as delivered.

These figures are one of the few pieces of hard evidence available, because (not surprisingly) organizations are rather secretive about this issue. Whatever the exact figures, it seems that a large proportion of systems do not meet the needs of their users and are therefore not used as supplied. It may be, of course, that smaller systems are more successful.

We might go further and deduce that the *main* problem of software development lies in requirements analysis rather than in any other areas, such as reliability or cost, which are discussed below.

The task of trying to ensure that software does what its users want is known as *validation*.

1.3 ● The cost of software production

Examples of costs

First of all, let us get some idea of the scale of software costs in the world. In the USA it is estimated that about $500 billion are spent each year on producing software. This amounts to 1% of the gross national product. The estimated figure for the world is that $1,000 billion is spent each year on software production. These figures are set to rise by about 15% each year. The operating system that IBM developed for one of its major range of computers (called OS 360) is estimated to have cost $200 million. In the USA, the software costs of the manned space program were $1 billion between 1960 and 1970.

These examples indicate that the amount spent on software in the industrialized nations is of significant proportions.

Programmer productivity

The cost of software is determined largely by the productivity of the programmers and the salaries that they are paid. Perhaps surprisingly, the productivity of the average programmer is only about 10–20 programming language statements per day. To the layperson, a productivity of 20 lines of code per day may well seem disgraceful. However, this is an average figure that should be qualified in two ways. First, enormous differences between individual programmers – factors of 20 – have been found in studies. Second, the software type makes a difference: applications software can be written more quickly than systems software. Also, this apparently poor performance does not just reflect the time taken to carry out coding, but also includes the time required to carry out clarifying the problem specification, software design, coding, testing and documentation. Therefore, the software engineer is involved in many more tasks than just coding. However, what is interesting is that the above figure for productivity is independent of the programming language used – it is similar whether a low-level language is used or a high-level language is used. It is therefore more difficult than it initially appears to attribute the level of productivity to laziness, poor tools or inadequate methods.

SELF-TEST QUESTION

1.1 A well-known word processor consists of a million lines of code. Calculate how many programmers would be needed to write it, assuming that it has to be completed in five years. Assuming that they are each paid $50,000 per year, what is the cost of development?

Predicting software costs

It is very difficult to predict in advance how long it will take to write a particular piece of software. It is not uncommon to underestimate the required effort by 50%, and hence the cost and delivery date of software is also affected.

Hardware versus software costs

The relative costs of hardware and software can be a lively battleground for controversy. In the early days of computers, hardware was costly and software relatively cheap. Nowadays, thanks to mass production and miniaturization, hardware is cheap and software (labor intensive) is expensive. So the costs of hardware and software have been reversed. These changes are reflected in the so-called "S-shaped curve", Figure 1.2, showing the relative costs as they have changed over the years. Whereas, in about 1955, software cost typically only about 10% of a project, it has now escalated to 90%, with the hardware comprising only 10%. These proportions should be treated carefully. They hold for certain projects only and not in each and every case. In fact, figures of this kind are derived largely from one-off large-scale projects.

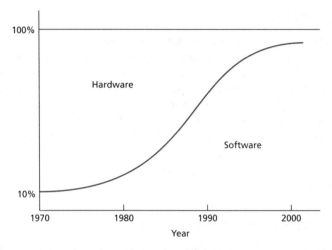

Figure 1.2 Changes in the relative costs of hardware and software

SELF-TEST QUESTION

1.2 Someone buys a PC, with processor, monitor, hard disk and printer. They also buy an operating system and a word processing package. Calculate the relative costs of hardware and software.

We will now look at a number of issues that affect the popular perception of software and its costs.

The impact of personal computers

Perhaps the greatest influence on popular perceptions of software costs has come about with the advent of personal computing. Many people buy a PC for their home, and so come to realize very clearly what the costs are.

First is the "rock and roll" factor. If you buy a stereo for $200, you don't expect to pay $2,000 for a CD. Similarly, if you buy a PC for $1,000, you don't expect to pay $10,000 for the software, which is what it would cost if you hired a programmer to write it for you. So, of course, software for a PC either comes free or is priced at about $50 or so. It can be hard to comprehend that something for which you paid $50 has cost millions of dollars to develop.

Second is the teenager syndrome. Many school students write programs as part of their studies. So a parent might easily think, "My kid writes computer programs. What's so hard about programming? Why is software so expensive?"

Software packages

There has been another significant reaction to the availability of cheap computers. If you want to calculate your tax or design your garden, you can buy a program off the shelf to do it. Such software packages can cost as little as $50. The reason for the remarkably low price is, of course, that the producers of the software sell many identical copies – the mass production of software has arrived. The problem with an off-the-shelf package is, of course, that it may not do *exactly* what you want it to do and you may have to resort to tailor-made software, adapt your way of life to fit in with the software, or make do with the inadequacies.

Nonetheless, the availability of cheap packages conveys the impression that software is cheap to produce.

Application development tools

If you want to create certain types of applications software very quickly and easily, several development tools are available. Notable examples of these tools are Visual Basic and Microsoft Access. These tools enable certain types of program to be constructed very easily, and even people who are not programmers can learn to use tools like a spreadsheet (e.g. Microsoft Excel). Thus a perception is created that programming is easy and, indeed, that programmers may no longer be necessary.

The truth is, of course, that some software is very simple and easy to write, but most commercially used software is large and extremely complex.

The IT revolution

The sophistication of today's software far outstrips that of the past. For example, complex graphical user interfaces (GUI's) are now seen as essential, systems are commonly implemented on the web, and the sheer size of projects has mushroomed. People and organizations expect ever more facilities from computers. Arguably, as hardware becomes available to make previously impractical software projects feasible, software costs can only continue to escalate.

In summary, what we see today is that software is expensive:

- relative to the gross national product
- because developers exhibit apparently low productivity
- relative to the cost of hardware
- in popular perception.

How is the cost made up?

It is interesting to see which parts of a software development project cost most money. Figure 1.3 shows typical figures.

Clearly the cost of testing is enormous, whereas coding constitutes only a small part of software development. One interpretation of this is that if a new magical development

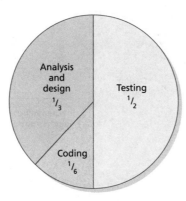

Figure 1.3 Relative costs of the stages of software development

method was devised that ensured the software was correct from the start, then testing would be unnecessary, and therefore only half the usual effort would be needed. Such a method would be a discovery indeed!

If mistakes are a major problem, when are they made? Figure 1.4 shows figures showing the number of errors made at the various stages of a typical project:

However, this data is rather misleading. What matters is how much it costs to *fix* a fault. And the longer the fault remains undiscovered, the more a fault costs to fix. Errors made during the earlier stages of a project tend to be more expensive, unless they are discovered almost immediately. Hence Figure 1.5 showing the relative costs of fixing mistakes in a typical project is probably more relevant.

A design flaw made early in the project may not be detected until late on in system testing – and it will certainly involve a whole lot of rework. By contrast, a syntax error in a program made late in the project will be automatically detected on a first compilation and then easily corrected.

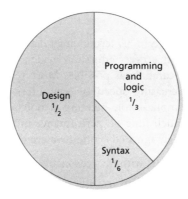

Figure 1.4 Relative numbers of errors made during the stages of software development

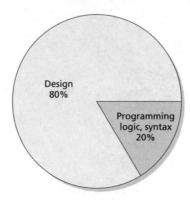

Figure 1.5 Relative cost of fixing different types of fault

1.4 ● Meeting deadlines

Meeting deadlines has always been a headache in software production. For example, sur-veys have consistently shown that this is the worst problem faced by project managers. The problem is related to the difficulty of predicting how long it will take to develop something. If you do not know how long it is going to take, you cannot hope to meet any deadline. It is a common experience for a software project to run late and over budget, disappointing the client and causing despair among the software team. Evidence suggests that around 60% of projects exceed their initial budgets and around 50% are completed late. Whatever the exact figures, meeting deadlines is clearly a problem.

Back in the 1980s, IBM's major new operating system (called OS 360) for its prime new range of computers was one year late. The computers themselves languished in warehouses waiting to be shipped. Microsoft's NT operating system was allegedly also a year late.

1.5 ● Software performance

This is sometimes called efficiency. This terminology dates from the days when the cost and speed of hardware meant that every effort was made to use the hardware – primarily memory and processor – as carefully as possible. More recently a cultural change has come about due to the increasing speed of computers and the fall in their cost. Nowadays there is more emphasis on meeting people's requirements, and conse-quently we will not spend much time on performance in this book. Despite this, per-formance cannot be completely ignored – often we are concerned to make sure that:

■ an interactive system responds within a reasonably short time

■ a control signal is output to a plant in sufficient time

■ a game runs sufficiently fast that the animation appears smooth

■ a batch job is not taking 12 hours when it should take one.

1.3   Identify two further software systems in which speed is an important factor.

The problem with fast run time and small memory usage is that they are usually mutually contradictory. As an example to help see how this comes about, consider a program to carry out a calculation of tax. We could either carry out a calculation, which would involve using relatively slow machine instructions, or we could use a lookup table, which would involve a relatively fast indexing instruction. The first case is slow but small, and the second case is fast but large. Generally, of course, it is necessary to make a judgment about what the particular performance requirements of a piece of software are.

1.6 ● Portability

The dream of portability has always been to transfer software from one type of computer to another with the minimum expenditure of effort. With the advent of high-level languages and the establishment of international standards, the prospects looked bright for the complete portability of applications programs.

The reality is that market forces have dominated the situation. A supplier seeks to attract a customer by offering facilities over and above those provided by the standard language. Typically these may lessen the work of software development. An example is an exotic file access method. Once the user has bought the system, he or she is locked into using the special facilities and is reliant on the supplier for developments in equipment that are fully compatible. The contradiction is, of course, that each and every user is tied to a particular supplier in this way, and can only switch allegiance at a considerable cost in converting software. Only large users, like government agencies, are powerful enough to insist that suppliers adopt standards.

Given this picture of applications software, what are the prospects for systems software, like operating systems and filing systems, with their closer dependence on specific hardware?

1.7 ● Maintenance

Maintenance is the term for any effort that is put into a piece of software after it has been written and put into operation. There are two main types:

- *remedial maintenance*, which is the time spent correcting faults in the software (fixing bugs)
- *adaptive maintenance*, which is modifying software either because the users' needs have changed or because, for example, the computer, operating system or programming language has changed

Remedial maintenance is, of course, a consequence of inadequate testing. As we shall see, effective testing is notoriously difficult and time-consuming, and it is an accepted fact of life in software engineering that maintenance is inevitable.

It is often difficult to predict the future uses for a piece of software, and so adaptive maintenance is also rarely avoided. But because software is called soft, it is sometimes believed that it can be modified easily. In reality, software is brittle, like ice, and when you try to change it, it tends to break rather than bend.

In either case, maintenance is usually regarded as a nuisance, both by managers, who have to make sure that there are sufficient people to do it, and by programmers, who regard it as less interesting than writing new programs.

Some idea of the scale of what has been called the "maintenance burden" can be appreciated by looking at a chart, Figure 1.6, showing typical figures for the amount of time spent in the different activities of developing a particular piece of software.

In a project like this, the maintenance effort is clearly overwhelming. It is not unusual for organizations that use well-established computer systems to be spending three-quarters of their programming time on maintenance.

Here are some more estimates:

■ world-wide, there are 50 billion lines of Cobol in use today

■ in the United States, 2% of the GNP is spent on software maintenance

■ in the UK, £1 billion (about $1.5 million) annually are spent on software maintenance

The millions of lines of program written in what many people consider to be outdated programming languages (like Cobol) constitute what are known as *legacy systems*. These are software systems that are up to 30 years old, but in full use in organizations today. They are often poorly documented, either because there was no documentation

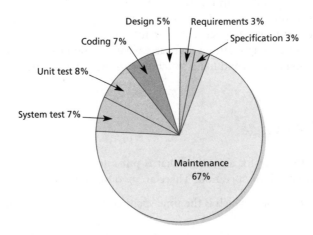

Figure 1.6 Relative costs of the stages of software development

in the first place or because the documentation is useless because it has not been kept up to date as changes have been made. Legacy systems have been written using expertise in tools and methods that are rarely available today. For these reasons, it is expensive to update them to meet ever-changing requirements. Equally, it would be expensive to rewrite them from scratch using a contemporary language and methods. Thus legacy systems are a huge liability for organizations.

Another major example of the problems of maintenance was the *millennium bug*. A great deal of software was written when memory was in short supply and expensive. Dates were therefore stored economically, using only the last two digits of the year, so that, for example, the year 1999 was stored as 99. After 2000, a computer could treat the date value 99 as 1999, 2099 or even 0099. The problem is that the meaning that is attached to a year differs from one system to another, depending on how the individual programmer decided to design the software. The only way to make sure that a program worked correctly after the year 2000 (termed year 2000 compliance) was to examine it line by line to find any reference to a date and then to fix the code appropriately. This was an immensely time-consuming, skilled and therefore costly process. The task often needed knowledge of an outdated programming language and certainly required an accurate understanding of the program's logic. The penalties for not updating software correctly are potentially immense, as modern organizations are totally reliant on computer systems for nearly all of their activities.

1.8 ● Reliability

A piece of software is said to be reliable if it works, and continues to work, without crashing and without doing something undesirable. We say that software has a bug or a fault if it does not perform properly. We presume that the developer knew what was required and so the unexpected behavior is not intended. It is common to talk about bugs in software, but it is also useful to define some additional terms more clearly:

- *error* – a wrong decision made during software development
- *fault* – a problem that may cause software to depart from its intended behavior
- *failure* – an event when software departs from its intended behavior.

In this terminology, a fault is the same as a bug. An error is a mistake made by a human being during one of the stages of software development. An error causes one or more faults within the software, its specification or its documentation. In turn, a fault can cause one or more failures. Failures will occur while the system is being tested and after it has been put into use. (Confusingly, some authors use the terms fault and failure differently.) Failures are the symptom that users experience, whereas faults are a problem that the developer has to deal with. A fault may never manifest itself because the conditions that cause it to make the software fail never arise. Conversely a single fault may cause many different and frequent failures.

The job of removing bugs and trying to ensure reliability is called *verification*.

There is a close but distinct relationship between the concept of reliability and that of meeting users' needs, mentioned above. Requirements analysis is concerned with establishing clearly what the user wants. *Validation* is a collection of techniques that try to ensure that the software does meet the requirements. On the other hand, reliability is to do with the technical issue of whether there are any faults in the software.

Currently testing is one of the main techniques for trying to ensure that software works correctly. In testing, the software is run and its behavior checked against what is expected to happen. However, as we shall see later in this book, there is a fundamental problem with testing: however much you test a piece of software, you can never be sure that you have found every last bug. This leads us to assert fairly confidently the unsettling conclusion that every large piece of software contains errors.

The recognition that we cannot produce bug-free software, however hard we try, has led to the concept of *good enough software*. This means that the developer assesses what level of faults are acceptable for the particular project and releases the software when this level is reached. By level, we mean the number and severity of faults. For some applications, such as a word processor, more faults are acceptable than in a safety critical system, such as a drive-by-wire car. Note that this means that good enough software is sold or put into productive use knowing that it contains bugs.

On the other hand, another school of thought says that if we can only be careful enough, we can create *zero defect software* – software that is completely fault free. This approach involves the use of stringent quality assurance techniques that we will examine later in this book.

One way of gauging the scale of the reliability problem is to look at the following series of cautionary tales.

In the early days of computing – the days of batch data-processing systems – it used to be part of the folklore that computers were regularly sending out fuel bills for (incorrectly) enormous amounts. Although the people who received these bills might have been seriously distressed, particularly the old, the situation was widely regarded as amusing. Reliability was not treated as an important issue.

IBM's major operating system OS 360 had at least 1,000 bugs each and every time it was rereleased. How is this known (after all we would expect that IBM would have corrected all known errors)? The answer is that by the time the next release was issued, 1,000 errors had been found in the previous version.

As part of the US space program, an unmanned vehicle was sent to look at the planet Venus. Part way through its journey a course correction proved necessary. A computer back at mission control executed the following statement, written in the Fortran language:

```
DO 3 I = 1.3
```

This is a perfectly valid Fortran statement. The programmer had intended it to be a repetition statement, which is introduced by the word DO. However, a DO statement should contain a comma rather than the period character actually used. The use of the period makes the statement into assignment statement, placing a value 1.3 into the variable named DO3I. The space probe turned on the wrong course and was never seen again. Thus small errors can have massive consequences. Note that this program had been compiled successfully without errors, which illustrates how language notation can be important. Bugs can be syntactically correct but incorrect for the job they are required for. The program had also been thoroughly tested, which demonstrates the limitations of testing techniques.

In March 1979, an error was found in the program that had been used to design the cooling systems of nuclear reactors in the USA. Five plants were shut down because their safety became questionable.

Some years ago, the USA's system for warning against enemy missiles reported that the USA was being attacked. It turned out to be a false alarm – the result of a computer error – but before the error was discovered, people went a long way into the procedures for retaliating using nuclear weapons. This happened not just once, but three times in a period of a year.

Perhaps the most expensive consequence of a software fault was the crash, 40 seconds after blast-off, of the European Space Agency's Ariane 5 launcher in June 1996. The loss was estimated at $500 million, luckily without loss of life.

In 1999, the website for eBay, the internet auction site went down for 22 hours. As the markets began to doubt that eBay could adequately maintain its key technology, $6 billion was wiped off the share value of the company.

The incidents related above are just a few in a long catalog of expensive problems caused by software errors over the years, and there is no indication that the situation is improving.

How does the reliability of software compare with the reliability of hardware? Studies show that where both the hardware and software are at comparable levels of development, hardware fails three times as often as software. Although this is grounds for friendly rivalry between software and hardware designers, it can be no grounds for complacency among software people.

There are particular applications of computers that demand particularly high reliability. These are known as *safety-critical systems*. Examples are:

- fly-by-wire control of an aircraft
- control of critical processes, such as a power station
- control of medical equipment

In this book, we will look at techniques that can be used in developing systems such as these.

It is not always clear whether a piece of software is safety related. The example mentioned earlier of the faulty software used in designing a power plant is just one example. Another example is communications software that might play a critical role in summoning help in an emergency.

The conclusion is that, generally, software has a poor reputation for reliability.

SELF-TEST QUESTION

1.4   Identify three further examples of software systems that are safety critical and three that are not.

1.9 ● Human–computer interaction

The user interface is what the human user of a software package sees when they need to use the software. There are many examples of computer systems that are not easy to use:

- many people have difficulty programming a video cassette recorder (VCR)
- some people find it difficult to divert a telephone call to another user within an organization

In recent years, many interfaces have become graphical user interfaces (GUIs) that use windows with features like buttons and scroll bars, together with pointing devices like a mouse and cursor. Many people saw this as a massive step in improving the user interface, but it remains a challenging problem to design a user interface that is simple and easy to use.

SELF-TEST QUESTION

1.5   Think of two computer-based systems that you know of that are difficult to use in some way or another. Alternatively, think of two features of a program you use that are difficult to use.

1.10 ● A software crisis?

We have discussed various perceived problems with software:

- it fails to do what users want it to do
- it is expensive
- it isn't always fast enough
- it cannot be transferred to another machine easily
- it is expensive to maintain
- it is unreliable
- it is often late
- it is not always easy to use.

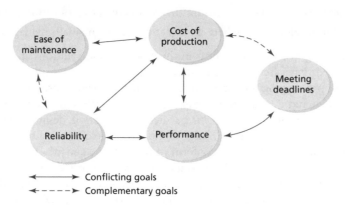

Figure 1.7 Complementary and conflicting goals in a software project

Of these, meeting users' needs (validation), reducing software costs, improving reliability (verification) and delivery on time are probably the four most important present-day problems.

Many people argue that things have been so bad – and continue to be so bad – that there is a continuing real "crisis" in software development. They argue that something must be done about the situation, and the main remedy must be to bring more scientific principles to bear on the problem – hence the introduction of the term software engineering. Indeed, the very term software engineering conveys that there is a weightier problem than arises in small-scale programming.

One of the obstacles to trying to solve the problems of software is that very often they conflict with each other. For example, low cost of construction and high reliability conflict. Again, high performance and portability are in conflict. Figure 1.7 indicates the situation.

Happily, some goals do not conflict with each other. For example, low cost of maintenance and high reliability are complementary.

1.11 ● A remedy – software engineering?

As we have seen, it is generally recognized that there are big problems with developing software successfully. A number of ideas have been suggested for improving the situation. These methods and tools are collectively known as software engineering. Some of the main ideas are:

■ greater emphasis on carrying out all stages of development systematically.

■ computer assistance for software development – software tools.

■ an emphasis on finding out exactly what the users of a system really want (requirements engineering and validation)

■ demonstrating an early version of a system to its customers (prototyping)

■ use of new, innovative programming languages

■ greater emphasis on trying to ensure that software is free of errors (verification).

■ incremental development, where a project proceeds in small, manageable steps

We will be looking at all of these ideas in this book. These solutions are not mutually exclusive; indeed they often complement each other.

Verification, prototyping and other such techniques actually address only some of the problems encountered in software development. A large-scale software project will comprise a number of separate related activities, analysis, specification, design, implementation, and so on. It may be carried out by a large number of people working to strict deadlines, and the end product usually has to conform to prescribed standards. Clearly, if software projects are to have any chance of successfully delivering correct software on time within budget, they must be thoroughly planned in advance and effectively managed as they are executed. Thus the aim is to replace ad hoc methods with an organized discipline.

One term that is used a lot these days in connection with software is the word *quality*. One might argue that any product (from a cream bun to a washing machine) that fulfills the purpose for which it was produced could be considered to be a quality product. In the context of software, if a package meets, and continues to meet, a customer's expectations, then it too can be considered to be a quality product. In this perspective, quality can be attained only if effective standards, techniques and procedures exist to be applied, and are seen to be properly employed and monitored. Thus, not only do good methods have to be applied, but they also have to be seen to be applied. Such procedures are central to the activity called "quality assurance".

The problem of producing "correct" software can be addressed by using appropriate specification and verification techniques (formal or informal). However, correctness is just one aspect of quality; the explicit use of project management discipline is a key factor in achieving high-quality software.

Summary

We have considered a number of goals and problem areas in software development. Generally, software developers have a bad image, a reputation for producing software that is:

■ late

■ over budget

■ unreliable

■ inflexible

■ hard to use.

Because the problems are so great, there has been widespread talk of a crisis in software production. The general response to these problems has been the creation of a number of systematic approaches, novel techniques and notations to address the software development task. The different methods, tools and languages fit within a plan of action (called a process model). This book is about these approaches. Now read on.

Exercises

These exercises ask you to carry out an analysis and come to some conclusion about a situation. Often there is no unique "right answer". Sometimes you will have to make reasonable assumptions or conjectures. The aim of the exercises is to clarify your understanding of the goals of software engineering and some of the problems that lie in the path of achieving these goals.

1.1   Write down a list of all of the different items of software that you know about, then categorize them within types.

1.2   What are your own personal goals when you develop a piece of software? Why? Do you need to re-examine these?

1.3   Is software expensive? What criteria did you use in arriving at your conclusion?

1.4   Is programming/software development easy? Justify your answer.

1.5   The evidence suggests that there are enormous differences between programmers in terms of productivity. Why do you think this is? Does it matter that there are differences?

1.6   For each of the applications described in Appendix A assess the importance of the various goals identified in this chapter. For each application, rank the goals in order.

1.7   What would you expect the relative costs of hardware and software development to be in each of the cases above?

1.8   How do you personally feel about software maintenance? Would you enjoy doing it?

1.9   Think of an example of a program in which the aims of minimizing run time and memory occupancy are mutually contradictory. Think of an example where these two are in harmony.

1.10 Analyze the conflicts and consistencies between the various goals of software engineering.

1.11 In addition to the goals described in this chapter, are there any other goals that software engineering should strive for? What about making sure that it is fun to do it? What about exercising creativity and individuality?

Answers to self-test questions

1.1 50 people at a cost of $12.5 million.

1.2 Hardware: $1,000.
Software: $100.
To buy, the hardware is approximately ten times the cost of the software.

1.3 Examples are a Web browser and a telephone switching system.

1.4 Examples of safety critical systems: an ABS braking system on a car, a fire alarm system, a patient record system in a health center.

Examples of systems that are not safety critical are a payroll system, a word processor, a game program.

1.5 Some well-known word processor programs incorporate the facility to search for a file. This facility is not always easy to use, especially when it fails to find a file that you know is there somewhere.

The DOS operating system provides a command-line command to delete a file or any number of files. Coupled with the "wild card" feature, denoted by an asterisk, it is easy to delete more files than you plan, for example:

```
del *.*
```

 Further reading

Accounts of failed projects are given in Stephen Flowers, *Software Failure: Management Failure: Amazing Stories and Cautionary Tales*, Stephen Flowers, John Wiley, 1996, and in Robert Glass, *Software Runaways*, Prentice Hall, 1998.

This is a good read if you are interested in how software projects really get done and what life is like at Microsoft. G. Pasacal Zachary, *Show-Stopper: The Breakneck Race to Create Windows NT and the Next Generation at Microsoft*, Free Press, a division of Macmillan, Inc., 1994.

A very readable and classic account of the problems of developing large-scale software is given in the following book, which was written by the man in charge of the development of the software for an IBM mainframe range of computers. It has been republished as a celebratory second edition with additional essays. Frederick P. Brooks, *The Mythical Man-Month*, Addison-Wesley, 2nd edn, 1995.

One of the key design goals of Java is portability. A compelling account of the arguments for portable software is given in Peter Van Der Linden, *Not Just Java*, Sun Microsystems Press; Prentice Hall, 1998.

Analyses of the costs of the different stages of software development are given in the following classic book, which is still relevant despite its age: B.W. Boehm, *Software Engineering Economics*, Prentice Hall International, 1981.

A fascinating review of disasters caused by computer malfunctions (hardware, software and human error) is given in Peter G. Neumann, *Computer-Related Risks*, Addison-Wesley; ACM Press, 1995.

In conjunction with the ACM, Peter Neumann also moderates a USENET newsgroup called comp.risks, which documents incidents of computer-related risks. Archives are available at http://catless.ncl.ac.uk/Risks/

For an up-to-date look at how software professionals see their role, look at the newsletter of the ACM Special Interest Group in Software Engineering, called Software Engineering Notes (SEN), published bi-monthly. Its Web address is http://www.acm.org/sigs/sigsoft/SEN/

The equivalent periodical from the IEEE is simply called *Software*. This is produced by and for practitioners, reflecting their current concerns and interests, such as software costs.

CHAPTER 2

The tasks of software development

This chapter:

- identifies the activities within software development
- explains the idea of a process model
- explains the term methodology
- explains the term hacking.

2.1 ● Introduction

In this chapter we identify the significant tasks of software development. The bulk of this book describes techniques for carrying out these tasks. As part of the story, we clarify the nature of two important activities that take place throughout software development – validation and verification.

If you have ever written a program, there a number of activities that you know you are going to have to carry out, for example, testing. The same is true of larger developments, but for big programs and large software systems, there are additional elements. The activities are:

- a feasibility study
- requirements engineering
- user interface design
- architectural design
- detailed design
- programming
- system integration
- validation
- verification (testing)
- production

- documentation
- maintenance
- project management.

A process model is a plan that makes provision for all these required activities and seeks to incorporate the stages in a methodical way. At the end of this chapter, we introduce the idea of process model, which is an overall strategy for accomplishing software development. However, while it may seem obvious that they are carried out in a certain order, we shall see that this is not always the best strategy. For example, it may not be ideal to carry out validation as the final step. Similarly, not all process models incorporate the activities as distinct steps.

2.2 ● The tasks

Feasibility study

Before anything else is done, a feasibility study establishes whether or not the project is to proceed. It may be that the system is unnecessary, too expensive or too risky. One approach to a feasibility study is to perform cost-benefit analysis. The cost of the proposed system is estimated, which may involve new hardware as well as software, and compared with the cost of likely savings. This comparison then determines whether the project goes ahead or not.

Requirements engineering (specification)

At the start of a project, the developer finds out what the user (client or customer) wants the software to do and records the requirements as clearly as possible. The product of this stage is a requirements specification.

User interface design

Most software has a graphical user interface, which must be carefully designed so that it is easy to use.

Architectural (large-scale) design

A software system may be large and complex. It is sometimes too large to be written as one single program. The software must be constructed from modules or components. Architectural, or large-scale design breaks the overall system down into a number of simpler modules. The products of this activity are an architectural design and module specifications.

Detailed design

The design of each module or component is carried out. The products are detailed designs of each module.

Programming (coding)

The detailed designs are converted into instructions written in the programming language. There may be a choice of programming languages, from which one must be selected. The product is the code.

System integration

The individual components of the software are combined together, which is sometimes called the build. The product is the complete system.

Verification

This seeks to ensure that the software is reliable. According to Barry Boehm (one of the all-time greats of software engineering), verification answers the question: Are we building the product right? A piece of software that meets its specification is of limited use if it crashes frequently. Verification is concerned with the developer's view – the internal implementation of the system.

Two types of verification are *unit testing* and *system testing*. In unit testing, each module of the software is tested in isolation. The inputs to unit testing are:

1. the unit specification
2. the unit code
3. a list of expected test results.

The products of unit testing are the test results. Unit testing verifies that the behavior of the coding conforms to its unit specification.

In system testing or integration testing, the modules are linked together and the complete system tested. The inputs to system testing are the system specification and the code for the complete system. The outcome of system testing is the completed, tested software, verifying that the system meets its specification.

Validation

This seeks to ensure that the software meets its users' needs. According to Boehm, validation answers the question: Are we building the right product? Validation is to do with the client's view of the system, the external view of the system. It is no use creating a piece of software that works perfectly (that is tested to perfection) if it doesn't do what its users want.

An important example of a validation activity is *acceptance testing*. This happens at the end of the project when the software is deemed complete, is demonstrated to its client and accepted by them as satisfactory. The inputs to acceptance testing are the client and the apparently complete software. The products are either a sign-off document and an accepted system or a list of faults. The outcome is that the system complies with the requirements of the client or it does not.

Current evidence suggests that many computer systems do not meet the needs of their users, and that therefore successful validation is a major problem in software engineering today. It is a common experience that users think they have articulated their needs to the software engineer. The engineer will then spend months or even years developing the software only to find, when it is demonstrated, that it was not what the user wanted. This is not only demoralizing for both users and developers, but it is often massively costly in terms of the effort needed to correct the deficiencies. As an extreme alternative the system is abandoned.

It is too easy to blame the requirements analysis stage of development, when in reality the basic problem is the quality of the communication between users and developers. Users do not know (and usually do not care) about technicalities, whereas the software engineer expects detailed instructions. Worst of all is the problem of some common language for accurately describing what the user wants. The users are probably happiest with natural language (e.g. English), whereas the software engineer would probably prefer some more rigorous language that would be incomprehensible to the users. There is a cultural gap.

Production

The system is put into use. (This is sometimes, confusingly, termed implementation.) The users may need training.

Maintenance

When the software is in use, sooner or later it will almost certainly need fixing or enhancing. Making these changes constitutes maintenance. Software maintenance often goes on for years after the software is first constructed. The product of this activity is the modified software.

Documentation

Documentation is required for two types of people – users and the developers.

Users need information about how to install the software, how to de-install the software and how to use it. Even in the computer age, paper manuals are still welcome. For general purpose software, such as a word processor, a help system is often provided. User documentation concentrates on the "what" (the external view) of the software, not the "how" (the internal workings).

Developers need documentation in order to continue development and to carry out maintenance. This typically comprises the specification, the architectural design, the detailed design, the code, annotation within the code (termed comments), test schedules, test results and the project plan.

The documentation is typically large and costly (in people's time) to produce. Also, because it is additional to the product itself, there is a tendency to ignore it or skimp on it.

Project management

Someone needs to create and maintain plans, resolve problems, allocate work to people and check that it has been completed.

Database design

Many systems use a database to store information. Designing the database is a whole subject in its own right and is not normally considered to be part of software engineering. Consequently, we don't tackle this topic within this book.

SELF-TEST QUESTION

2.1   Which stages of software development, if any, can be omitted if the required software is only a small program?

We will see that, in dividing the work into a series of distinct activities, it may appear that the work is carried out strictly in sequence. However, it is usual, particularly on large projects, for many activities to take place in parallel. In particular, this happens once the large-scale (or architectural) design is complete. It is at this stage that the major software components have been identified. Work on developing the components can now proceed in parallel, often undertaken by different individuals.

2.3 ● Process models

We have seen (Chapter 1) that software systems are often large and complex. There is a clear need to be organized when embarking on a development. What do you need when you set about a software project? You need:

■   a set of methods and tools

■   an overall plan or strategy.

The plan of action is known as a *process model*. It is a plan of what steps are going to be taken as the development proceeds. This term is derived as follows: a process is a step or a series of steps; a process model is a model in the sense that it is a representation of reality. Like any model, a model is only an approximation of reality. A process model has two distinct uses:

- it can be used as a basis for the plan for a project. Here the aim is to predict what will be done.
- it can be used to analyze what actually happens during a project. Here the aim is to improve the process for the current and for future projects.

There are several mainstream process models:

- waterfall
- prototyping
- incremental
- agile
- rational
- open source
- seat of the pants, do it yourself or ad hoc.

Each of these approaches will be discussed later in this book, except for the last in the list. An ad hoc approach is no plan at all, and no organization would admit to using such an approach. A software development project can take several years and involve tens or even hundreds of people. Moreover, software development is a complex task. To avoid catastrophe, some way of organizing a project must be established. Thus most approaches identify a series of distinct stages within a project, along with a plan of what order they will occur in.

2.4 ● Methodology

In common language, the word methodology means the study of method. It answers such questions as: What is the basis of method x? How good is method y? However, in software development, the term methodology has been kidnapped and come to mean a complete package of techniques, tools and notations. Such a package is given a name, say the XYZ methodology, and is often marketed by a corporation, together with books, manuals and training. Consultants are also on hand to guide an organization in using the methodology.

In this book, we have avoided describing any particular methodology, but we do explain all the ingredients that go into making the mainstream methodologies available today.

2.5 ● Hacking

There is one notorious approach to software development, called hacking. There are actually two types of hacker:

■ the malicious hacker who breaks into computer systems, often using the internet, to commit fraud, to cause damage or simply for fun

■ the programmer hacker, who uses supreme skills, but no obvious method, to develop software.

It is the second of these meanings that we will use in this book. Hacking is often disparaged in software development circles because it appears to be out of control. However, the display of skill also earns hackers praise. Hackers also obviously enjoy what they do and relish their skills. We will return to the subject of hacking in the chapter on open source development.

Summary

We have identified a list of tasks that are part of software development. All of them must be carried out somehow during development.

A process model is a strategic plan for the complete process. Different process models offer alternative suggestions as to exactly how and when tasks are carried out. As we shall see, in some process models all of the stages are visible, while in other process models some of the stages vanish or become part of some other stage.

A methodology is a complete (often proprietary) package of methods, tools and notations.

Hacking is an approach to development that is highly skilled but ill-disciplined.

Exercises

2.1 Discussion question on validation and verification: What do the following mean, what is the difference between them, and which is better?

■ a program that works (but doesn't meet the specification)

■ a program that meets the specification (but doesn't work).

2.2 Discussion question on validation and verification: What do the following terms mean and how do they relate to one another (if at all):

■ correctness

■ working properly

- error free
- fault
- tested
- reliable
- meet the requirements.

Answer to self-test question

2.1 Architectural design, unit testing, project management, configuration management and version control.

3

The feasibility study

This chapter:

- explains the role of a feasibility study
- suggests how to go about conducting a feasibility study.

3.1 ● Introduction

Every software project begins with a judgment as to whether the project is worthwhile or not. This is called a feasibility study. Sometimes this assessment is carried out in a detailed and systematic fashion; and sometimes it is carried out in a hurried and ad hoc fashion; and sometimes it is not carried out at all. In this chapter we outline a framework for assessing whether a software system is worthwhile.

There are two types of computer system:

- a system that replaces an existing computer-based system
- a brand new system that replaces or enhances work that is not currently computer-assisted.

Another categorization is:

- a general purpose system, such as a word processor or a game. This is written and then sold in the market place
- a tailor-made one-off system for a specific application.

Remember also that there is often the choice between writing the software and buying it off the shelf.

3.2 ● Technical feasibility

Before beginning a project, there is a crucial decision that must be made: Is the proposal technically feasible? That is, will the technology actually work? We know, for example, that a system to predict lottery results cannot work. But a system to recognize voice commands is borderline. A system to download and play DVD-quality movies into people's homes is also borderline.

3.3 ● Cost-benefit analysis

In engineering, there has long been a tradition of assessing available technology, for example, the use of reinforced concrete in building. Similarly in computer-based information systems, a number of techniques have been used in advance of building a system in order to determine whether the system will be worthwhile.

Money provides the ready-made metric for measuring value. This kind of investigation is called *investment appraisal* or a *cost-benefit analysis*. The organization expects a *return on investment*. In this approach two quantities are calculated:

1. the cost of providing the system
2. the money saved or created by using the system – the benefit.

If the benefit is greater than the cost, the system is worthwhile; otherwise it is not.

If there is some other way of accomplishing the same task, which may be manually, then it is necessary to compare the two costs. Whichever technique gives the smaller cost is the one to select, provided that the benefit is greater than the cost.

Costs and benefits are usually estimated over a five year period. This means that the initial start-up costs are spread over the expected useful life of the system. Five years is the typical lifetime of a computer-based system. Beyond this time, changes in technology as well as changes in requirements make predictions uncertain.

Many evaluation criteria are common to all computer systems – and indeed to all products designed for some useful purpose. Thus motor cars, buildings and televisions need to be reliable, robust, easy to maintain, easy to upgrade. The obvious, central consideration is the construction cost. With each of these criteria we can associate a cost, though for some it is less easy:

- cost to buy equipment, principally the hardware
- cost to develop the software
- cost of training
- cost of lost work during switchover

- cost to maintain the system
- cost to repair the equipment in the event of failure
- cost of lost work in the event of failure
- cost to upgrade, in the event of changed requirements.

The upgrade cost is part of the cost of some future system and not strictly part of the current costing, but is worth bearing in mind at the evaluation stage.

While all of these costs *should* be estimated in advance of developing a system, it is in practice very difficult to estimate the cost of construction and of maintenance.

3.4 ● Other criteria

It is easy to be drawn into judging everything on the basis of costs, but there are other approaches.

Many people develop software purely for fun. Open source programmers are a prime example. Their motivations include providing useful tools, enjoying the act of programming and collaborating with others.

Large military projects are sometimes funded because they are considered necessary (militarily or politically), whatever the cost.

Some people, perhaps seduced by technology, take the view that a computer system is obviously better than a manual system.

Some systems are, arguably, socially useful and, perhaps, outside the scope of a costing-based approach. How can we meaningfully assess the value of a system that allows a patient to book a medical appointment, or a system that provides information on bus arrival times at bus stops?

SELF-TEST QUESTION

> **3.1** Suggest another system for which cost-benefit analysis is probably not appropriate.

3.5 ● Case study

We will examine carrying out a feasibility study of the software for an ATM, outlined in Appendix A. An ATM is part hardware, part software, so we could either carry out a feasibility study for the complete system or limit ourselves to the software component. However, if we are assessing the viability on the basis of cost, we must look at the complete system.

We first look at costs of construction. We expect that the ATM is not just a one-off but that a number of them will be built and deployed. Let us assume that 200 machines will be needed.

The hardware cost includes the processor, the card reader, the display, the screen, the key pad, the printer, a cash dispenser and a modem. We presume that these can be bought off the shelf rather than specially designed and made. We could estimate the cost of the hardware for each ATM at $10,000. In addition there is the cost of installing the machines in a secure fashion. There will probably be a need for extra server capacity at the bank in order to handle the requests from ATMs. An estimate for the total hardware costs is $20,000 per ATM.

Running costs include the telephone line charge, replacing printer paper, stocking the ATM with cash.

Now we attempt to estimate the software cost. The software is relatively complex because it uses a number of special devices. There is software in each ATM, plus the software at the bank to handle requests from ATMs. The ATM software must be robust and reliable because it is used by members of the public. We *could* adopt such techniques as those explained in Chapter 30 to predict the software cost, but these techniques are poor, and anyway, as we shall see, we only need a ball park figure. Suppose we guess two person years for the software. Suppose that this equates to $100,000. But this cost must be shared across the 200 machines, which is $500 per machine. This is about 2–5% of the cost of each ATM – an insignificant component. This is typical of software costs in embedded systems, where the software is simply one component among many others.

What about the benefits of providing ATMs? No doubt ATMs are convenient, available 24/7 hours in stations, stores and public buildings. But most banks are not philanthropists – their mission is not to serve the public, but to make a profit. The provision of ATMs might attract customers to the bank and this benefit could be costed. This would probably be only a temporary advantage, until other banks caught up. However, most banks in the industrialized world have reduced jobs by computerization and this is probably the significant cost benefit. We might estimate that a single 24-hour ATM would replace two full-time cashiers. This is a saving of, say, $40,000 each per year. (This is not simply salaries, but includes other costs, such as office space.)

So, in summary, over a five-year period for each ATM:

Costs		Benefits	
cost of hardware	$20,000	staff costs	$400,000
cost of software	$500		
cost of maintenance	$4,500		
total	$25,000	total	$400,000

Should the ATMs be developed? The conclusion speaks for itself.

Now, all these figures are indicative, but the point is to see how to go about cost-benefit analysis. We can see that assessing the costs and the benefits of a system is complicated and time-consuming. It is not an exact science and some guesses usually have to be made.

3.6 ● Discussion

It is notoriously difficult to predict the cost of a system and therefore it is very difficult to carry out a feasibility study. This may explain why it is common to ignore it. There is, however, another common reason for avoiding a feasibility study: once an idea for a system has been suggested, the project generates its own momentum, people become committed to it and it cannot be stopped. Instead people talk about a *business case* for the system, which tends to emphasize the positive aspects while minimizing the negative.

Bear in mind that sometimes the feasibility study plays a large part in deciding that the project should be abandoned.

Summary

A feasibility study is an investigation to check that a development is worthwhile. It is carried out at the start of a project. It assesses technical feasibility and costs.

Cost-benefit analysis compares the cost of developing the system with the money saved by using it. The costs include development, additional hardware, maintenance and training.

● Exercises

3.1   Suggest how a feasibility study would be conducted for each of the systems outlined in Appendix A.

3.2   Discuss the validity of using cost-benefit analysis, especially in socially useful applications.

Answers to self-test questions

3.1 There are a number of possible systems. For example, aids for disabled people.

3.2 Yes. The software cost is only a small part of the cost. The benefits overwhelm the costs.

Further reading

A collection of papers that looks at the topic from a variety of perspectives is the following title. Some non-computer case studies are presented. Richard Layard and Stephen Glaister (eds), *Cost-Benefit Analysis*, Cambridge University Press, 1994.

Requirements engineering

This chapter:

- explains what happens during requirements engineering
- explains the nature of a requirements specification
- explains how to employ use cases in specifying requirements
- explains how to draw use case diagrams
- suggests guidelines and checklists for writing good specifications.

4.1 ● Introduction

Logically the first stage of software development is to establish precisely what the users of the system want. The dominant part of this stage is communication between the users and the software developer or engineer. When the engineers are dealing with requirements, they are normally referred to as systems analysts or, simply, "analysts". This is the term we shall use. As far as the users are concerned, they are sometimes known as clients or customers. We will use the term "user".

The story begins when a user has an idea for a new (or enhanced) system. He or she summons the analyst and thereafter they collaborate on drawing up the requirements specification. The user's initial idea may be very vague and ill-defined, but sometimes clear and well-defined.

Arguably, establishing the requirements is the single most important activity in software development. It typically consumes 33% of the project development effort. If we cannot accurately specify what is needed, it is futile to implement it. Conversely, we could implement the most beautiful software in the world, but if it is not what is needed, we have failed. In the real world of software development there are strong indications that many systems do not meet their users' needs precisely because the needs were not accurately specified in the first place.

Establishing the requirements for a software system is the first step in trying to ensure that a system does what its prospective users want. This endeavor continues throughout the software development and is called validation.

The requirements specification has a second vital role. It is the yardstick for assessing whether the software works correctly – that it is free from bugs. The job of striving to ensure that software is free from errors is a time-consuming and difficult process that takes place throughout development. It is called verification.

Errors in specification can contribute hugely to testing and maintenance costs. The cost of fixing an error during testing can be 200 times the cost of fixing it during specification. It is estimated that something like 50% of bugs arise from poor specification. The remedy of course is to detect (or prevent) bugs early, that is, during specification.

It is easy to write poor requirements specifications for software; it is difficult to write good specifications. In this chapter we will examine guidelines for writing specifications.

Remember that specifications are not usually written once and then frozen. More typically, requirements change during the software development as the users' requirements are clarified and modified.

4.2 ● The concept of a requirement

The task of analyzing and defining the requirements for a system is not new or peculiar to software. For generations, engineers have been carrying out these activities. For example, the following is part of the requirements specification for a railway locomotive:

On a dry track, the locomotive must be able to start a train of up to 100 tonnes on an incline of up to 30% with an acceleration of at least 30 km/h/h.

This statement serves to emphasize that a requirement tells us *what* the user (in this case the railway company) wants. It says nothing about *how* the locomotive should be built. Thus, it does not state whether the locomotive is diesel, coal or nuclear powered. It says nothing about the shape or the wheel arrangements.

One of the great controversies in computing is whether it is desirable (or even possible) to specify what a system should do without considering how the system will do it. This is the relationship between specification and implementation. We will now look at both sides of this argument.

On the one hand, there are several reasons why the requirements specification should avoid implementation issues. The prime reason is that the user cannot reasonably be expected to understand the technical issues of implementation and cannot therefore be expected to *agree* such elements of the specification. To emphasize the point, how many users of a word processor really understand how software works? A second reason for minimizing implementation considerations is to avoid unduly constraining the implementation. It is best if the developer has a free reign to use whatever tools and techniques he or she chooses – so long as the requirements are met.

On the other hand, some people argue that it is impossible to divorce specification and implementation. Indeed, in several major approaches to specification they are intermixed. In such a method, the first task is to understand and to document the workings of an existing system. (This might be a manual or a computer-based system, or some combination.) This investigation serves as the prelude to the development of a new computer system. Thus the implementation of one system (the old) acts as a major ingredient in the specification for the new system. For example, suppose we wished to develop a computer system for a library that currently does not use computers. One approach would be to investigate and document all the current manual procedures for buying books, cataloging, shelving, loaning, etc. Having accomplished this task, the next step is to decide which areas of activity are to be computerized (for example, the loans system). Finally, the specification of the new system is derived from the design (implementation) of the old system. This approach to development seems very appealing and logical. However, it does mean that implementation and specification are intertwined.

There are several, additional and powerful reasons why the analyst must think about implementation during specification. First, they must check that a requirement is technically possible. For example, is it possible to achieve a response time of 0.1 second? Second, it is vital to consider implementation in order to estimate the cost and delivery date of the software. In order to estimate figures for performance and cost it will almost certainly be necessary to carry out some outline development at least as far as architectural design.

So, an ideal specification stipulates what, not how. But this is not always practical.

4.3 ● The qualities of a specification

We have seen that, ideally, a specification should confine itself to what is needed. We now present a list of desirable qualities for a specification. A good specification should exhibit the following characteristics:

- implementation free – what is needed, not how this is achieved
- complete – there is nothing missing
- consistent – no individual requirement contradicts any other
- unambiguous – each requirement has a single interpretation
- concise – each requirement is stated once only, without duplication
- minimal – there are no unnecessary ingredients
- understandable – by both the clients and the developers
- achievable – the requirement is technically feasible
- testable – it can be demonstrated that the requirements have been met.

This list of desirable features can be used as a checklist when a specification is drawn up. Additionally it can be used as a checklist to examine and improve an existing specification.

A requirements specification should also be able to provide clear guidance as to how to check that the system meets its users' needs. In the specification for the locomotive given above there is plenty of quantitative information that would allow an objective judgment of the success of the locomotive by using measuring instruments like stopwatches.

We will examine some common deficiencies in specifications. We have seen that the locomotive specification has the following positive characteristics:

1. it specifies requirements, not implementation

2. it is testable

3. it is clear.

However, the specification suffers from at least one deficiency: it is incomplete. For example, there is no mention of cost or a deadline.

Let us now look at the requirements specification for a simple piece of software:

> *Write a Java program to provide a personal telephone directory. It should implement functions to look up a number and to enter a new telephone number. The program should provide a friendly user interface.*

and apply the checklist above.

On the issue of implementation, the specification says that the program is to be written in Java, which is definitely to do with the "how" of implementation. Second, the specification gives no detail about the detail of the two functions; it is incomplete. Often a requirement is simply unclear or susceptible to alternative interpretations, and this, of course, may well be due to the use of natural language in the specification. Vagueness is a common problem. Thus the requirement to provide a user-friendly interface is hopelessly vague, thereby making the specification incomplete and untestable.

Some words are vague and therefore should be avoided within a specification. Some typical examples are the words "flexible", "fault tolerant", "fast", "adequate", "user friendly".

Sometimes requirements contradict each other, as in these two:

> *the data will be stored on magnetic tape*
> *the system will respond in less than 1 second.*

because magnetic tape cannot provide a one-second response time.

Omissions or incompleteness can be difficult to identify. A typical area of specification that is omitted is that of how to deal with faults, for example, input errors by a user of the system.

All in all, constructing a successful specification is a demanding activity that needs the clearest of thinking. It needs effective communication between client and developer. It needs the most precise use of natural language. A review of the specification by a number of people can help improve it.

4.4 ● How to elicit requirements

The activity of eliciting requirements involves the analysts and users talking together, with the former trying to understand the latter. It necessitates the clearest form of communication. The skills involved on the part of the analyst are not the usual, technical skills that are associated with developing software. It is beyond the scope of this book to explore the issues of human communication that are involved, and we shall largely concentrate on the notations and format of specifications. We will, however, touch on the issue of viewpoints.

We can distinguish three activities that lead to a requirements specification:

1. listening (or requirements elicitation)
2. thinking (or requirements analysis)
3. writing (or requirements definition).

Elicitation involves listening to users' needs or requirements, asking questions that assist the users in clarifying their goals and constraints and finally recording the users' viewpoint of the system requirements.

Requirements analysis is the stage where the software engineer simply thinks! He or she transforms the users' view of the system into an organized representation of the system as seen by the analyst. And this may be complicated by the fact that there may be a number of different users with different views of what is wanted.

Requirements definition is the writing of a clear statement, often in natural language, of what the system is expected to provide for its user. This information is called the requirements specification.

As in any complex process of communication and negotiation, these three activities will usually take place repetitively and sporadically.

The conversation between clients and analysts will often be long and complicated. There is primarily the need to communicate clearly and then to record the requirements clearly. But then there is also the negotiating ingredient, during which the user may baulk at the price quoted for a particular feature. Eventually, we hope, agreement can be reached on the final requirement specification.

From the outset of any project there are at least two viewpoints – that of the users and that of the developers. As we shall see, there are cultural differences between these two groups, but also there will often be differences of view within the group of users. For example, consider a computer system that is to be used by cashiers in a bank. The cashiers may be concerned with giving good customer service, job satisfaction and with enriching their jobs. They may resent any attempt to speed up or intensify their work. They may object to any facilities in the system to monitor their work rate. The management in the bank, however, will probably be concerned with costs, performance and effectiveness. There may very well be a conflict of interest between the cashiers and the managers. This paints an extreme picture, but illustrates that the users will not necessarily present a single, uniform view.

Another example of a potential gulf between users and analysts is to do with the level of expectation of users. Some users have seen science fiction films and come to believe that computers can do anything – or at least can offer a high level of artificial intelligence. Others, perhaps, are naive in the opposite direction and believe that computers can carry out only the most mundane tasks.

To sum up, the role of the analyst is:

- to elicit and clarify the requirements from the users
- to help resolve possible differences of view amongst the users and clients.
- to advise users on what is technically possible and impossible.
- to document the requirements (see the next section).
- to negotiate and to gain the agreement of the users and clients to a (final) requirements specification.

The journey from the users' initial idea to an agreed requirements specification will often be long and tortuous.

4.5 ● The requirements specification

The end product of requirements elicitation and analysis is the requirements specification. It is a vital piece of documentation that is crucial to the success of any software development project. If we cannot precisely state what the system should do, then how can we develop the software with any confidence, and how can we hope to check that the end product meets its needs? The specification is the reference document against which all subsequent development is assessed.

Three important factors to be considered are:

1. the level of detail
2. to whom the document is addressed
3. the notation used.

The first factor is about the need to restrict the specification as much as possible to specify *what* the system should do rather than *how* it should do it. As we have seen, the specification should ideally be the users' view of the system rather than anything about how the system is to be implemented.

The second factor arises because the specification has to be understood by two different sets of people – the users and the developers. The people in these two sets have different backgrounds, expertise and jargon. They share the common aim of clearly describing what the system should do, but they will each be inclined to use a different language. The users will have a preference for non-technical descriptions expressed in natural language. Unfortunately, while natural language is excellent for poetry and love letters, it is a poor vehicle for achieving a precise, consistent and unambiguous specification. On the other hand, the analysts, being of a technical orientation, will probably want to use precise (perhaps mathematical) notation in order to specify a system. This brings us to the question of the notation.

Several notations are available for writing specifications:

■ *informal*, writing in natural language, used as clearly and carefully as possible. In this chapter we will concentrate on this approach.

■ *formal*, using mathematical notation, with rigor and conciseness. This approach is outside the scope of this book. Formal methods tend to be used only in safety critical systems.

■ *semi-formal*, using a combination of natural language together with various diagrammatic and tabular notations. Most of these notations have their origins in methods for software design, that is, in methods for the implementation of software. Thus there is a potential problem of including information about the implementation. These notations are discussed later in this book and include pseudo-code, data flow diagrams and class diagrams.

At the present time, most requirements specifications are written in natural language, assisted by use case diagrams.

One approach is to draw up two documents:

1. a requirements specification written primarily for users, describing the users' view of the system and expressed in natural language. This is the substance of the contract between the users and the developers.

2. a technical specification that is used primarily by developers, expressed in some more formal notation and describing only a part of the information in the full requirements specification.

If this approach is adopted, there is then the problem of ensuring that the two documents are compatible.

4.6 ● The structure of a specification

Given that a requirements specification will usually be written in natural language, it is useful to plan the overall structure of the specification and to identify its component parts. We can also identify those ingredients that, perhaps, should not be included at all, because they are concerned with the implementation rather than the requirement. The remainder of this section presents one way of structuring specifications.

One approach to giving a clear structure to a specification is to partition it into parts. Software essentially consists of the combination of data and actions. In specifications, the corresponding elements are called functional and data requirements. One of the major debates in computing is about which of these two main elements – data or function – is primary. Some approaches to development, notably the object-oriented approach, are holistic, treating function and data with equal importance. However, our concern here is with specification, not with development approaches. However, the format of a specification will tend to reflect the system development method being employed.

A checklist for the contents of a requirements specification is:

1. the functional requirements
2. the data requirements
3. performance requirements
4. constraints
5. guidelines.

We shall now look at these in turn.

Functional requirements

The functional requirements are the real essence of a requirements specification. They state what the system should *do*. Examples are:

The system will display the titles of all the books written by the specified author.
The system will continuously display the temperatures of all the machines.

Functional requirements are characterized by verbs that perform actions.

Data requirements

Data requirements have three components:

1. users' data that is input to or output from the system via screen, keyboard or mouse.
2. data that is stored within the system, usually in files on disk, for example, information about the books held in a public library.
3. information passed to or from another computer system, for example, to a server.

Performance requirements

These are measures of performance, some of which are quantitative, and some of which can be used as part of testing. Examples are:

- cost
- delivery date
- response times (e.g. *the system will respond to user requests within one second.*)

- data volumes (e.g. *the system must be able to store information on 10,000 employees.*)
- loading levels to be coped with (e.g. *the system must be able to cope with 100 transactions per minute from the point-of-sale terminals*).
- reliability requirements (e.g. *the system must have a mean time between failure of six months.*)
- security requirements.

Constraints

These are influences on the implementation of a system. An example is:

The system must be written in Java.

Constraints deal with such items as:

- the computer hardware that is to be used
- the amount of memory available
- the amount of backing store available
- the programming language to be used
- interoperability constraints (e.g. the software must run under the latest version of Windows).

Constraints often address implementation (e.g. the specification of the programming language) and therefore should be included with caution. For example, this might be unnecessarily constraining:

The search must use a binary chop method.

Guidelines

A guideline provides useful direction for the implementation in a situation where there may be more than one implementation strategy. For example:

The response times of the system to mouse clicks should be minimized.

Or, as an alternative:

The usage of main memory should be as small as possible.

Many specifications mix up the areas identified above, so that, for example, design guidelines are sometimes confused with functional requirements.

4.7 ● Use cases

One widely used approach to documenting requirements is "use cases". These are textual descriptions which can be augmented by UML use case diagrams. Use cases take the point of view of the user or users of the system. A user who is carrying out a particular role is called an *actor*. A use case is a task that an actor needs the system to carry out.

For example, in the ATM system (Appendix A), one of the things that a user does is withdraw cash. This is a use case. As part of withdrawing cash, the user will have to carry out subtasks, such as offering up their card and entering a PIN, but these smaller tasks are not use cases. It is the overall user task that constitutes a use case.

A use case both specifies what the user does and what the system does, but says nothing about how the system performs its tasks. In the ATM system, the use case for withdrawing cash is:

> **withdraw cash**. *The user offers up their card. The system prompts for the PIN. The user enters the PIN. The system checks the PIN. If the card and PIN are valid, the system prompts the user for their choice of function. The user selects dispense cash. The user prompts for the amount. The user enters the amount. The system ejects the card. When the user has withdrawn the card, the system dispenses the cash.*

We see that the user's task requires a whole number of detailed steps. Sometimes the user's objective is not achieved, for example, if the PIN is wrong. However, the overall name of the use case describes what normally happens.

Other use cases for the ATM are check balance and transfer money.

SELF-TEST QUESTION

4.2 Write a use case for checking a balance.

You will see that sometimes different use cases have parts in common. This is no problem.

In the above example, and in most cases, the actor is a person, but an actor can be anything that interacts with the system. This could be, for example, another software system or another computer communicating across the internet. For example, in a web server (program), the actor is a web browser program running on another computer.

It is sometimes difficult to identify distinct use cases. In the ATM, for example, is entering and validating the PIN a use case? The answer is no because it is not a useful function from the user's point of view, whereas withdrawing cash is. Suppose a person carries out a series of transactions, inserting their card, withdrawing cash, checking their balance and then transferring money. Is this collection a single use case? No, because it constitutes a number of useful user functions.

One way to identify distinct use cases is to identify a goal that an actor wishes to accomplish. Another viewpoint is identifying some outcome of value to the user. The task of correctly entering a PIN is neither a goal nor a valuable outcome. It is only a part of some complete and useful function. It is therefore not a valid use case in itself.

For a large system, there will be many use cases. In order to control complexity, use cases are grouped into *use case packages*. Each package contains a set of related use cases. For example, a word processor has many commands, but the commands are in groups, such as filing, editing text, setting styles and printing.

The set of use cases constitutes the functional specification of a system. This in itself is valuable, but, as we shall see, use cases can also be used to:

■ derive the software structure

■ create test cases

■ help write a user manual

■ predict software cost.

In some approaches to development, such as Agile Methods and the Unified Process (both discussed later in this book), use cases are the driving force behind the development process.

4.8 ● Use case diagrams

We can document use cases, such as those we have met, as a UML use case diagram. Figure 4.1 shows the use case diagram for the ATM. There is a single actor, shown as a stick figure. The name of the role of the user is shown below. Arrows lead from the actor to the use cases, shown as ovals with their function named beneath.

You will see that a use case diagram does not contain the detail associated with a (textual) use case. However, it does give an overall picture of the actors and the use cases. Thus a use case diagram is an informal graphical representation of requirements.

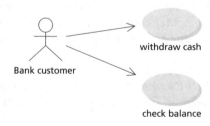

Figure 4.1 Use case diagram for the ATM

Summary

The ideal characteristics of a requirements specification are that it is:

- implementation free
- complete
- consistent
- unambiguous
- concise
- minimal
- understandable
- achievable
- testable.

A number of notations and approaches are available to carry out requirement specification. The notations range from informal (use case diagrams) through semi-formal (e.g. use cases) to formal (mathematics).

A useful checklist for the ingredients of a specification is:

1. functional requirements
2. data requirements
3. performance requirements
4. constraints
5. guidelines.

A major vehicle for describing functional requirements are use cases and UML use case diagrams. A use case is a textual description of a small, but complete user task. A use case diagram shows all the actors and all the use cases for a system.

The main issue with specifications is good communication, both in discussions and in writing.

Exercises

4.1 Appendix A gives specifications for several systems. For each specification identify the functional, data and performance components of the specification. Use the guidelines and checklists given above to rewrite and thereby improve the specification.

4.2 Appendix A gives specifications for several systems. For each specification identify and write the use cases. Draw a use case diagram.

4.3 Appendix A gives specifications for several systems. For each specification identify any problems with the specification, such as ambiguities, inconsistencies and vagueness.

4.4 Group exercise. One way of understanding more clearly the difficulties of carrying out requirements elicitation is to carry out a role-playing exercise. Students can split up into groups of four people, in which two act as users (or clients), while the other two act as software analysts.

The users spend ten minutes in deciding together what they want. Meanwhile the analysts spend the ten minutes deciding how they are going to go about eliciting the requirements from the users.

The users and analysts then spend 15 minutes together, during which the analysts try to elicit requirements. At the end of this period an attempt is made to get all parties to sign the requirements specification.

After the role play is complete, everyone discusses what has been learned from the exercise.

Possible scenarios are the systems already specified in Appendix A.

4.5 Requirements specifications are sometimes very long – they can be as long as a book. Suggest a software tool that could be used (in addition to a word processor) to assist in writing, checking, browsing and maintaining a specification. Consider, for example, using a web browser and including hyperlinks in a specification to promote cross-referencing.

4.6 Who should be consulted when collecting the requirements of a computer-based system to replace an existing information system?

4.7 Who should be consulted when collecting the requirements for a process control system or an embedded system? (It is not immediately obvious who the users of these systems will be.)

4.8 Define the terms completeness and consistency in a specification. How can we achieve them?

4.9 What are the skills required to collect, analyze and record software requirements?

4.10 Explain the difficulties in using natural language for describing requirements.

4.11 Why is requirements engineering so important and why is it so difficult?

Answers to self-test questions

4.1 If something is ambiguous it cannot be clearly understandable. So ambiguity has to be removed to help achieve an understandable specification.

4.2 Check balance. The user offers up their card. The system prompts for the PIN. The user enters the PIN. The system checks the PIN. If the card and PIN are valid, the system prompts the user for their choice of function. The user selects check balance. The system displays the current balance.

● Further reading

A comprehensive and wide-ranging account of requirements analysis and specification is given in: A.M. Davis, *Software Requirements Analysis and Specification*, Prentice Hall, 1990.

The widely used approach called structured analysis is described in: E. Yourdon, *Modern Structured Analysis*, Yourdon Press; Prentice Hall, 1989.

The object-oriented approach is described in: P. Coad and E. Yourdon, *Object-Oriented Analysis*, Yourdon Press; Prentice Hall, 1990.

A wide ranging review of approaches to system development is given in: D.E. Avison and G. Fitzgerald, *Information Systems Development: Methodologies, Techniques and Tools*, Blackwell Scientific Publications, 1988.

A good review of approaches to analyzing and specifying data is: H.F. Korth and Silberschatz, *Database System Concepts*, McGraw-Hill, 1986.

DESIGN

CHAPTER

5

User interface design

This chapter explains:

- the principles, techniques and guidelines for designing a user interface.

5.1 ● Introduction

The interface that the user sees when they use the computer is the single, paramount aspect of the system. The interface is the packaging for software. The user does not know and probably does not care how the system works (provided that it is reliable and fast), but they do care what it does and how to use it. If it is easy to learn, simple to use, straightforward and forgiving, the user will be encouraged to make good use of what's inside. If not, they won't. The user interface is often the yardstick by which a system is judged. Interfaces can be hard to learn, difficult to use, unforgiving and sometimes totally confusing. An interface which is difficult to use will, at best, result in a high level of user errors. At worst, it will cause the software to be discarded, irrespective of its functionality. These are the challenges of user interface design.

User interface design offers the software engineer:

- some principles to guide interface design (e.g. simplicity, learnability)
- some guidelines for good interfaces
- a process for developing good interfaces, based on prototyping
- methods for evaluating interfaces.

Today prototyping (Chapter 23) is considered essential for user interface development – a prototype is made available to users and the resulting feedback used to improve the interface design.

It is common in user interface design to distinguish between principles and guidelines (or rules):

- principles are high level and general. An example of a principle is: maintain consistency throughout the interface.
- guidelines are specific and detailed. An example of a guideline is: black text on a white background is clearer than white text on a black background.

Guidelines are direct, immediate and therefore easy to apply, but principles have to be interpreted and applied to the specific system.

5.2 ● An inter-disciplinary field

User interface design or human–computer interaction (HCI) is very much an inter-disciplinary subject, with contributions from computer science, cognitive psychology, sociology and ergonomics. Cognitive scientists are concerned with how human beings perceive the world, think and behave at an individual level. Sociologists study groups of people and their interactions. Ergonomics is about designing systems that are easy to use. Software engineers must often take responsibility for user interface design as well as the design of the software to implement that interface. These different disciplines bring different perspectives to bear on designing the human–computer interface.

User interface design has as much to do with the study of people as it does with technology. Who is the user? How does the user learn to interact with a new system? How does the user interpret information produced by the system? What will the user expect of the system? These are just a few of the questions that must be answered as part of user interface design. User interface design must take into account the needs, experience and capabilities of the user. It is nowadays considered important that potential users should be involved in the design process.

The different specialisms reflect different views about the interaction between people and computers. At one level it is possible to view HCI as the interaction between one individual and the computer. At this level, the concerns are about such things as the amount of information displayed on the screen and the colors chosen. In the workplace, however, the computer system is often part of the wider context of the work being carried out. Usually, other people are also involved in the work, so that the sociology of the workplace has a role. The questions here may be: Who does what? How can person A and person B communicate most effectively?

5.3 ● Styles of human–computer interface

The manner in which users tell the computer what they want to do has changed dramatically over the last ten years. Broadly, there have been three types of interface: command line, menu and GUI (graphical user interface).

In the early days of computing, the only mode of HCI was the *command line interface*. Communication was purely textual and was driven either via commands or by responses to system-generated queries. If we take as an example the instruction to delete a file, the command to do it typically looks like this:

```
del c:\file.txt
```

where the user has to key in this text (accurately), following a prompt from the system. This type of command is associated with such operating systems as Unix. This kind of interaction is error prone, very unforgiving if an error occurs, and relatively difficult to learn. Clearly, command line interfaces are not suitable for casual and inexperienced users. On the other hand, experienced users often prefer a command line interface.

A development of the command line is the *menu* interface. The user is offered a choice of commands, like this:

```
To delete the file, key D
To display the file, key L
To open a file, key O
To save the file, key S
```

after which the user makes their selection by pressing the appropriate key.

Menu-based systems have several advantages over a command line interface:

- users do not need to remember what is on offer
- users do not need to know command names
- typing effort is minimal
- some kinds of user error are avoided (e.g. invalid menu options can be disabled)
- syntax errors are prevented
- context-dependent help can be provided.

The ATM, specified in Appendix A and designed later in this chapter uses a menu interface. The user uses buttons to select options. Use of a mouse is inappropriate since it is not sufficiently robust for use in open-air, public situations.

Developments in user interfaces have been largely enabled by more sophisticated technology – early computers only had facilities for text input and output, whereas modern computers have high-resolution bit mapped displays and pointing devices. As hardware became more sophisticated, and software engineers learned more about human factors and their impact on interface design, the modern *window-oriented, point and pick* interface evolved – with a GUI or WIMP (windows, icons, menus and pointing devices). Such an interface presents the user with a set of controls or *widgets* (window gadgets), such as buttons, scroll bars and text boxes. Instead of typing an option the user makes a selection using the mouse and mouse button.

The advantages of GUIs include:

- they are relatively easy to learn and use
- the user can use multiple windows for system interaction
- fast, full-screen interaction is possible with immediate access to anywhere on the screen

- different types of information can be displayed simultaneously, enabling the user to switch contexts

- the use of graphical icons, pull-down menus, buttons and scrolling techniques reduce the amount of typing.

One way of helping to achieve interface consistency is to define a consistent model or metaphor for user–computer interaction, which is analogous to some real world domain that the user understands. A *direct manipulation* interface presents users with a visual model of their information space. The best known of these is the *desktop metaphor*, familiar to users of Microsoft and Apple Macintosh operating systems. Another example is a WYSIWYG (what you see is what you get) word processor.

While there is a massive trend towards multitasking, window-oriented, point and pick interfaces which can make HCI easier, this only happens if careful design of the interface is conducted. Using a GUI is, in itself, no guarantee of a good interface.

5.4 ● Different perspectives on user interface design

In designing a user interface it is as well to realize that there are several potentially different viewpoints. The perspectives are:

- the end-user who will eventually get to use the software
- different end-users with different personalities
- the novice or occasional user
- the experienced or power user
- users with different types of skill
- the software developer who designs and implements the system.

Most people do not apply any formal reasoning when confronted with a problem, such as understanding what a computer is displaying. Rather, they apply a set of guidelines, rules and strategies based on their understanding of similar problems. These are called heuristics. These heuristics tend to be domain specific – an identical problem, encountered in entirely different contexts, might be solved by applying different heuristics. A user interface should be developed in a manner that enables the human to develop heuristics for interaction.

The problem is that different people often have different perspectives of the user interface; they also have different skills, culture and personalities. Each person has some model of how the system works and what it does. These different perspectives are sometimes called *mental models*.

An interface used by two individuals with the same education and background but entirely different personalities may seem friendly to one and unfriendly to the other. Therefore, the ideal user interface would be designed to accommodate differences in personality, or, alternatively, would be designed to accommodate a typical personality among a class of end users. A third possibility is to create an interface that is flexible and can be used in different ways according to personality differences.

A novice user or an occasional user is not likely to remember much about how to use the system. Thus a direct manipulation interface may be the most suitable approach. But an experienced and frequent user may be frustrated by an interface designed for novices and may prefer shortcut commands and/or a command line interface. For example, a number of applications provide a *macro facility*, in which a series of commands can be grouped together, parameterized and invoked as a single command. Again the need for flexibility in the interface becomes apparent.

The skill level of the end user has a significant impact on the ability to extract meaningful information from the user interface, respond efficiently to tasks that are demanded by the interaction, and effectively apply heuristics that create a rhythm of interaction. It seems that context- or domain-specific knowledge is more important than overall education or intelligence. For example, an engineer who uses a computer-based diagnostic system to find faults in automobiles understands the problem domain and can interact effectively through an interface specifically designed to accommodate users with an engineer's background. This same interface might confuse a physician, even though the physician has considerable experience of using a computer for diagnosing illnesses in patients.

The software developer may unconsciously incorporate into the user interface some assumptions about the implementation that are irrelevant or even confusing for the users. Consider a word processor, for example. What the user wants is to create and edit documents, and they know that documents reside in files on a disk. The user probably understands the concept of opening a file, because this is a familiar concept in using manual files, but the idea of saving a file may well be completely mysterious to them. The reason is that the concept of saving a file derives from the developer's mental model of how a word processor works, that is, it keeps all or part of the document in main memory. This example illustrates how the designer can get it wrong and therefore the importance of the involvement of the user in design.

In conclusion, there are a number of different viewpoints taken by the users and developers of a user interface. There is scope for either conflict or harmony between these views. Conflict between the users' perception and the developers' concepts can make for a system that is difficult to use, but involving the users in the design can assist in recognizing users' views, and flexibility in the interface can help cater for different users.

5.5 ● Design principles and guidelines

Design principles are high-level principles that can guide the design of a user interface. Three overall principles are:

- learnability – how easily can new users learn to use the system?
- flexibility – does the interface support a variety of interaction styles? (We have already seen why this is an important consideration.)
- robustness – how much feedback does the system give the user to confirm what is going on?

Each of these qualities can be specified in greater detail as follows:
Learnability involves:

■ predictability – is the effect of any of the user actions predictable? A user should never be surprised by the behavior of a system.

■ synthesizability – can the user see the effect of their actions? A counter-example of this characteristic is some Unix commands, which give the user no information or even a confirmation of what they have accomplished.

■ familiarity – are the facilities familiar to the user from their previous experience? The interface should use terms and concepts which are drawn from the anticipated class of user. This attribute will clearly be more easily achieved with an direct manipulation interface.

■ generalizability – can the user safely assume that the same operation in different circumstances gives the same outcome? For example, does clicking the mouse button on a folder icon have the same effect as clicking on a file icon?

■ consistency – are comparable operations activated in the same way? For example, in a word processor, is the selection of a single character, a word, a line or a paragraph achieved in a consistent manner?

Flexibility involves:

■ user initiative – can the user initiate any valid task whenever they desire? This is an issue of who is in control, the user or the machine.

■ multi-threading – can several tasks be carried out concurrently? For example, carrying out text editing while printing is in progress?

■ task migratability – can particular tasks be undertaken either by the user or the system, or some combination of the two? For example, some e-mail systems provide for automatic response to e-mail while the user is on vacation.

■ substitutivity – can a facility be used in different ways? For example, selecting font size either from a menu or by typing font size explicitly.

■ customizability – can the user change the user interface? For example, hiding an unwanted tool bar, adding macros or scripts.

Robustness involves:

■ observability – does the system display information that allows the user fully to know what is going on? Again, this attribute will clearly be more easily achieved with a direct manipulation interface.

■ recoverability – does the system allow the user to recover from an unintended situation? For example, the provision of an undo button can help rectify certain user mistakes.

■ responsiveness – does the system respond in a reasonable time? Response time has two characteristics, length and variability. Variability refers to the deviation from average response time, and is in some ways more important than length, because it can affect the user's rhythm. So it is sometimes better to have equal length response times (even if they are long) in preference to response times that are unpredictable.

■ task conformance – does the system do everything that the user needs to do? Is some facility missing?

It should be emphasized that this list of principles, useful though it is, constitutes just one of several possible categorizations of desirable attributes. Alternative factors that might be considered equally important include user error prevention, minimizing the user's memory requirements and maximizing productivity.

Principles like these are distilled from practical experience, controlled experiments and an understanding of human psychology and perception. They serve as goals to aim for during development. They can also act as quality factors (see Chapter 29 on metrics and quality assurance) that can be used to assess the quality of a completed design. For example, if recoverability is important for a particular application, an assessment of this quality can be made in order to evaluate the success of the product.

Let us see how a principle, such as those above, differs from a guideline. The principle of task conformance, for example, tells us what to look for, what to aim for, but not how to achieve it – and it can sometimes be difficult to identify something that is missing. By contrast, a guideline, such as "black text on a white background is easier to read than the opposite", is immediately useful and applicable.

The drawback of principles is that they are not immediately applicable, but have to be interpreted and applied (as with real life principles). The last example of a principle, task conformance, illustrates a major problem with using these principles for user interface design – it is not always obvious how or when to use them. The designer could post the principles up above their desk so that they can see them and use them while they carry out design, but there is no explicit way of using the principles as part of a well-defined design methodology. Thus they are more akin to goals than principles.

Design guidelines or rules give the designer more detailed and specific advice during the process of designing an interface. There are many long lists of guidelines in the literature and we give here only a sample of typical guidelines. If you were asked to design an interface for an application running under Microsoft Windows, for example, you would be provided with a comprehensive manual of guidelines specific to the look and feel of Windows applications. Among the many guidelines this would stipulate, for example, that the icon to close an application must be displayed at the top right of the window as a cross. Using guidelines such as these promotes the principle of consistency mentioned above.

Here, for illustration, are some examples of guidelines for designing GUI interfaces:

■ ask the user for confirmation of any non-trivial destructive action (e.g. deleting a file)

■ reduce the amount of information that must be memorized in between actions

■ minimize the number of input actions required of the user, e.g. reduce the amount of typing and mouse travel that is required

■ categorize activities by function and group related controls together

■ deactivate commands that are inappropriate in the context of current actions

- display only the information that is relevant to the current context
- use a presentation format that enables rapid assimilation of information, e.g. graphs and charts to present trends
- use upper and lower case, indentation and text grouping to aid understanding
- use windows to compartmentalize different types of activity
- consider the available geography of the display screen and use it efficiently
- use color sparingly. (Designers should take account of the fact that a significant number of people are color-blind.)

These guidelines are more detailed and specific than the rather more generalized principles given earlier.

SELF-TEST QUESTION

5.1   Distinguish between user interface design guidelines and principles.

5.6 ● Interface design

The process for designing a user interface begins with the analysis of the tasks that the user needs to carry out. The human- and computer-oriented tasks are then delineated, general design principles and guidelines are considered, tools are used to prototype a system, and the result is evaluated for quality. The prototype is then refined repeatedly until it is judged satisfactory. This can be visualized as shown in Figure 5.1.

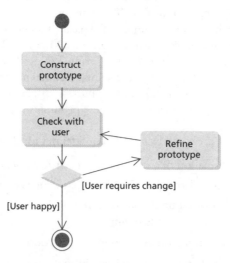

Figure 5.1 Using prototyping in user interface design

In Chapter 2 we identified requirements analysis as an important early part of any software development project. The process of user interface design, described above, is similar to the requirements analysis phase. In interface design, the user of a system plays a central role and thus user evaluation of prototypes is probably essential.

SELF-TEST QUESTION

5.2   What problems can you see with this approach to design?

Once a user interface prototype has been created, it is evaluated to determine whether it meets the needs of the user. Evaluation can range from an informal test drive to formally designed studies that use statistical methods for the evaluation of questionnaires completed by a population of end users.

The evaluation cycle proceeds as follows. After a preliminary design has been completed, a first prototype is created. The prototype is evaluated by the user or users, who provide the designer with comments about the efficacy of the interface. Design modifications based on the user comments are then made and the next prototype is created. The cycle continues until no further modifications to the interface design are necessary.

A user interface evaluation is concerned with assessing the usability of the interface and checking that it meets user requirements. Ideally, an evaluation is conducted against a usability specification – the specification of a system should include, wherever possible, quantitative values for usability attributes. Possible usability attributes are:

- learnability – the time taken to achieve a specified level of performance
- throughput – the speed at which the user can carry out tasks
- robustness when confronted with user errors
- recoverability from user errors
- adaptability – the extent to which the system can accommodate tasks that were not envisaged during design

Metrics for each of these usability attributes can be devised. For example, a learnability metric might state "a user who is familiar with the work supported by the system will be able to use 80% of the system functionality after a three-hour training session". A recoverability metric might state that "a user who is familiar with the computer system will be able to recover from an error that they made in less than two seconds".

There are a number of techniques for user interface evaluation. Some involve directly monitoring users as they use the system. There are several techniques:

- observation – someone watches users as they use the system
- video recording – users are video recorded as they use the system
- software monitoring – monitoring software is included to collect information as the system is used
- verbalizing – the user speaks aloud as they use the system, relating what they are doing and what they are thinking.

Most large software development organizations maintain dedicated usability laboratories in which numbers of users are monitored while using prototypes of software products under development.

An alternative approach is to use questionnaires or rating sheets to elicit views after people have used the system. Questions may ask for:

■ a simple yes or no response. For example, "Is the clear button easy to use?"

■ a numerical score on a scale of, say 1 to 10. For example, "How easy is the clear button to use?"

If desired the designer can extract quantitative feedback from this information, for example, "70% of users found the clear button easy to use."

5.7 ● Case study

As an example we will look at the development of the ATM software specified in Appendix A. We start with the specification, which describes the functions that the ATM must carry out when requested by a bank customer. These functions are to withdraw cash and display a balance. The specification also tells us that part of the dialog with the user is the entry of a PIN and its authentication.

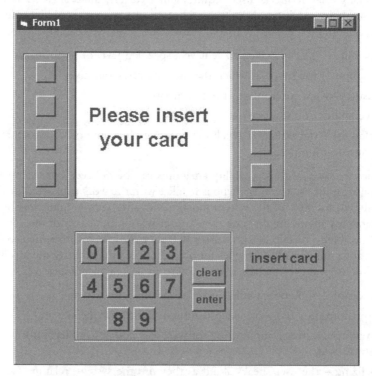

Figure 5.2 Simulated ATM user interface

Our plan is to use prototyping to design the user interface. We assume that a decision has been taken to provide a screen that displays characters, a keyboard (with numeric keys, a cancel key and an enter key), a card reader, a printer and a cash dispenser.

We assume that the system is for occasional untrained users rather than experts. We should also realize that some users will be visually impaired and/or have difficulty pressing keys.

We begin by roughly sketching an interface on paper. In constructing this first prototype we note a list of guidelines. For example, in order to minimize overloading the user with information, we design a number of screens. We can then easily translate this into a simulated ATM using Visual Basic (or similar). One possible design is shown in Figure 5.2. This prototype user interface does everything a real system would do except read a card, dispense cash and print statements.

We now show several users the proposed interface. As they use the system, we observe them, noting their difficulties, frustrations and annoyances.

5.8 ● Help systems

Help systems are just one aspect of user guidance, which deals with three areas:

1. the messages produced by the system in response to user actions
2. the on-line help system
3. the documentation provided with the system.

The design of useful and clear information for users should be taken seriously and should be subject to the same quality process as designs or programs.

Here are some guidelines for error messages. Error messages should always be polite, concise, consistent and constructive. They must not be abusive and should not have associated beeps or other noises which might embarrass the user. Error messages should:

- describe the problem in jargon the user can understand
- provide constructive advice for recovering from the error
- spell out any negative consequences of the error
- be accompanied by a visual cue
- not blame the user.

Help facilities may be either *integrated* or *add-on*. An integrated help facility is designed into the software from the beginning. It is usually context-sensitive, providing information relevant to what the user is doing. An add-on help facility is added to the software after the system has been built. It is often merely an on-line manual with query capability. A number of design issues should be considered when a help facility is considered:

- will help be available for all system functions at all times?
- how will the user request help – help menu, function key, HELP command?

- how will help be represented – separate window, reference to printed document, one-line suggestion in a fixed screen location?
- how will the user return to normal interaction – return button, function key, control sequence?
- how will the information be structured – flat, layered, hypertext?

Summary

There are a number of different views of the user interface – the software engineer's, the user's, the psychologist's, the sociologist's.

A number of design guidelines and principles are available to assist in user interface design.

Prototyping is currently the most effective method for user interface design. It means repeated evaluation of an interface until it meets usability standards

A set of guidelines is available to assist in the design of help systems.

● Exercises

5.1   Identify a set of functions that might be provided by a word processor (Appendix A). Design an interface. Suggest how the interface could be evaluated.

5.2   Design a user interface for a desk calculator. It must include at least one display to show the number currently being used. It must have buttons for the functions provided. These include a button for each of the digit buttons and buttons for the common arithmetic operations. It should also have a clear button and an undo button. Use the guidelines and principles from the text during the design, construct a prototype and carry out an evaluation of the design.

5.3   Design a user interface for a website that allows the user to browse a catalog of books and choose to buy selected books by entering a credit card number, a name and address.

5.4   Perhaps the most notorious example of a poor user interface is the VCR. Design a user interface for programming a VCR to record one or more television programs using a remote control device. Assume that the television can be used as a display device during programming.

5.5 Design a user interface for a mobile phone. Design suitable buttons and assume that a small display is available as part of the phone. Make assumptions about the tasks that users of the phone want to carry out. Suggest criteria for evaluating your design and suggest how the design could be evaluated (and thereby improved).

5.6 Suggest features for a web browser. Design a user interface for the browser. Suggest how the interface of the browser could be evaluated.

5.7 "User interface design is in its infancy." Discuss.

5.8 "User interface design methods are little more than a set of guidelines. There is no proper methodology for user interface design." Discuss.

5.9 Suggest features for a toolkit to assist in the development of graphical user interfaces.

5.10 Assess the strengths and weaknesses of user interface design methods.

5.11 Suggest a future for user interface devices and methods.

Answers to self-test questions

5.1 A principle is general, abstract; a guideline is specific, concrete and applicable.

5.2 Who is the user? How many users do you involve? How many times should you go round the loop?

Further reading

Wilbert O. Galitz, *The Essential Guide to User Interface Design*, John Wiley, 2nd edn, 2002.

Susan Weinschenk, Pamela Jamar and Sarah C. Yeo, *GUI Design Essentials*, John Wiley, 1997.

This book by one of the gurus gives good accounts of guidelines for user interface design: B. Schneiderman, *Designing the User Interface: Strategies for Effective Human–Computer Interaction*, Addison-Wesley, 2nd edn, 1998.

A widely used and liked textbook on the subject is: Alan Dix, Janet Findlay, Gregory Abowd and Russell Beale, *Human–Computer Interaction*, Prentice Hall, 2nd edn, 1998.

Another popular textbook book is wide-ranging, readable and comprehensive. It presents the views of a variety of people from different disciplines: Jenny Preece *et al.*, *Human–Computer Interaction*, Addison-Wesley, 1994.

Some light reading, guidelines and practical advice on designing GUI interfaces from the creator of Visual Basic: Alan Cooper, *About Face: The Essentials of User Interface Design*, IDG Books, 2003.

Alan Cooper has also written this valuable book: *The Inmates Are Running the Asylum: Why High Tech Products Drive Us Crazy and How To Restore The Sanity*, Sams, 1999.

Well worth a read, an oldie but a goodie is: Donald Norman, *The Psychology of Everyday Things*, Perseus Books, 1988.

This book shows how to implement GUIs using statecharts: Ian Horrocks, *Constructing the User Interface with Statecharts*, Addison-Wesley, 1999.

CHAPTER

6

Modularity

6.1 ● Introduction

Modularity is one of the key issues in software design. Modularity is to do with the structure of software. This structure is the end product of all of the major current design methods, such as functional decomposition, object-oriented design and data structure design. A perfect design is the almost unobtainable Holy Grail.

If we were asked to design an automobile, we would probably design it in terms of several subsystems – engine, transmission, brakes, chassis, etc. Let us call these subsystems components. In identifying these particular components for an automobile, we have selected items that are as independent of each other as possible. This is the essence of good modularity.

The guidelines we shall describe in this chapter help to answer questions like:

- how big should a component be?
- is this component too complex?
- how can we minimize interactions between components?

Before we embark on these questions, we should identify what a "component" is. Usually this is dictated by practical considerations, such as the facilities provided in the available programming language and operating system.

Java is a typical modern language. At the finest level of granularity, a number of statements and variable declarations can be placed in a method. A set of methods can be grouped together, along with some shared variables, into a class. A number of classes can be grouped into a package. Thus a component is a fairly independent piece of program that has a name, some instructions and some data of its own. A component is used, or called, by some other component and, similarly, uses (calls) other components.

There is a variety of mechanisms for splitting software into independent components, or, expressed another way, grouping together items that have some mutual affinity. In various programming languages, a component is:

■ a method

■ a class

■ a package.

In this chapter we use the term component in the most general way to encompass any current or future mechanism for dividing software into manageable portions.

6.2 ● Why modularity?

The scenario is software that consists of thousands or even hundreds of thousands of lines of code. The complexity of such systems can easily be overwhelming. Some means of coping with the complexity are essential. In essence, the desire for modularity is about trying to construct software from pieces that are as independent of each other as possible. Ideally, each component should be self-contained and have as few references as possible to other components. This aim has consequences for nearly all stages of software development, as follows.

Architectural design

This is the step during which the large-scale structure of software is determined. It is therefore critical for creating good modularity. A design approach that leads to poor modularity will lead to dire consequences later on.

Component design

If the architectural design is modular, then the design of individual components will be easy. Each component will have a single well-defined purpose, with few, clear connections with other components.

Debugging

It is during debugging that modularity comes into its own. If the structure is modular, it should be easier to identify which particular component is responsible for the observed fault. Similarly, the correction to a single component should not produce "knock-on" effects, provided that the interfaces to and from the component are not affected.

Testing

Testing a large system made up of a large number of components is a difficult and time-consuming task. It is virtually impossible to test an individual component in detail once it has been integrated into the system. Therefore testing is carried out in a piecemeal fashion – one component at a time (see Chapter 19 on testing). Thus the structure of the system is crucial.

Maintenance

This means fixing bugs and enhancing a system to meet changed user needs. This activity consumes enormous amounts of software developers' time. Again, modularity is crucial. The ideal would be to make a change to a single component with total confidence that no other components will be affected. However, too often it happens that obvious or subtle interconnections between components make the process of maintenance a nightmare.

Independent development

Most software is implemented by a team of people, often over months or years. Normally each component is developed by a single person. It is therefore vital that interfaces between components are clear and few.

Damage control

When an error occurs in a component, the spread of damage to other components will be minimized if it has limited connections with other components.

Software reuse

A major software engineering technique is to reuse software components from a library or from an earlier project. This avoids reinventing the wheel, and can save enormous effort. Furthermore, reusable components are usually thoroughly tested. It has long been a dream of software engineers to select and use useful components, just as an electronic engineer consults a catalog and selects ready-made, tried-and-tested electronic components.

However, a component cannot easily be reused if it is connected in some complex way to other components in an existing system. A heart transplant from one human being to another would be impossible if there were too many arteries, veins and nerves to be severed and reconnected.

There are therefore three requirements for a reuseable component:

- it provides a useful service
- it performs a single function
- it has the minimum of connections (ideally no connections) to other components.

6.3 ● Component types

Components can be classified according to their roles:

- computation-only
- memory
- manager
- controller
- link.

A computation-only component retains no data between subsequent uses. Examples are a math method or a filter in a Unix filter and pipe scheme.

A memory component maintains a collection of persistent data, such as a database or a file system. (Persistent data is data that exists beyond the life of a particular program or component and is normally stored on a backing store medium, such as disk.)

A manager component is an abstract data type, maintaining data and the operations that can be used on it. The classical examples are a stack or a queue.

A controller component controls when other components are activated or how they interact.

A link component transfers information between other components. Examples are a user interface (which transfers information between the user of a system and one or more components) and network software.

This is a crude and general classification, but it does provide a language for talking about components.

6.4 ● Component size and complexity

How big should a software component be? Consider any piece of software. It can always be constructed in two radically different ways – once with small components and again with large components. As an illustration, Figure 6.1 shows two alternative structures for the same software. One consists of many small components; the other a few large components.

If the components are large, there will only be a few of them, and therefore there will tend to be only a few connections between them. We have a structure which is a network with few branches and a few very big leaves. The complexity of the interconnections is minimal, but the complexity of each component is high.

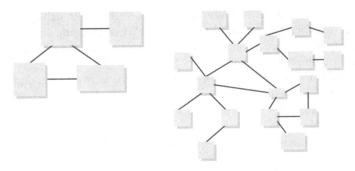

Figure 6.1 Two alternative software structures

If the components are small, there will be many components and therefore many connections between them in total. The structure is a network with many branches and many small leaves. The smaller the components, the easier an individual component should be to comprehend. But if the components are small, we run the risk of being overwhelmed by the proliferation of interconnections between them.

The question is: Which of the two structures is the better? The alternatives are large components with few connections, or small components with many connections. However, as we shall see, the dilemma is not usually as simple as this.

A common point of view is that a component should occupy no more than a page of coding (about 40–50 lines). This suggestion takes account of the difficulty of under-standing logic that spills over from one page of listing (or one screen) to another.

A more extreme view is that a component should normally take up about seven lines or less of code, and in no circumstances more than nine. Arguments for the "magic number" seven are based on experimental results from psychology. Research indicates that the human brain is capable of comprehending only about seven things (or con-cepts) at once. This does not mean that we can remember only seven things; clearly we can remember many more. But we can only retain in short-term memory and study as a complete, related set of objects, a few things. The number of objects ranges from about five to nine, depending on the individual and the objects under study. The implication is that if we wish to understand completely a piece of code, it should be no more than about seven statements in length. Relating lines of code to concepts may be oversimpli-fying the psychological basis for these ideas, but the analogy can be helpful. We shall pursue this further later in the chapter.

Clearly a count of the number of lines is too crude a measure of the size of a com-ponent. A seven-line component containing several `if` statements is more complex than seven ordinary statements. The next section pursues this question.

We have already met an objection to the idea of having only a few statements in a component. By having a few statements we are only increasing the number of compo-nents. So all we are doing is to decrease complexity in one way (the number of state-ments in a component) at the cost of increased complexity in another way (the number of components). So we gain nothing overall.

Do we need a few, large components or many small components? The answer is that we need both. We pose the question of how a piece of software is examined. Studying a program is necessary during architectural design, verification, debugging and maintenance, and it is therefore an important activity. When studying software we cannot look at the whole software at once because (for software of any practical length) it is too complex to comprehend as a whole.

When we need to understand the overall structure of software (e.g. during design or during maintenance), we need large components. On other occasions (e.g. debugging) we need to focus attention on an individual component. For this purpose a small component is preferable. If the software has been well designed, we can study the logic of an individual component in isolation from any others. However, as part of the task of studying a component we need to know something about any components it uses. For this purpose the power of abstraction is useful, so that while we understand *what* other components do, we do not need to understand *how* they do it. Therefore, ideally, we never need to comprehend more than one component at a time. When we have completed an examination of one component, we turn our attention to another. Therefore, we conclude, it is the size and complexity of individual components and their connections with other components that is important.

This discussion assumes that the software has been well constructed. This means that abstraction can be applied in understanding an individual component. However, if the function of a component is not obvious from its outward appearance, then we need to delve into it in order to understand what it does. Similarly, if the component is closely connected to other components, it will be difficult to understand in isolation. We discuss these issues later.

Small components can give rise to slower programs because of the increased overhead of method calls. But nowadays a programmer's time can cost significantly more than a computer's time. The question here is whether it is more important for a program to be easy to understand or whether it is more important for it to run quickly. These requirements may well conflict and only individual circumstances can resolve the issue. It may well be better, however, first to design, code and test a piece of software using small components, and then, if performance is important, particular methods that are called frequently can be rewritten in the bodies of those components that use them. It is, however, unlikely that method calls will adversely affect the performance of a program. Similarly, it is unlikely that encoding methods in-line will give rise to significant improvement. Rather, studies have shown that programs spend most of their time (about 50%) executing a small fraction (about 10%) of the code. It is the optimization of these small parts that will give rise to the best results.

In the early days of programming, main memory was small and processors were slow. It was considered normal to try hard to make programs efficient. One effect of this was that programmers often used tricks. Nowadays the situation is rather different – the pressure is on to reduce the development time of programs and ease the burden of maintenance. So the emphasis is on writing programs that are clear and simple, and therefore easy to check, understand and modify.

What are the arguments for simplicity?

■ it is quicker to debug a simple program
■ it is quicker to test a simple program

- a simple program is more likely to be reliable
- it is quicker to modify a simple program.

If we look at the world of design engineering, a good engineer insists on maintaining a complete understanding and control over every aspect of the project. The more difficult the project the more firmly the insistence on simplicity – without it no one can understand what is going on. Software designers and programmers have frequently been accused of exhibiting the exact opposite characteristic: they deliberately avoid simple solutions and gain satisfaction from the complexities of their designs. Perhaps programmers should try to emulate the approach of traditional engineers.

Many software designers and programmers today strive to make their software as clear and simple as possible. A programmer finishes a program and is satisfied that it both works correctly and is clearly written. But how do we know that it is clear? Is a shorter program necessarily simpler than a longer one (that achieves the same end), or is a heavily nested program simpler than an equivalent program without nesting? People tend to hold strong opinions on questions like these; hard evidence and objective argument are rare.

Arguably, what we perceive as clarity or complexity is an issue for psychology. It is concerned with how the brain works. We cannot establish a measure of complexity – for example, the number of statements in a program – without investigating how such a measure corresponds with programmers' perceptions and experiences.

6.5 ● Global data is harmful

Just as the infamous `goto` statement was discredited in the 1960s, so later ideas of software engineering came to regard global data as harmful. Before we discuss the arguments, let us define some terms. By *global data* we mean data that can be widely used throughout a piece of software and is accessible to a number of components in the system. By the term *local data*, we mean data that can only be used within a specific component; access is closely controlled.

For any particular piece of software, the designer has the choice of making data global or local. If the decision is made to use local data, data can, of course, be shared by passing it around the program as parameters.

Here is the argument against global data. Suppose that three components named A, B and C access some global data as shown in Figure 6.2. Suppose that we have to study component A in order, say, to make a change to it. Suppose that components A and B both access a piece of global data named X. Then, in order to understand A we have to understand the role of X. But now, in order to understand X we have to examine B. So we end up having to study a second component (B) when we only wanted to understand one. But the story gets worse. Suppose that components B and C share data. Then fully to understand B we have to understand C. Therefore, in order to understand component A, we have to understand not only component B but also component C. We see that in order to comprehend *any* component that uses global data we have to understand *all* the components that use it.

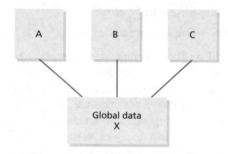

Figure 6.2 Global data

In general, local data is preferable because:

- it is easier to study an individual component because it is clear what data the component is using
- it is easier to remove a component to use in a new program, because it is a self-contained package.
- the global data (if any) is easier to read and understand, because it has been reduced in size.

So, in general, the amount of global data should be minimized (or preferably abolished) and the local data maximized. Nowadays most programming languages provide good support for local data and some do not allow global data at all.

Most modern programming languages provide a facility to group methods and data into a component (called variously a component, class or package). Within such a component, the methods access the shared data, which is therefore global. But this data is only global within the component.

6.6 ● Information hiding

Information hiding, data hiding or *encapsulation* is an approach to structuring software in a highly modular fashion. The idea is that for each data structure (or file structure), all of the following:

- the structure itself
- the statements that access the structure
- the statements that modify the structure

are part of just a single component. A piece of data encapsulated like this cannot be accessed directly. It can only be accessed via one of the methods associated with the data. Such a collection of data and methods is called an abstract data type, or (in object-oriented programming) a class or an object.

The classic illustration of the use of information hiding is the stack. Methods are provided to initialize the stack, to push an item onto the stack top and to pop an item from the top. (Optionally, a method is provided in order to test whether the stack is empty.) Access to the stack is only via these methods. Given this specification, the implementer of the stack has freedom to store it as an array, a linked list or whatever. The user of the stack need neither know, nor care, how the stack is implemented. Any change to the representation of the stack has no effect on the users (apart, perhaps, from its performance).

Information hiding meets three aims:

1. Changeability

If a design decision is changed, such as a file structure, changes are confined to as few components as possible and, preferably, to just a single component.

2. Independent development

When a system is being implemented by a team of programmers, the interfaces between the components should be as simple as possible. Information hiding means that the interfaces are calls on methods which are arguably simpler than accesses to shared data or file structures.

3. Comprehensibility

For the purposes of design, checking, testing and maintenance it is vital to understand individual components independently of others. As we have seen, global and shared data weaken our ability to understand software. Information hiding simply eliminates this problem.

Some programming languages (Ada, C++, Modula 2, Java, C#, Visual Basic .Net) support information hiding by preventing any references to a component other than calls to those methods declared to be public. (The programmer is also allowed to declare data as publicly accessible, but this facility is only used in special circumstances because it subverts information hiding.) Clearly the facilities of the programming language can greatly help structuring software according to information hiding.

In summary, the principle of information hiding means that, at the end of the design process, any data structure or file is accessed only via certain well-defined, specific methods. Some programming languages support information hiding, while others do not. The principle of information hiding has become a major concept in program design and software engineering. It has not only affected programming languages (see Chapter 15), but led to distinctive views of programming (see below) and design (see Chapter 11).

In object-oriented programming, data and actions that are strongly related are grouped together into entities called objects. Normally access to data is permitted only via particular methods. Thus information hiding is implemented and supported by the programming language. Global data is entirely eliminated.

6.7 ● Coupling and cohesion

The ideas of coupling and cohesion are a terminology and a classification scheme for describing the interactions between components and within components. Ideally, a piece of software should be constructed from components in such a way that there is a minimum of interaction between components (low coupling) and, conversely, a high degree of interaction within a component (high cohesion). We have already discussed the benefits that good modularity brings.

The diagrams in Figure 6.3 illustrate the ideas of coupling and cohesion. The diagrams show the same piece of software but designed in two different ways. Both structures consist of four components. Both structures involve 20 interactions (method calls or accesses to data items). In the left-hand diagram there are many interactions between components, but comparatively few within components. In contrast, in the right-hand diagram, there are few interactions between components and many interactions within components. The left-hand program has strong coupling and weak cohesion. The right-hand program has weak coupling and strong cohesion.

Coupling and cohesion are opposite sides of the same coin, in that strong cohesion will tend to create weak coupling, and vice versa.

The ideas of coupling and cohesion were suggested in the 1970s by Yourdon and Constantine. They date from a time when most programming languages allowed the programmer much more freedom than modern languages permit. Thus the programmer had enormous power, but equally had the freedom to write code that would nowadays be considered dangerous. In spite of their age, the terminology of coupling and cohesion is still very much alive and is widely used to describe interactions between software components.

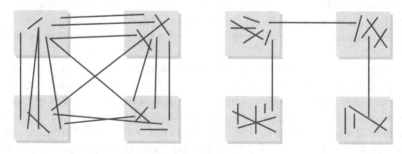

Figure 6.3 Coupling and cohesion in two software systems

6.8 ● Coupling

We are familiar with the idea of one component making a method call on another, but what other types of interaction (coupling) are there between components? Which types are good and which bad?

First, an important aspect of the interaction between components is its "size". The fewer the number of elements that connect components, the better. If components share common data, it should be minimized. Few parameters should be passed between components in method calls. It has been suggested that no more than about 2–4 parameters should be used. Deceit should not be practiced by grouping together several parameters into a record and then using the record as a single parameter.

What about the *nature* of the interaction between components? We can distinguish the following ways in which components interact. They are listed in an order that goes from strongly coupled (least desirable) to weakly coupled (most desirable):

1. altering another component's code
2. branching to or calling a place other than at the normal entry point
3. accessing data within another component
4. shared or global data
5. method call with a switch as a parameter
6. method call with pure data parameters
7. passing a serial data stream from one component to another.

We now examine each of these in turn.

1. Altering another component's code

This is a rather weird type of interaction and the only programming language that normally allows it is assembler. However, in Cobol the **alter** statement allows a program to essentially modify its own code. The problem with this form of interaction is that a bug in one component, the modifying component, appears as a symptom in another, the one being modified.

2. Entering at the side door

In this type of interaction, one component calls or branches to another at a place other than the normal entry point of the component. Again, this is impossible in most languages, except assembler, Cobol and early versions of Basic.

The objection to this type of interaction is part of the argument for structured programming. It is only by using components that have a single entry (at the start) and one exit (at the end) that we can use the power of abstraction to design and understand large programs.

3. Modifying data within another component

Allowing one component to alter another component's data seems rather less harmful than changing another component's code. However, the objection is the same and the coupling is strong because a fault that appears in one component may be caused by another.

4. Shared or global data

Shared data is data that two or more components have access to. The data is in a distinct component. Global data means a collection of data that is accessible to a large number of, perhaps all, components. The facility to access data in this way is present in nearly all widely used programming languages.

We have already seen why this is undesirable.

SELF-TEST QUESTION

6.1   Give one reason why global data is undesirable.

---

5. A method call with a parameter that is a switch

We have seen that both shared data and unusual transfers of control result in strong coupling between components. The solution is, of course, to use method calls with their attendant parameters. Even so, it is possible to worsen the coupling by passing as a parameter not pure data but an element of control. An example is where a component is passed an indicator telling the method which action to take from among a number of available actions. (This indicator is sometimes called a switch.) Here is an example of a method call on a general-purpose input-output method:

```
inputOutput(command, device, buffer, length);
```

The parameter `command` has values 0, 1, 2, etc. that specify whether the operation is a read, write, open, etc. This is undesirable simply because it is unnecessarily complicated. This method can be divided into several methods – each carrying out a single action. As an alternative to calling a single method and passing it a switch, we can instead call the individual appropriate method, like this:

```
read(device, buffer, length);
```

We have eliminated a parameter from the interaction and at the same time created well-defined methods, each with a specific function. This contrasts with a single, multi-purpose method. Arguably this modularization is easier to understand and maintain.

6. Method calls with parameters that are pure data

Here we have a form of coupling that is nearly ideal. The components interact in a well-defined manner, suffering none of the weaknesses discussed in the schemes described above. In particular, it is quite clear what information is being communicated between components. Remember, though, that for weak coupling the number of parameters should be few.

7. Passing a serial data stream

The weakest (best) coupling is achieved without any transfer of control between components. This is where one component passes a serial stream of data to another. We can visualize this by imagining that one component outputs information as if to a serial file, and the second component reads it, again as if from a file. The important feature is that the outputting component has no access to the data once it has released it.

This type of interaction is available in some programming languages and most operating systems. Within the Java library, the classes **java.io.PipedInputStream** and **java.io.PipedOutputStream** allow a producer object (data source) to send a serial stream of data to a consumer object (data sink). Ada allows software to be constructed from concurrent tasks that communicate by message passing. In the Unix system, programs called filters communicate via pipes, which again are serial data streams.

Conclusion

The conclusion from this review of the types of coupling is that the weakest (best) coupling is to be achieved by using components that communicate by either

- method calls with a small number of data parameters
- passing a serial stream of data from one to the other.

6.9 ● Cohesion

Cohesion is about unity. How do we group actions together in the best way? Cohesion describes the nature of the interactions *within* a method. A scheme has been drawn up for classifying the various types of cohesion. These range from low cohesion (undesirable) at the top of the list to high cohesion (desirable) at the bottom. Some of these types of cohesion are now only of historical interest; current design methods ensure that they just don't arise. The list of categories is:

1. coincidental
2. logical
3. temporal

4. communicational
5. functional.

We will now look in turn at each of the different types of cohesion. In each case our analysis will be based on a statement of what a method will do. We will see that if a method does a mixture of things, then it has poor cohesion. On the other hand, if a method carries out one specific action, then it has good cohesion.

1. Coincidental cohesion

In coincidental cohesion the elements are in the method purely by coincidence. There is no relationship between the elements; their coexistence is purely arbitrary. This type of modularity would arise if someone had taken, say, an existing method and arbitrarily chopped it up into methods each of one page in length. It would then be impossible to write down a meaningful statement of what each method accomplishes.

2. Logical cohesion

In logical cohesion the method performs a set of logically similar functions. As an example, we could during the design of a piece of software identify all of the output activities of the system and then combine them into a single method whose function could be described as

```
output anything
```

Such a method is clearly multi-functional. It performs any of a range of (output) operations, such as:

- `display text on screen`
- `output line to printer`
- `output record to file`

On the face of it such a method is rational, even logical. It seems like an act of housekeeping has been carried out to collect together logically related activities.

Another example of a logically cohesive method is one that is described by the name:

```
calculate
```

and which carries out any of a range of mathematical calculations (log, sine, cosine, etc.).

The problem with a logically cohesive method is that it is multifunctional; it carries out any of a menu of actions rather than one single well-defined action. It is unnecessarily complex. If we need to modify any one ingredient within the method, we will find it hard to ignore the other elements.

3. Temporal cohesion

In temporal cohesion the method performs a set of actions whose only relationship is that they have to be carried out at the same time. The classic example is a set of initialization operations. Thus a method that carried out the following collection of actions:

```
clear screen
open file
initialize total
```

would exhibit temporal cohesion.

A sequence of initialization actions like this is such a common feature of most programs and systems that it is hard to see how to avoid it. But as we can see in our example, the ingredients are not related to each other at all. The solution is to make the initialization method call other, specialized components. In the above example the initialization method would be improved if it consisted of the sequence of calls:

```
initialize terminal
initialize files
initialize calculation
```

Initialization plays a role in object-oriented programming. Whenever a new object is created, a constructor method is executed to carry out any initialization of the object. A constructor method is written as part of the class to which it belongs and has a very specific remit.

4. Communicational cohesion

In communicational cohesion, functions that act on the same data are grouped together. For example, a method that displays and logs temperature is carrying out two different actions on the temperature data. A similar example is a method that formats and prints a number.

Thus a communicationally cohesive method is described by several verbs and one noun. The weakness of such a method is, again, that it is unnecessarily complex – too many things are being grouped together. The actions can be distinguished and designed as separate methods.

5. Functional cohesion

This is the best type of cohesion. A method with functional cohesion performs a single, well-defined action on a single subject. Thus a sentence that accurately describes the purpose of the method has only one verb and a single object that is acted upon by the verb. Here are examples of descriptions of such methods:

- calculate average
- print result

- input transaction
- open valve
- obtain date

As with the ideas of coupling, if we find that the methods in our software exhibit poor cohesion, the concepts of cohesion do not provide us with a method for improving our structure – they merely tell us how poor our structure is. Another problem with the classification scheme is that it is sometimes very difficult to identify which type of cohesion is present.

SELF-TEST QUESTION

6.2   A library method draws a line from one set of coordinates to another. What type of cohesion does it exhibit?

6.10 ● Object-oriented programming

In this form of programming, methods and data that are strongly related are grouped together into an object. This matches exactly the ideas of information hiding and encapsulation discussed above. The items within an object are strongly coupled and the object as a whole possesses high cohesion. A well-designed object presents a few simple interfaces to its clients. The interfaces are those public methods that are declared to be accessible outside of the object. Thus a well-designed object displays loose coupling with other objects – method calls with pure data parameters to methods with functional cohesion. It is possible to code an object that allows clients direct access to its variables, but this is regarded as poor practice and is heavily discouraged because it is essentially making data global.

Object-oriented languages encourage the programmer to describe classes rather than individual objects. For example, here is the description, in Java, of a graphical object, a ball, which has *x* and *y* screen coordinates:

```java
class Ball {

    protected int x, y;
    private int radius;

    public void setRadius(int newRadius) {
        radius = newRadius;
    }

    public void setX(int newX) {
        x = newX;
    }
```

```
        public void setY(int newY) {
            y = newY;
        }
    }
```

Here the private and public elements are clearly distinguished. A third description, protected, means that the item is not accessible to clients but is accessible to subclasses, as we shall see shortly. Not shown in this example are private methods that are used by a class as necessary to carry out its work.

It is of course possible to misuse objects, by grouping ingredients that are not related. However it is the purpose of a good design approach to ensure that this does not arise (see Chapter 11).

Object-oriented programming (OOP) completely eliminates global data; all data is encapsulated within objects.

The open-closed principle

If you need to modify a class (or object), there is no need to make a separate edited copy. Instead you can use the inheritance mechanism of OOP. So the original copy of the class remains intact, but is reused with additional or changed methods. This is called the open-closed principle. Using the example above, we can create a new class called **MovingBall** with additional methods that cause the ball to move left and right:

```
    class MovingBall extends Ball {

        public void moveLeft(int distance) )
            x = x - distance;
        }

        public void moveRight(int distance) {
            x = x + distance;
        }
    }
```

The new class **MovingBall** has all the features of the class **Ball**, but as the keyword **extends** denotes, the new class has additional methods. The variables **x** and **y** in the superclass are accessible in this subclass because they were declared as protected. **MovingBall** makes use of **Ball** without altering it. Thus the modularity and integrity of the original component remain intact.

There is a snag: inheritance creates an additional type of coupling between a class and its superclasses. Thus if a subclass is changed, the programmer needs to re-examine all the superclasses.

6.11 ● Discussion

In this chapter we have discussed a range of considerations about the design of components. The ideas can be grouped into two areas:

1. those that deal with interactions within components – length, cohesion
2. those that deal with interactions between components – information hiding, coupling, shared components.

These guidelines help us in three ways:

1. they help us decide what to do during the act of design, guiding us to software that is clear, simple and flexible
2. they provide us with criteria for assessing the structure of some completed software
3. they assist us in refactoring (restructuring) software in order to improve it.

This book describes a number of methods for software design – creating a structure for the software. Unfortunately no method can claim to lead the designer to an ideal structure, and so guidelines for modularity supplement design methods in providing guidance during the process of design. In addition, they enable us to make judgments on the quality of a piece of software that has been designed. They may enable the designer to improve the software structure.

A problem with these guidelines is that they are largely qualitative rather than quantitative. In Chapter 29 on metrics we look at one attempt to establish a quantitative measure for the complexity of a component.

We shall see more on the nature of the relationships between components in Chapter 12 on patterns.

Summary

Modularity is important throughout software development including design, testing and maintenance.

Restricting component size is one crude way of reducing complexity. An extreme view is to restrict all components to no more than seven statements.

The principle of information hiding is that data should be inaccessible other than by means of the methods that are specially provided for accessing the data.

Coupling and cohesion are terms that describe the character of the interaction between components and within components, respectively. Coupling and cohesion are complementary. Strong coupling and weak cohesion are bad; weak coupling and strong cohesion are good. Thus coupling and cohesion provide a terminology and a qualitative analysis of modularity.

Object-oriented programming explicitly supports information hiding, weak coupling and strong cohesion.

Exercises

6.1 What is modularity and why is it important?

6.2 Argue for and against restricting components to about seven statements.

6.3 Look at the way that the library methods are called within a library available to you – say the Java or C# library. Assess what forms of coupling are demonstrated by the methods.

6.4 Examine any software or software design that you have available. How are the components coupled? What forms of coupling and cohesion are present? Analyze the component types. Is information hiding in use? Can the structure be improved?

6.5 Is there any correspondence between:

(a) any one form of cohesion and information hiding?

(b) any form of coupling and information hiding?

6.6 Does functional decomposition tend to lead to components that possess a particular form of cohesion? If so, which?

6.7 In functional decomposition, the components are functionally independent but they may act upon shared data. Is functional decomposition compatible with information hiding?

6.8 Does the data structure design method lead to a program structure that exhibits any particular types of coupling and cohesion? How does information hiding relate to, or contrast with, data structure design?

6.9 Does data flow design create a program structure that exhibits any particular types of coupling and cohesion?

6.10 Does object-oriented design tend to create software structures that exhibit any particular types of coupling and cohesion?

6.11 Consider a programming language with which you are familiar. What types of coupling are allowed? What types are not permitted?

6.12 Compare and contrast the features for modularity provided by C++, Ada, Java and Unix.

Answers to self-test questions

6.1 In order to understand one component, we are forced into studying them all.

6.2 The method performs a single well-defined action. The parameters are pure data. This is functional cohesion.

Further reading

This is the paper that suggests the small capacity of the human brain when comprehending a set of items as a complete whole: G. A. Miller, The magical number seven, plus or minus two; limits on our capacity for processing information, *The Psychological Review*, **63** (2) (March 1956), pp. 81–97.

This classic paper introduced the idea of information hiding: D.L. Parnas, On the criteria to be used in decomposing systems into component modules, *Communications of ACM*, 15 (December 1972), pp. 1053–8. This paper is reprinted in P. Freemen and A.I. Wasserman, *Tutorial on Software Design Techniques*, IEEE, 4th edn, 1983.

This is the book that first introduced the ideas of coupling and cohesion. There is also treatment of the issue of the optimal size of a component: E. Yourdon and Larry L. Constantine, *Structured Design*, Prentice Hall, 1979.

This book gives a more recent presentation of the ideas of coupling and cohesion: M. Page-Jones, *The Practical Guide to Structured Systems Design*, Yourdon Press, 1980.

One of the first books on design patterns (architectures) – general software structures that can be applied to a whole number of software systems. The book also analyses the different mechanisms available for connecting components: Mary Shaw and David Garlan, *Software Architecture: Perspectives on an Emerging Discipline*, Prentice Hall, 1966.

CHAPTER 7

Structured programming

This chapter explains:

- the principles of structured programming
- the arguments surrounding the **goto** statement.

7.1 ● Introduction

Structured programming is now part and parcel of most approaches to programming. It is widely accepted that it is not only the best, but the only way to carry out programming. This was not always the case. At one time there was a great debate about structured programming, what it meant and whether it was a good idea. This chapter reviews the principles and practice surrounding structured programming.

Once upon a time most programming languages provided a **goto** statement that allowed control to be transferred to any desired place in a program. Here is an example of **goto** in action:

```
        ------
        ------
label:
        ------
        ------
goto label
        ------
        ------
```

A label can be placed anywhere within a program. The **goto** statement transfers control to the specified label. The venerable language C provides a **goto** statement. Among modern languages, Java does not support a **goto** but C# does.

This chapter seeks to answer questions like: What is the essence of structured programming? What is the role of the **goto** statement? Why are certain control structures favored?

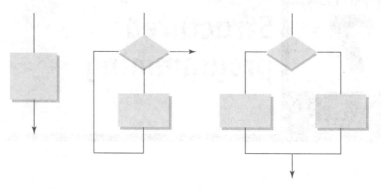

Figure 7.1 The three structures of structured programming

One view of structured programming is that it holds that programs should only be built from three components: sequences (normally written in the order in which the statements are to be executed), selections (normally written as **if-then-else**), and repetitions (written as **while-do**). The **goto** statement is, by implication, banned. In this chapter we begin by examining the controversy about the **goto** statement. The outcome of the argument is that **goto**s are an irrelevancy; the argument is about something else, good program structure. We go on to explore the significant principles of structured programming.

There are some other principles. We will explore these using flowcharts, which describe flow of control. A flowchart is read from the top downwards or in the direction of the arrows. Flowchart decisions (corresponding to **if** or **while** statements in code) are drawn as diamonds. Flowchart activities are shown as rectangular boxes. A flowchart is very similar to a UML activity diagram and conveys the same information. If the three structures of structured programming are diagrammed as flowcharts (Figure 7.1), the following characteristics become clear:

1. they have only one entry and exit
2. none of the constructs consists of more than three boxes

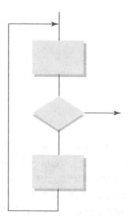

Figure 7.2 A control structure that is not structured

If we visualize any one of the three constructs as they are used, then a third characteristic is evident:

3. the entry is at the start and the exit is at the end.

Why is it that these characteristics are important? Why are other constructs that have the same characteristics (Figure 7.2) ruled out? We now go on to look at these questions.

SELF-TEST QUESTION

7.1 Write a loop that repeats ten times, first using a **while** statement, then using **goto**.

7.2 ● Arguments against goto

gotos are unnecessary

Fortunately there is a mathematical theorem (thanks to Bohm and Jacopini) guaranteeing that any program written using **goto** statements can be transformed into an equivalent program that uses only the structured constructs (sequence, selection and iteration). The converted program will, in general, need additional data items that are used as flags to control the actions of the program. Indeed the new program may look rather contrived; nonetheless, it can be done. On the face of it, therefore, there is no need for programs with **goto**s in them.

Note, as an interesting side issue, that the theorem does not tell us how to transform the unstructured program; only that it can be done.

Experimental evidence

Structured programming is well established and widely regarded as the best approach to programming. You might think, therefore, that there would be clear evidence from real software projects that it is beneficial, but this is not so; there are no convincing results from real projects, largely because a carefully controlled experiment would be difficult and expensive to mount. It would be necessary to develop a particular piece of software in two ways: once using structured programming and again using "unstructured" programming. All other variables, like the expertise of the programmers, would have to be held constant. The two versions of the software could be compared according to criteria like development time and number of errors. Regrettably, there are no results of this type.

However, experimenters have carried out small-scale studies comparing how easily people can understand and debug small structured programs compared with unstructured ones. In a typical experiment, each of a group of subjects is presented with the listing of a program that is written in a structured way and asked a series of questions that are designed to assess their comprehension of it. The accuracy of the replies and the time taken to reply are both measured. These are measures of the ease with which the program could be debugged or changed. A second group of subjects are given copies of the same program rewritten in an unstructured way. The accuracy and response times of the two groups are compared. The results of these experiments generally indicate that structured programs are superior to unstructured ones.

The results of empirical studies are reviewed in the literature given at the end of the chapter. In a review published in 1984, long after the dust had settled on the structured programming debate, Vessey and Weber concluded that "the evidence supporting [structured programming] is weak". This conclusion largely stems from the difficulty of carrying out experiments that give trustworthy results.

Clarity and expressive power

Compare the following two equivalent program fragments:

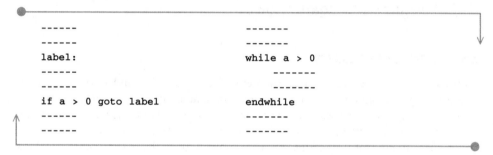

```
        ------                        -------
        ------                        -------
        label:                        while a > 0
        ------                        -------
        ------                        -------
        if a > 0 goto label           endwhile
        ------                        -------
        ------                        -------
```

As we read down the first program fragment, we are not immediately sure what the roles of the label and **goto** are. It would take us some time to read and study the program in order to discover that they are being used to create the repetition of a piece of code. This is made immediately obvious by the **while** statement in the second program. Worse, there is a remaining doubt in the first program that there may be another **goto** aimed at this same label from some other point in the program.

The facilities of a programming language should allow people to describe what they want to do in a meaningful way. If we examine a typical program written using **goto**s we see that the **goto**s are used for a variety of purposes, for example:

- to avoid a piece of code (which is to be executed in different circumstances)
- to perform repetition
- to exit from the middle of a loop
- to invoke a shared piece of code.

When we see a **goto**, there are few clues that allow us to decide the purpose for which the **goto** is being used. The alternative is, of course, a unique language construct for use in each of these different circumstances. These are, respectively:

- `if-then-else`

- `while-do` or `repeat-until`

- `exit`

- method call

It is as if the `goto` is too primitive an instruction – like a machine instruction to load a register – that can be used in a whole variety of circumstances, but does not clearly convey its meaning in any of them.

In summary, the `goto` lacks expressive power and it is therefore difficult to understand the logic of a program that is written using a lot of `goto`s. When we look at a piece of coding, words like `while` and `if` give us a strong clue as to what is intended; `goto`s do not.

How many pencils?

Suppose we want to read a program in order to understand it by tracing through it as if we were a computer executing it. Suppose we have available a supply of pencils (or fingers) to help us. The pencils will be used as markers, and are to be placed on the program listing to point to places of interest.

If we are following a simple sequence, then we will only need one pencil to keep track of our position. If we encounter a method call, we need two pencils, one to leave at the point of the call (in order to know where to return) and another to proceed into the method.

If we encounter a `while` statement or a `for` loop, then we need an integer, a counter, to keep count of the number of times we have repeated the loop.

To summarize, if the program has been written in a structured way, we need:

- one pencil to point to the current position

- one pencil to point to each method call that has been executed but not returned from

- a counter for every uncompleted loop.

This may seem like a lot of equipment, but consider the alternative of a program that contains a lot of `goto`s. As before, we will need to indicate the position of the current statement. Next, we need a pencil to point at every `goto` that has been executed. But now, whereas in the structured program we can remove a pencil whenever we return from a method, finish a loop or complete an `if` statement, we can never dispense with pencils; instead we need ever more. The increased number of pencils reflects the increased complexity of the `goto` program.

The real problem becomes evident when we want to refresh our memory about what happened *before* we arrived at the current point in the program. In the program without `goto`s we simply look back up the program text. In the unstructured program, when we look backwards we are defeated as soon as we reach a label, because we have no way of knowing how we reached it.

Ease of reading (static and dynamic structures)

In the Western world we are used to reading left to right and top to bottom. To have to begin by reading forwards and then to have to go backwards in the text is rather unnatural; it is simpler if we can always continue onwards. It is an important feature of a structured program that it can always be read from top to bottom – provided it has no methods. The exception to this rule arises in comprehending a **while** loop, during which repeated references back to the terminating condition at the start of the loop are necessary.

Programs are essentially dynamic beings that exhibit a flow of control, while the program listing is a static piece of text. To ease understanding, the problem is to bring the two into harmony – to have the static text closely reflect the dynamic execution. In a structured program, the flow of control is always down the page, which exactly corresponds to the way that text is normally read.

Proving programs correct

Formally to prove all programs correct is not a practical proposition with present-day techniques. Nonetheless there are some lessons that can be learned from proving.

In one technique of program proving, assertions are made at strategic points in the program. An assertion is a statement of what things are true at that point in the program. More exactly, an assertion describes the relationships that hold between data items that the program acts upon. Assertions at the start and end of a piece of program are called the input and output assertions respectively. Proving consists of rigorously demonstrating that if the input assertion is true, then the action of the program will lead to the output assertion being true.

A structured program consists solely of components that have a single entry and a single exit point. This considerably aids the process of reasoning about the effect of the program. In contrast, it is usually impossible to isolate single-entry, single-exit structures within a program with **goto**s in it.

Even when formal proof techniques are not being used, but where an informal study of the program is being made, the single-entry and single-exit character of programs aids checking and understanding.

7.3 ● Arguments in favor of goto

Deskilling

The **goto** statement is one tool among many provided by the programming language. To take it away from the programmer is to deprive him or her of a tool that can be validly used in certain circumstances.

Consider a craftsperson who is an expert at making delicate objects from wood. Suppose that we remove from that person a tool that we consider to be inappropriate, say an ax. The skill of making a discriminating selection among the available tools is reduced, because the choice is narrower. Furthermore, the skill in using the tool is no longer required. (Remember, however, that there may occasionally be circumstances in which an ax is the most suitable tool.)

Exceptions

Often a program is required to detect an error and to take some special action to deal with it. Suppose that such an error is detected many levels down in a chain of method calls. One way of handling the error is to create an additional parameter associated with each method call. This approach can become very unwieldy as methods receive and merely pass on parameters that they do not need to act on.

An alternative is for the method detecting the error to simply **goto** a suitable place in the program where the error can be dealt with. This can result in a significant simplification to the program. The essence of the argument is that an exceptional situation in the program demands an exceptional solution – a **goto**.

Some programming languages, such as Java, have solved this problem using a special mechanism for handling exceptional situations.

Program performance

On occasions it is possible to write a program that will run more quickly using **goto** statements. An example is a program to search an array **a** for an item **x**:

```
for i = 1 to tableSize
    if a[i] = x then goto found endif
endfor

notfound:
    ----
    ----

found:
    ----
    ----
```

The nearest we can get to writing this as a structured program is to write:

```
i = 1
while i <= tableSize and a[i] not = x
    i = i+1
endwhile

if i > m then
    -----
    -----
else
```

```
          -----
          -----
     endif
```

which requires an additional test. Although both programs achieve the same end – finding (or not finding) the desired item – the steps taken by the two programs differ. The first (unstructured) program takes fewer steps, and there is no way of writing a structured program that works in the same way. Thus it is possible to write `goto` programs that run more quickly than structured ones.

Naturalness

Consider the table searching program above. Arguably the unstructured solution is the best in the sense that it is the solution that solves the problem most naturally. Any transformation of this program, or any other solution, is a distortion of the natural solution. In other words, getting rid of `goto`s in existing programs (as can always be done), will sometimes needlessly destroy a good program.

The trouble is deciding what is natural. It surely differs from person to person, depending on individual psychology and cultural experiences. So it is a rather subjective judgment.

7.4 ● Selecting control structures

Rather than take part in a parochial debate about the merits of a particular control structure, let us take a constructive approach. If we had a free choice and a blank piece of paper, what control structures would we choose to use in programming? Perhaps our first consideration should be to establish the principles that govern the selection. Let us examine the following criteria:

- standardization
- abstraction
- expressive power
- orthogonality
- minimality.

We shall see that some of these conflict with each other. Note also that in our examination we are confining ourselves to sequential, imperative programming, in contrast to concurrent or declarative programming (as in logic or functional programming).

Standardization

Domestic appliances exhibit enormous variety and yet all plug into a standard socket. Similarly, it is desirable to build software from components that all exhibit the same external interface.

The simplest interface comprises one entry point, at the start, and one exit point at the end. This has the strength of being consistent with the essence of sequential programming. It also conforms to the important idea of calling a method. We are used to the idea of calling a method as a sequential step and returning from it to the next instruction in sequence. (We do not, for example, expect to supply a label as a parameter to which control is returned.)

Abstraction

This is probably the most important idea in structured programming. The human mind cannot devise or understand the whole of a complex system. Instead we can only understand one part of the system at a time. Nonetheless it is vital to understand the whole system. The only way to resolve these contradictory statements is to be able to perceive the overall structure in a digestible way. The solution is to use *abstraction*, that is, the system must be described in a notation that allows subsystems to be seen as black boxes whose task is readily understood but whose detail is invisible. In programming, the method has long been a mechanism that fulfills this role.

Other constructs that possess the same single-entry at the start, single-exit at the end property, are `if-then-else` and `while-do.`

Expressive power

In discussing the arguments against the `goto` statement, we saw that the `goto` is too primitive. It has more to do with describing what a machine will do than what a programmer intends. Instead we look at the range of structures on offer, tempted on the one hand to seize every mechanism available, while at the same time conscious of the need for minimality.

Certainly we need some mechanism for repetition, and either a `while` statement or recursion is sufficient to provide this facility. Many languages provide both a `while` statement and a `repeat-until` statement. Most languages also support recursion.

Arguably we also require a statement to carry out a choice of actions following a test. The `if-then-else` fulfills this requirement, but others are equally valid, including the `case` statement. Again, we are torn between expressive power and minimality.

Orthogonality

When designing a set of facilities, a good design principle is to create features that are each as different from each other as possible. If this is so, we can more easily satisfy the goal of a minimum number of functions, while at the same time ensuring that the facilities are sufficiently powerful for all our needs.

Minimality

The principle of minimality curbs our tendency to include too many facilities. A consequence of Bohm and Jacopini's theorem is that we know that the three control structures (sequence, selection and iteration) are sufficient. (Strictly, a construct for iteration, such as a `while`, is also unnecessary, because any loop that can be written iteratively can also, in theory, be achieved using only recursion.) Consider the flowcharts of various control structures. Sequence has one box, `while` has two, and `if` has three boxes. There are other control structures that involve only three or less boxes; but from amongst them all, these are the minimal feasible set.

7.5 ● What is structured programming?

It is easy to become engrossed in the arguments about the `goto` statement, but is this the central issue of structured programming?

Can a program that is written using only the three structures claim to be well structured? The answer is no; it is possible to create a bad program structure using the three structures, just as it is possible (with greater difficulty) to create a good structure that uses `goto` statements. To illustrate why this is so, consider a badly structured program that has been written using many `goto`s. If we now transform this into a program that uses the three structures, we still have a badly structured program, since we have done nothing significant to improve it.

As a second example, consider a program to search a table for a required item. Two alternative solutions, one structured, the other not, were compared earlier. However, arguably, neither of these is the best solution. Here is another, in which the item being sought is first placed at the end of the table:

```
a[tableSize + 1] = x
i = 1
while a[i] not = x
    i = i + 1
endwhile

if i = tableSize + 1
then
    ----
else
    ----
endif
```

This is arguably the best of the solutions because it is less complex (the condition in the while statement is simpler) and would execute more quickly on a conventional computer (for the same reason that there is only one condition to test). This example illustrates that the use of the approved structures does not necessarily guarantee the best design.

A structured program is essentially one that can be understood easily, and the most useful tool in understanding is abstraction. Abstraction is concerned with identifying the major elements of what is being studied, and ignoring detail. Such is the complexity of software that we have to do this in order to stand a chance of understanding it.

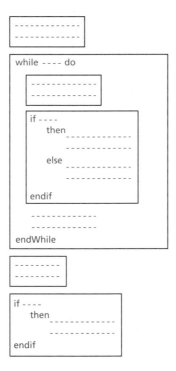

Figure 7.3 A structured program, showing self-contained components

Abstraction can only be achieved if the control flow constructs are used in a disciplined way, so that part of structured programming is the avoidance of **goto**s. For example, consider the program in Figure 7.3.

We can draw boxes around components as shown. Because it is built from limited control structures, we can view the program at all levels of detail as consisting of abstract components that have only one entry and one exit. If we examine any subsystem of the program, it is totally contained – the boxes do not overlap. If we look in detail at its contents, it does not suddenly sprout connections with other subsystems. When we uncover the nested contents of a traditional Russian wooden doll, we do not expect suddenly to encounter a doll that affects any of those we have already seen. (Structured programs are, of course, more complex than these dolls; it is as if, when we open a doll, not just one, but several more are revealed.)

Suppose that in the above program we inserted a **goto** as shown in Figure 7.4. We have now ruined the structure, since we can no longer view the program at different levels of abstraction.

As an analogy compare the problems of understanding a plate of spaghetti as compared with a plate of lasagna. In order to understand the spaghetti, we have to understand it all; we cannot employ abstraction. With the lasagna, we can peel off layers, one by one, uncovering the interesting detail of successive layers and understanding each separately from the others.

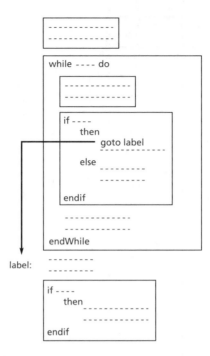

Figure 7.4 An unstructured program

Notice, though, that throughout our discussion we have concentrated almost exclusively on *control* structures and have neglected references to data. Although a program that uses the three structures may have abstraction of control, it may well have global data. This seriously weakens the abstraction, since at any level of detail all of the data has to be considered. Thus control abstraction is only one side of the coin; the other side is data abstraction – an important theme that is developed in the chapters on modularity, object-oriented design and object-oriented programming later in this book.

The idea of abstraction is a powerful tool in constructing software that is understandable, but, by itself, it is inadequate. In order to create programs that are well structured, we need a systematic *method* that takes us from the statement of the problem to the structure of the program. There are a variety of methods, discussed in later chapters.

Summary

The arguments against the `goto` are:

1. it is unnecessary

2. the experimental evidence

3. the lack of expressive power of `gotos`

4. the difficulty of finding out where you came from in a program constructed using **gotos**

5. the need to read backwards in a program with **gotos** in it.

6. the difficulty of proving the correctness of programs that use **gotos**.

The arguments for **gotos** are:

1. to ban them is to deskill programming

2. they have a use in exceptional circumstances

3. **gotos** are sometimes necessary in order to make programs perform well

4. it is sometimes "natural" to use **gotos**.

Much of the debate about structured programming has been conducted in this way. Throughout the arguments, the need for clarity in programs is the dominant idea.

The avoidance of **gotos** does not necessarily lead to a structured program. The central idea of structured programming is abstraction. Indeed, we can define structured programming as:

"the systematic use of (control) abstraction in programming"

(Abstraction can be applied not just to control, but to data as well. This is the subject of other chapters.)

Abstraction requires not only the use of suitable control structures but also a systematic design method.

Exercises

7.1 Review the arguments for and against **goto** statements and criticize their validity.

7.2 State in your own words what structured programming is. Imagine that you meet a friend who is used to programming using **goto**s. Explain in simple clear language what structured programming is.

7.3 A **while** statement can be used instead of an **if** statement, because the statement:

```
if bool then s endif
```

can be rewritten as:

```
while bool do s bool = false endwhile
```

Show how an **if-then-else** statement can similarly be rewritten using **while** statements. If the **if** statement is superfluous, why have it?

7.4 Convert the following into a structured program.

```
    i = start
loop:
  if x = a[i] then goto found endif
  if i = end then goto notFound endif
  i = i + 1
  goto loop

notFound:
    display 'not found'
    action1
    goto end

found:
    display 'found'
    action2

end:
```

Compare and contrast the two programs.

7.5 Recursion can be used to accomplish repetition, as in the following example of a method to skip spaces in a stream of input information:

```
method skipSpaces
    read(char)
    if char = space then skipSpaces endif
endmethod
```

Convert this example to a method that uses a **while** statement for repetition. Compare and contrast the two solutions. What is the role of recursion in the programmer's toolkit?

7.6 Argue for and against providing the following constructs in a programming language:

■ case
■ repeat-until
■ until-do

Answer to self-test question

```
7.1  count = 0
     while count < 10 do
          count = count + 1
     endwhile
```

```
count = 0
loop:
count = count + 1
if count < 10 goto loop
```

Further reading

The famous article that launched the debate about structured programming is: E.W. Dijkstra, Go To statement considered harmful, *Communications of the ACM*, **11**(3) (March 1968), pp. 147–48.

It is widely agreed that structured programming is a vital ingredient of software development. For a review of the (inconclusive) experimental evidence about the effectiveness of structured programming, see: I. Vessey and R. Weber, Research on structured programming: an empiricist's evaluation, *IEEE Trans on Software Engineering*, **10** (4) (1984), pp. 397–407.

A vigorous exposition of the argument that structured programming is de-skilling is given in: P. Kraft, *Programmers and Managers*, Springer-Verlag, 1977.

CHAPTER

8

Functional decomposition

This chapter explains:

- how to use functional decomposition
- the principles behind the method.

8.1 ● Introduction

Functional decomposition is a technique for designing either the detailed structure or the large-scale structure of a program or module. As its name suggests, functional decomposition is a method that focuses on the functions, or actions, that the software has to carry out. To use the method we first write down, in English, a single-line statement of what the software has to do. If the software performs several functions (as most GUI-driven software does) write down a single line for each function. For example, suppose we want to write a program to direct a robot to make a cup of instant coffee. We could begin by writing:

```
make a cup of coffee
```

Then we express the problem solution in terms of a sequence of simpler actions:

```
boil water
get a cup
put coffee in cup
add water
add milk
add sugar to taste
```

Next we take each of these statements and write down what it does in greater detail. This process of decomposition or refinement is continued until the solution is expressed in sufficient detail. Usually this is when the solution corresponds to the statements provided by the programming language to be used.

A statement that is to be broken down may be regarded as a method call. The set of more elementary steps into which it is decomposed can be viewed as the implementation of the method.

The language that is used to express the solution is called pseudo-code (because it is similar in some ways to programming language code), or program design language (PDL). It consists of sequences of (natural language) sentences, each beginning with a verb. It also involves the usual control structures – **if-then-else** for selection and **while** for repetition. For example, the statement **boil water** above can be refined to:

```
boil water

        switch on kettle
        while water not boiling do
            watch tv
        endwhile
        switch off kettle
```

Again we can refine **add sugar to taste** as:

```
add sugar to taste

        if sugar required
        then
            put sugar in cup
            stir
        endif
```

We can restrict ourselves just to **while** and **if** or we can make use of the **repeat**, **for** and **case** constructs.

8.2 ● Case study

In order to illustrate the use of functional decomposition, we will design the software for a simple game called cyberspace invaders. The screen is shown in Figure 8.1. The specification of the program (also given in Appendix A) is as follows:

A window displays a defender and an alien (Figure 8.1). The alien moves sideways. When it hits a wall, it reverses its direction. The alien randomly launches a bomb that moves vertically downwards. If a bomb hits the defender, the user loses and the game is over. The defender moves left or right according to mouse movements. When the mouse is clicked, the defender launches a laser that moves upwards. If a laser hits the alien, the user wins and the game is over.

A button is provided to start a new game.

Figure 8.1 Cyberspace invaders

The program responds to events from the play button, a timer, mouse clicks and mouse move events. To create animation, we move all the objects and redisplay them whenever the timer produces an event. So the overall logic is:

```
timer event

    move all the objects
    display all the objects
    check hits

mouse clicked event

    create laser

mouse moved event

    move defender
```

```
start button event

    create defender
    create alien
    start timer
```

We have hidden the detail in such statements as:

```
move all the objects
```

and we can study and check the high-level design without worrying about detail.

When we are satisfied with the high-level design, we choose one of the statements and write down what it does in more detail. An obvious first candidate is:

```
move all the objects

    move alien
    move bomb
    move laser
    check boundaries
```

and then:

```
display all the objects

    display background
    display defender
    display alien
    display laser
    display bomb
```

At this stage we have expressed the design in terms of a number of methods. The most complex of these are **check hits** and **check boundaries**. So we now design their detail:

```
check hits

    if collides(laser, alien)
    then
        endOfGame(userWins)
    else
        if collides(bomb, defender)
        then
            endOfGame(alienWins)
        endif
    endif
```

```
check boundaries

    if bomb is outside window
    then
        destroy bomb
    endif

    if laser is outside window
    then
        destroy laser
    endif
```

This completes some of the detail. The next item that has some complexity is the method **collides**. It has two parameters, the objects to be tested for impact. It returns either **true** or **false**. It uses the *x* and *y* coordinates of the objects, together with their heights and widths. We use the notation **a.x** to mean the **x** coordinate of object **a**. (The joy of pseudo-code is that you can use any notation that is convenient.)

```
collides(a, b)

    if      a.x > b.x
        and a.y < b.y + b.height
        and a.x + a.width < b.x + b.width
        and a.y + a.width > b.y
    then
        return true
    else
        return false
    endif
```

This illustrates how we have used the tool of abstraction to hide this complexity within a method.

There is still some way to go with this particular design, but this much gives the flavor of the design and of the method. Notice how the design is refined again and again. Notice how, throughout, we can check the design without having to take account of a lot of unnecessary detail. Notice the informality of the statements used; we can simply make up new actions as necessary, but still within the discipline of the control structures – sequence, **if** and **while**, supplemented with methods.

SELF-TEST QUESTION

8.1 Write method **move alien** assuming it is at window coordinates **x** and **y**.

8.3 ● Discussion

Abstraction

One way of visualizing functional decomposition is to see that at any stage of decomposition the solution is expressed in terms of operations that are assumed to be available and provided by an abstract (or virtual) machine, like a very high-level programming language. This is the idea of "levels of abstraction". In order to design and understand a solution at any one level of detail, it is not necessary to understand anything about how the levels beneath work. We know *what* they do, but not *how* they do it. Thus the human mind has a much better chance of understanding the solution and therefore of getting it right.

One approach to using functional decomposition is to refine the software design level by level. The software structure can be visualized as an upside-down tree – always with a very flat top that grows downwards uniformly. This is the *breadth-first* approach to design; it matches the strict, abstract machine view of software design described above.

An alternative approach is to pursue one of the branches of the tree, leaving the others stunted until later. (This is called *depth first*.) Our motive for doing this might be to explore what seems to be a difficult part of the software. We might thereby hope to gain insights that guide us in refining the rest of the structure.

This idea of trying to ignore the detail of lower levels of the design is easier said than done and takes some nerve. It is a real test of whether we believe software design is worthwhile and whether we can resist the temptation to rush on to coding pieces of the software.

What about data?

What is the role of data in the method? It does rather play second fiddle to the actions that have to be taken. The making of the cup of coffee illustrates that, by concentrating on what the software should do, considerations of data are ignored, or rather postponed. The idea is that the data emerges during the decomposition as it becomes evident what is necessary and what needs to be done with it. We defer decisions about pieces of data and the structure of information until we have a very clear knowledge of what operations have to be performed on them. When that stage is reached we can design data which is tailored precisely to the operations.

There is a possible problem here. Suppose a program is written in this way and later needs modifying. What happens if some new operation on the data is required? Remember that the data was designed with the old operations in mind, so it may not be in a convenient form for the new.

Another question about functional decomposition is whether it is actually possible to delay thinking about data in this way.

Alternative solutions

A major characteristic of functional decomposition is its flexibility, or (put another way) its lack of guidance. When you use the method you do not necessarily arrive at a unique solution. On the contrary, you can often see several solutions. According to functional decomposition they are all reasonable. The method gives us no guidance as to which design is best. The only way to find out is to refine all the solutions to a level of detail at which we can make a reasoned choice between them. The choice might be made on the basis of clarity and simplicity, performance or some other criteria, but functional decomposition, by itself, gives no guidance for selecting the best solution.

Because there is always more than one solution to a problem – more than one design that meets the specification – the user of functional decomposition is duty bound to find not just one solution, but to find the best solution. The criteria for the "best" solution will differ from program to program – sometimes it will be maximum clarity, sometimes it will be optimum performance. If in pursuing one design it turns out to be unsatisfactory, we can retrace the design level by level, considering alternatives at each level. It will often prove desirable to replace whole subtrees in this manner. This process is largely under control because we know which part of the structure we are looking at, and it has only one entry and exit point.

Review

Arguably functional decomposition was the first truly systematic method for software design. It is associated with the names Dijkstra and Wirth. It evolved hand-in-hand with the ideas of structured programming in the 1960s. Since then other methods that claim to involve structured programming have been devised, so that nowadays functional decomposition is just one variety of structured programming.

There is sometimes confusion about the terminology surrounding structured programming and top-down methods. Let us try to clarify the situation. Functional decomposition is a top-down method, since it starts with an overall task of the software, but it is not unique in this respect. Functional decomposition is also called *stepwise refinement*, though it is, of course, refinement of function.

Functional decomposition concentrates almost exclusively on defining the functions (the actions) that software must take. The flexibility of functional decomposition means that it can be used in the design of software for any type of application; it is generally applicable. But because it concentrates on the actions that the software has to take, it is perhaps most useful for problems in which the procedural steps are clearly evident. One such area is numerical computation, like a program to calculate a square root. Another is the control of a sequential process, like a washing machine.

Functional decomposition can be used either to design the detailed, low-level structure of a program. It can also be used to design the high-level or architectural structure of software. Thus it is applicable to both small- and large-scale software.

Functional decomposition assumes that the structure of software must be a collection of hierarchies (trees), one for each top-level function or use case. This distinguishes it from other approaches.

If we want a completely well-defined method that we can use almost without thinking, then functional decomposition is inadequate, since its use requires considerable skill. On the other hand, it is an excellent approach if we want a method that guides our thinking but allows us plenty of scope for creativity. In a sense, therefore, the method is not as advanced as some. For example, data structure design takes the programmer from a description of the structure of the data or files that the program is to act upon, via a number of fairly precise steps to the program design. By contrast, the use of functional decomposition encourages (some would say necessitates) the use of creativity and imagination in devising software structures. Its use also needs careful judgment in selecting the best structure from amongst any alternatives found.

In summary, functional decomposition is a general-purpose method for software design, based around structured programming, but in allowing the development of alternative designs for the same problem it poses several unanswered questions:

- where do we get the inspiration for alternative designs?
- how do we choose between designs?
- how do we know that we have arrived at the best possible design?

We have to look to other sources of ideas to answer these questions. These issues have led some to say that functional decomposition is not really a serious method.

Summary

Functional decomposition proceeds by starting with a single statement of each function of the software. Next these are rewritten as a series of simpler steps using pseudo-code (program design language) as a notation. Pseudo-code consists of natural language imperative sentences written as sequences, with **if** statements or with **while** statements. The designs are refined (rewritten as more primitive steps) until the required level of detail is achieved.

The method makes direct use of the power of abstraction provided by structured programming, while requiring significant creativity and judgment to be employed. It is applicable to the full range of computer application areas.

Exercises

8.1 Complete the design of the game program.

8.2 Write pseudo-code for the **withdraw cash** function in the ATM (Appendix A).

8.3 Use functional decomposition to design the software for each of the systems described in Appendix A.

8.4 What characteristics should a good software design method have? Does the functional decomposition exhibit them?

8.5 Evaluate functional decomposition under the following headings:

- special features and strengths
- weaknesses
- philosophy/perspective?
- systematic?
- appropriate applications
- inappropriate applications
- is the method top-down, bottom-up or something else?
- good for large-scale design?
- good for small-scale design?

8.6 Compare and contrast the principles behind the following design methods:

- functional decomposition
- data structure design
- data flow design
- object-oriented design

Answer to self-test question

```
8.1  move alien
        if x > window width or x < 0
        then
             stepSize = -stepSize;
        endif
        x = x + stepSize;
```

● Further reading

Arguably the most important book about structured programming is: O.J. Dahl, E.W. Dijkstra and C.A.R. Hoare, *Structured Programming*, Academic Press, 1997.

Data flow design

This chapter explains:

- how to use the data flow design method
- the principles behind the method.

9.1 ● Introduction

Data flow design is a method for carrying out the architectural (large-scale) design of software. Data flow design depends on identifying the flows of data through the intended software, together with the transformations on the flows of data. The method leads from a specification of the software to a large-scale structure for the software expressed in terms of:

- the constituent components of the software
- the interrelationships between the components

What is a component? A component is a collection of lines of code, usually involving variables (descriptions of data) and actions. A component is usually self-contained; it is somewhat separate from any other component or components. A component is called from some other component and, similarly, calls other components. Programming languages (nearly) always provide facilities for modularity – such features as methods, classes and packages. Ideally, a component is as independent as it can be. One of the goals of software design is to create software structures in which all of the components are as independent as possible. Chapter 6 discusses various general aspects of modularity.

We begin exploring data flow design method using an analogy. Suppose a chef works in a kitchen all day preparing plates of spaghetti bolognese. The principal inputs to the system are:

- spaghetti
- meat

The output from the system is:

■ plates of spaghetti bolognese

We can draw a diagram (Figure 9.1) to describe what is to happen in the kitchen.

In essence, data flows into the system, is transformed by actions (functions) and data then flows out of the system.

The diagram is called a *data flow diagram*. Each line with an arrow on it represents a stream of data flowing through the system. In this example there are three – spaghetti, meat and plates of spaghetti bolognese. Each bubble represents a transformation, an activity or a process that converts an input flow into an output flow. In this example there is only one transformation – prepare food. Note that the diagram shows data flows (which are dynamic), and does not show files (which are static objects).

We can now explore the detail that lies within the single bubble. We redraw it as Figure 9.2 so as to show more clearly the steps that are involved.

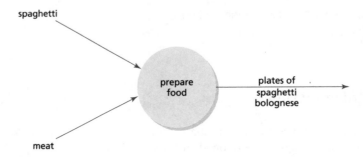

Figure 9.1 Data flow diagram for making spaghetti bolognese

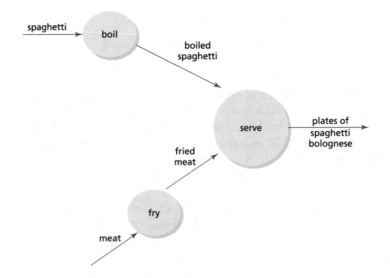

Figure 9.2 More detailed data flow diagram for making spaghetti bolognese

Notice again the essential components – data flows (lines) and functions (bubbles). Each line is labeled to describe exactly what data it is. Each bubble is labeled with a verb to describe what it does.

We could go on redrawing our data flow diagram for the chef in the kitchen, adding more and more detail. There are, for example, other ingredients, like tomatoes to consider (data flows) and more detailed actions (bubbles), such as mixing in the various ingredients.

We started with a single, high-level diagram in which all the detail was hidden. We end with a richer, more detailed diagram in which the components of the system (and their interrelationships) are revealed. In a computer system, the bubbles correspond to the software components. We have created a design for the kitchen system expressed in terms of components and the flows of data between the components.

9.2 ● Identifying data flows

We will use as a case study the design of software to monitor a patient in a hospital. The specification (Appendix A) for the software is:

A computer system monitors the vital signs of a patient in a hospital. Sensors attached to a patient send information continually to the computer:

- *heart rate*
- *temperature*
- *blood pressure*

Some of the readings require conversion to useful units of measurement (e.g. micro volts into degrees centigrade). The computer displays the information on a screen. It also logs the information in a file that can be retrieved and displayed. If any of the vital signs exceeds safe limits, the screen flashes a warning and an alarm sounds. The limits have default values, but can also be changed by the operator. If a sensor fails, the screen flashes a warning and the alarm sounds.

The data flow diagram of the major data flow for this software is shown in Figure 9.3. It is straightforward to draw this diagram simply by reading the specification closely and picking out the functional steps that need to be carried out.

This diagram also shows some data stores. These are drawn as open boxes and represent files or databases. The difference between a data store and a data flow is that a data store is static (it does not move).

Drawing the data flow diagram for a proposed piece of software is a vital step in the method. How do we do it? There are three alternative approaches.

Method 1 is to start with a single bubble like Figure 9.4 that shows the overall function of the software and its input and output data flows. We then refine the bubble, or break it down, into a set of smaller bubbles like Figure 9.5. We continue redrawing bubbles as sets of smaller ones until we can't do it any more.

In method 2 we start with the output data flow from the system and try to identify the final transformation that has to be done to it. Then we try to identify the transformation before that, and so on, until we have a complete diagram.

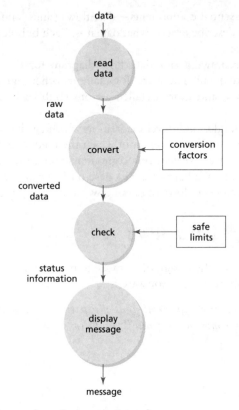

Figure 9.3 Data flow diagram for patient monitoring software

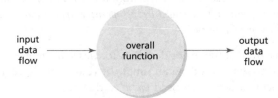

Figure 9.4 Initial data flow diagram

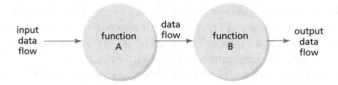

Figure 9.5 Refined data flow diagram

Method 3 is the same as method 2, except that we start from the input flow to the system and work out the sequence of transformations that should be applied to it.

There is no definite, systematic way of drawing these diagrams. Lots of paper, pencil and erasers (or a software tool) are needed – together with a lot of creativity.

Now that we have obtained the data flow diagram using one of these methods, what do we do with it? One option is to regard each bubble as a component that inputs a serial stream of data from one component and outputs a serial stream to another. Some operating systems (such as Unix) and some languages (such as the piped input and output streams facility in Java) support this "filter and pipe" software architecture. This means that we can directly implement a data flow diagram as a series of filters and pipes. However, if pipes are not available, a data flow diagram must be transformed into a structure in which components make method calls on each other.

SELF-TEST QUESTION

9.1 The data flow for the log file is omitted from the above data flow diagram. Add this data flow.

9.3 ● Creation of a structure chart

The first and most crucial step of data flow design is drawing the data flow diagram. Such a diagram shows the transformations and the flows of data between them. The next step is to convert the data flow diagram into a structure chart or structure diagram. A structure chart shows the components that comprise the software and how they call each other. Suppose, for example, that some software consists of three components named A, B and C. Suppose that component A calls component B and also component C. The structure chart for these components is shown in Figure 9.6.

A structure chart is thus a hierarchical diagram that shows components at the higher levels calling components at lower levels. A structure chart is a tree, with one single root at the top of the chart. Notice by contrast that a data flow diagram is not hierarchical.

Let us now consider the patient monitoring system and see how to convert the data flow diagram into its equivalent structure chart. In this data flow diagram, arguably the

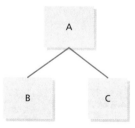

Figure 9.6 Structure chart in which component A calls B and C

central and most important bubble is the **check** bubble. We take this to be the main, most important component. Imagine that we can touch and move the objects within the diagram. Suppose that the bubbles are joined by pieces of string. Grasp the central component and lift it into the air. Let the other bubbles dangle beneath. Next change the bubbles into rectangles. We now have a structure chart that looks like Figure 9.7.

Each box is a software component. The components communicate by calls from higher components to lower components. The data that flowed along lines in the data flow diagram is now passed as parameters to and from the various components.

The **check** component calls the **convert** component which in turn calls the **read data** component to obtain data. Then it calls the **display message** component to display the output on the screen.

As we have illustrated, the steps for converting a data flow diagram into a structure chart are:

1. identify the most important bubble (transformation)
2. convert this into the top-level component in the structure chart
3. allow the other components to dangle beneath the top-level component, creating a hierarchical tree
4. convert the bubbles into rectangles and the data flows into lines representing method calls.

The patient monitoring example illustrates how to use the data flow design method. But the example chosen is simple and we have deliberately avoided drawing attention to complications. Data flow diagrams typically have tens of bubbles and can be quite complex. Often there are several input and output data flows. In more complex diagrams, it can be difficult to identify a single center of the diagram.

Notice that although the method leads us to a structure for a piece of software that is expressed in terms of well-defined, independent components, we still have to design the detail of each and every component; we have to carry out the low-level or detailed design. This emphasizes that data flow design is a method for high-level or architectural design.

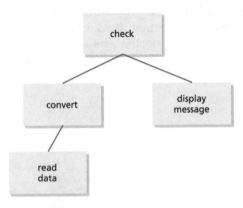

Figure 9.7 Structure chart for patient monitoring software

SELF-TEST QUESTION

9.2   Enhance the structure chart for the patient monitoring software so as to show the logging.

9.4 ● Discussion

Why does the data flow method prescribe these steps? There are two main ideas behind the method:

1.   the connection between data flows and modularity
2.   the idea of an idealized software structure.

The first concerns the data flow diagram. Why exactly do we draw a data flow diagram and what is its significance? The answer is that the central aim of this technique is to create a design with the best possible modularity. As described in Chapter 6, the different types of modularity have been analyzed and classified in an attempt to identify which is the best sort of modularity. Perfect modularity would mean that an individual component could be designed, tested, understood and changed when necessary without having to understand anything at all about any other component. The result of the analysis is that out of all the types of relationships, the most independent components are those that communicate with each other only by inputting and outputting serial streams of data – just like the bubbles in a data flow diagram. This type of interaction is termed data coupling.

The second idea behind the data flow design method is the observation that many software systems have a similar overall structure. Most software carries out some input, performs some action on the input data and then outputs some information. The most important of these three is the action or transformation on the data. Therefore, in general, the ideal structure for any software is as shown in Figure 9.8.

We have seen that the component that does the main processing should be at the top. If we now look at what the input component does, it is likely that it can be broken down into two components, one that inputs some raw data and another that converts it into a more convenient form. The corresponding structure diagram is shown in Figure 9.9.

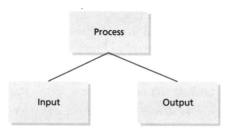

Figure 9.8 Idealized structure for software

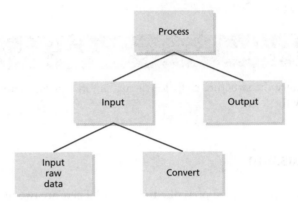

Figure 9.9 Converting raw data for input

In general, a piece of software will require that several transformations are carried out on its input data streams and that, after the main processing, several transformations are carried out on its output data streams. We can use an analogy from outside computing. To make wine, we have first to grow vines, pick the grapes, transport them to the farm, and then press them. Only then can we carry out the central task of fermentation. After this we have to pour the wine into bottles, store the bottles for some time, and finally transport them to the shop.

Data flow design recognizes this as the archetypal structure for software systems.

As we have seen, data flow design concentrates on modeling the flows of data within software. The essential ingredient is any application in which the flows of data are important and can be identified easily. Data flows are significant because nearly every software system involves data flows. In all computer systems information enters the computer as a serial stream of data, simply because time flows serially. Similarly any component within a software system is only capable of carrying out one task at any time. Thus the demands placed on any component are a serial data stream. Therefore data flows constitute a fundamental concept within software.

Summary

Data flow design proceeds by initially analyzing the data flows and transformations within a software system. The first task is to draw the data flow diagram (bubble diagram), consisting of arcs (data flows) and bubbles (transformations). This diagram can be arrived at by using any one of the following three methods:

1. starting with a single, large bubble, break it up into smaller bubbles
2. start with the output data stream from the software and trace it backwards
3. start with the input data stream to the system and trace it forwards.

During the second stage of data flow design, the data flow diagram is transformed into a structure chart, showing the constituent components of the software and their interrelationships, by:

1. identifying the most important or central transformation in the data flow diagram
2. lifting this transformation into the air, leaving the others dangling beneath it. This creates a hierarchical or tree-shaped structure for the software.

Arguably data flow design leads to the most modular structure for the software, since the design is based on "data coupling" (the best type) between the components.

Exercises

9.1 Complete the development of the patient monitoring system described in this chapter.

9.2 Apply data flow design to devising an architectural structure for each of the systems described in Appendix A.

9.3 What characteristics should a good software design method possess? Does data flow design exhibit them?

9.4 Suggest the facilities of a software tool that could assist in using data flow design.

9.5 Compare and contrast the principles behind the following design methods:

- functional decomposition
- data structure design
- data flow design
- object-oriented design.

9.6 Evaluate data flow design under the following headings:

- special features and strengths.
- weaknesses
- philosophy/perspective?
- systematic?
- appropriate applications
- inappropriate applications
- is the method top-down, bottom-up or something else?

- good for large-scale design?
- good for small-scale design?

9.7 Suggest features for a software toolkit to assist in using data flow design.

Answers to self-test questions

9.1 Arrow from the `convert` bubble to a `log` bubble. Then arrow from this bubble to a `log file` data store.

9.2 Line downwards from the `check` component to a component labeled `log`.

● Further reading

Data flow design is described in: E. Yourdon and Larry L. Constantine, *Structured Design,* Prentice Hall, 1979.

This chapter explains:

- how to use data structure design
- the principles behind the method.

10.1 ● Introduction

Starting with the specification of a program, this method, via a series of steps, leads to a detailed design, expressed in pseudo-code. The method is variously called the Michael Jackson program design method (after the name of its inventor), or Jackson Structured Programming (JSP), and data structure design.

The basic idea behind the data structure design method is that the structure of a program should match the structure of the information that the program is going to act on. To get a feel for how this can be done, let us look at a few simple examples.

First, suppose we want a program to add a set of numbers held in an array, and terminated by a negative number. Here's some sample data:

29 67 93 55 –10

With experience of programming, we can, of course, immediately visualize the structure of this program. Its main feature is a **while** loop. But a more rigorous way of looking at the design is to realize that because there is a repetition in the data, there must be a corresponding repetition in the program. Thus we have gone from the data structure to the program structure.

Consider a program that is to print a bank statement. The bank statement will be printed on a number of pages. Each page has a heading, a series of ordinary lines (representing transactions) and a summary line. Ignore, for the time being, the structure of any input data. Again, with some experience of programming, we can visualize that we will need statements to print a heading, print a transaction line and so on. But we can also see that we will need:

- a loop to print a number of pages
- a loop to print the set of transaction lines on each page.

You can see that this description of the program structure matches the structure of the report. What we have done is to derive the structure of the program from what we know about the structure of the report.

These small examples show how it is possible to approach program design using the structure of data. We will return to these examples later, showing exactly how the method treats them.

10.2 ● A simple example

Let us consider the design of a program to display the following pattern on a computer screen. We will assume that, in drawing this pattern, the only possible cursor movements are across the screen from left to right, and down to the beginning of a new line.

```
    *
   ***
  *****

  *****
   ***
    *
```

The first step in the method is to analyze and describe the structure of the information that the program is to create. The product of this step is called a *data structure diagram*. The diagram for the pattern is given in Figure 10.1.

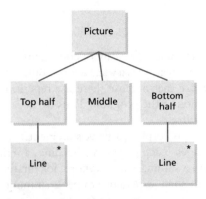

Figure 10.1 Data structure diagram for the asterisks pattern

In English, this reads:

■ the pattern consists of the top half followed by the middle, followed by the bottom half

■ the top half consists of a line of asterisks, which is repeated. The bottom half also consists of a line of asterisks which is repeated.

In general, the diagrammatic notation has the following meaning:

■ **consists of** – a line drawn downwards below a box means "consists of". Thus Figure 10.2 shows that A consists of B.

■ **sequence** – boxes at the same level denote a sequence. Figure 10.3 shows that A consists of B followed by C.

■ **repetition** – an "*" in a box signifies zero or more occurrences of the component. Figure 10.4 shows that A consists of B repeated zero or more times.

Having now described the data structure, the next step is to convert it into a program structure. This is easy because, remember, the program structure must correspond to the

Figure 10.2 A consists of B

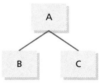

Figure 10.3 A consists of B followed by C

Figure 10.4 A consists of B repeated

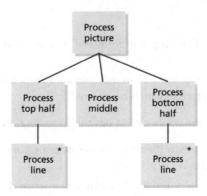

Figure 10.5 Program structure diagram for the pattern program

data structure, so all we have to do is to write "process" in every box of the data structure diagram. We thereby obtain a *program structure diagram*. For our program this is
shown in Figure 10.5.

A program structure diagram like this is interpreted as follows:

■ the program as a whole (represented by the box at the top) consists of (lines leading downwards) a sequence of operations (boxes alongside one another)

■ sometimes a program component is to be repeatedly executed (an "*" in the box).

The next step is to write down (in any order) a list of all the elementary operations
that the program will have to carry out. This is probably the least well-defined part of
the method – it does not tell us how to determine what these actions should be. For
the program we are working on they are:

```
1   display n asterisks
2   display blank line
3   display s spaces
4   increment s
5   decrement s
6   increment n
7   decrement n
8   initialize n and s
9   new line
```

For later reference, we number the operations, but the ordering is not significant.

Next each of these operations is placed in its appropriate position in the program
structure diagram. For example, operation 2 needs to be done once, for the middle
of the pattern. It is therefore associated with the box containing **process middle**.
Similarly, operation 1 is associated with the component **process line** (Figure 10.6).

This act of associating operations with positions is not automatic; instead, as indicated,
judgment has to be employed.

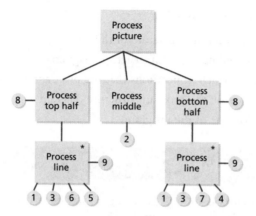

Figure 10.6 Annotated program structure diagram

Now comes the final step of transforming the program structure diagram into pseudo-code. Expressed in pseudo-code, the structure of our example program is:

```
initialize n and s
while more lines do
        display s spaces
        display n asterisks
        new line
        decrement s
        increment n
endwhile

display blank line

initialize n and s
while more lines do
        display s spaces
        display n asterisks
        new line
        decrement n
        increment s
endwhile
```

To derive this pseudo-code from the diagram, start with the box at the top of the diagram and write down its elementary operations. Then indent the code across the page and go down a level on the diagram. Now write down the operations and structures present at this level. Repeatedly go down a level, indenting the code for each new level. This transformation is straightforward and mechanical.

We have now arrived at a program design capable of being readily translated into most conventional programming languages.

To sum up, the steps we have taken are:

1. draw a diagram showing the structure of the file
2. derive the corresponding program structure diagram
3. write down the elementary operations that the program will have to carry out
4. place the operations on the program structure diagram
5. derive the pseudo-code of the program.

10.3 ● Processing input files

To understand how to input and process information from a file, consider the following problem:

A serial file consists of records. Each record describes a person. Design a program to count the number of males and the number of females.

The data structure diagram is given in Figure 10.7.

The new notation here is the boxes with the letter "o" in them (meaning or) to indicate alternatives. These boxes are drawn alongside each other. Depending on the application, there are sometimes a number of alternatives.

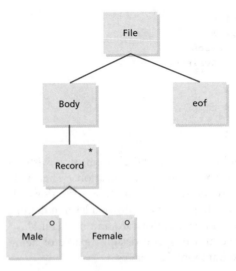

Figure 10.7 Data structure diagram for counting males and females

We now derive the program structure diagram as before (not shown).

After writing down operations and assigning them to the program structure diagram (not shown), we arrive at the following pseudo-code design:

```
open file
initialize counts
read record
while not end of file
do
    if record = male
    then increment male-count
    else increment female-count
    endif
    read record
endwhile
display counts
close file
```

This recognizes that the boxes with alternatives in them become **if-then-else** statements.

There is just one small point to note. Data structure design did not help us to realize that we would need an initial **read record** operation before the loop, followed by another at the end of each loop. Data structure design gave us the structure or skeleton in which we could place the elementary operations – it did not give us the fine detail.

We have now considered and used all the notations used by the data structure design method. They are: sequence, selection, repetition and hierarchy.

SELF-TEST QUESTION

10.2 Suppose that instead of counting both males and females, the program is only required to count males. How would the data structure diagram be different?

10.4 ● Multiple input and output streams

So far we have just looked at programs that process a single input or a single output stream. Now we turn to the more common situation of multiple streams. The method is basically the same, except that we will have to describe all of the streams and make the program structure reflect them all.

The basic principle, as always with the data structure design method, is that the program structure should reflect the structures of all the input and output streams. So we draw a data structure diagram for each input and output file and then devise a program structure that incorporates all aspects of all of the data structure diagrams.

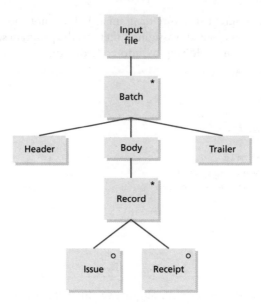

Figure 10.8 Data structure diagram for input file

Figure 10.9 Data structure diagram for report

Consider the following problem:

A serial file describes issues and receipts of stock. Transactions are grouped into batches. A batch consists of transactions describing the same stock item. Each transaction describes either an issue or a receipt of stock. A batch starts with a header record and ends with a trailer record. Design a program to create a summary report showing the overall change in each item. Ignore headings, new pages, etc. in the report.

The data structure diagrams are given in Figures 10.8 and 10.9.

We now look for correspondences between the two diagrams. In our example, the report (as a whole) corresponds to the input file (as a whole). Each summary line in the report matches a batch in the input file. So we can draw a single, composite program structure diagram as in Figure 10.10.

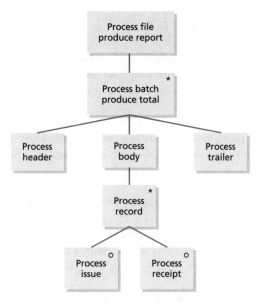

Figure 10.10 Program structure diagram for processing batches

Writing down operations, attaching them to the program structure diagram (not shown) and translating into pseudo-code, gives:

```
open files
read header record
while not end of file
do
        total = 0
        read record
        while not end of batch
        do
                update total
                read record
        endwhile
        display total
        read header record
endwhile
close files
```

Thus we have seen that, where a program processes more than one file, the method is essentially unchanged – the important step is to see the correspondences between the file structures and hence derive a single compatible program structure.

10.5 ● Structure clashes

In a minority of problems, the two or more data structures involved cannot be mapped onto a single program structure. The method terms this a *structure clash*. It happens if we try to use the method to design a program to solve the following problem.

> *Design a program that inputs records consisting of 80 character lines of words and spaces. The output is to be lines of 47 characters, with just one space between words.*

This problem looks innocuous enough, but it is more complex than it looks. (Have a go if you don't agree!) A problem arises in trying to fit words from the input file neatly into lines in the output file. Figures 10.11 and 10.12 show the data structure diagrams for the input and output files. Superficially they look the same, but a line in the input file does not correspond to a line in the output file. The two structures are fundamentally irreconcilable and we cannot derive a single program structure. This situation is called a *structure clash*.

Although it is difficult to derive a single program structure from the data structure diagrams, we can instead visualize two programs:

■ program 1, the **breaker**, that reads the input file, recognizes words and produces a file that consists just of words.

■ program 2, the **builder**, that takes the file of words created by program 1 and builds it into lines of the required width.

We now have two programs together with a file that acts as an intermediary between the programs.

Figure 10.11 Data structure diagram for input file

Figure 10.12 Data structure diagram for output file

Figure 10.13 Data structure diagram for the intermediate file (as seen by the **breaker**)

Figure 10.14 Program structure diagram for the **breaker** program

As seen by the **breaker**, Figure 10.13 shows the data structure diagram for the intermediate file, and it is straightforward to derive the program structure diagram (Figure 10.14).

Similarly, Figure 10.15 shows the structure of the intermediate file as seen by the second program, the **builder**, and again it is easy to derive the program structure diagram for program 2, the **builder** (Figure 10.16).

Thus, by introducing the intermediate file, we have eradicated the structure clash. There is now a clear correspondence both between the input file and the intermediate file and between the intermediate file and the output file. You can see that choosing a suitable intermediate file is a crucial decision.

From the program structure diagrams we can derive the pseudo-code for each of the two programs:

```
program 1 (the breaker)

open files
read line
while not end of file do
      while not end of line do
            extract next word
            write word
      endwhile
      read next line
endwhile
close files
```

Figure 10.15 Data structure diagram for the intermediate file (as seen by the **builder**)

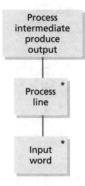

Figure 10.16 Program structure diagram for the **builder** program

To avoid being distracted by the detail, we have left the pseudo-code with operations such as **extract word** in it. Operations like this would involve detailed actions on array subscripts or on strings.

```
program 2 (the builder)

open files
read word
while more words
do
        while line not full
                and more words
        do
                insert word into line
                read word
        endwhile
        output line
endwhile
close files
```

We began with the need to construct a single program. In order to eliminate the structure clash, we have instead created two programs, plus an intermediate file, but at least we have solved the problem in a fairly systematic manner.

Let us review the situation so far. We drew the data structure diagrams, but then saw the clash between the structures. We resolved the situation by identifying two separate programs that together perform the required task. Next we examine the two file structures and identify a component that is common to both. (In the example program this is a word of the text.) This common element is the substance of the intermediate file and is the key to dealing with a structure clash.

What do we do next? We have three options open to us.

First, we might decide that we can live with the situation – two programs with an intermediate file. Perhaps the overhead of additional input-output operations on the intermediate file is tolerable. (On the other hand, the effect on performance might be unacceptable.)

The second option requires special operating system or programming language facilities. For example, Unix provides the facility to construct software as collections of programs, called filters, that pass data to and from each other as serial streams called pipes. There is minimal performance penalty in doing this and the bonus is high modularity.

For the above problem, we write each of the two programs and then run them with a pipe in between, using the Unix command:

```
breaker < InputFile | builder > OutputFile
```

or the DOS command:

```
InputFile | breaker | builder > OutputFile
```

in which the symbol | means that the output from the filter (program) **breaker** is used as input to the program (filter) **builder**.

The third and final option is to take the two programs and convert them back into a single program, eliminating the intermediate file. To do this, we take either one and transform it into a subroutine of the other. This process is known as *inversion*. We will not pursue this interesting technique within this book.

On the face of it, structure clashes and program inversion seem to be very complicated, so why bother? Arguably structure clashes are not an invention of the data structure design method, but a characteristic inherent in certain problems. Whichever method that was used to design this program, the same essential characteristic of the problem has to be overcome. The method has therefore enabled us to gain a fundamental insight into problem solving.

In summary, the data structure design method accommodates structure clashes like this. Try to identify an element of data that is common to both the input file and the output file. In the example problem it is a word of text. Split the required program into two programs – one that converts the input file into an intermediate file that consists of the common data items (words in our example) and a second that converts the intermediate file into the required output. Now each of the two programs can be designed according to the normal data structure design method, since there is no structure clash in either of them. We have now ended up with two programs where we wanted only one. From here there are three options open to us:

1. tolerate the performance penalties
2. use an operating system or programming language that provides the facility for programs to exchange serial streams of data
3. transform one program into a subroutine of the other (inversion).

10.6 ● Discussion

Principles

The basis of the data structure design method is this. What a program is to do, its specification, is completely defined by the nature of its input and output data. In other words, the problem being solved is determined by this data. This is particularly evident in information systems. It is a short step to saying that the *structure* of a program should be dictated by the structure of its inputs and outputs. Specification determines design. This is the reasoning behind the method.

The hypothesis that program structure and data structure can, and indeed should, match constitutes a strong statement about the symbiotic relationship between actions and data within programs. So arguably, this method not only produces the best design for a program, but it creates the *right* design.

The correspondence between the problem to be solved (in this case the structure of the input and output files) and the structure of the program is termed *proximity*. It has an important implication. If there is a small change to the structure of the data, there should only need to be a correspondingly small change to the program. And vice versa – if there is a large change to the structure of the data, there will be a correspondingly large change to the program. This means that in maintenance, the amount of effort needed will match the extent of the changes to the data that are requested. This makes a lot of sense to a client who has no understanding of the trials involved in modifying programs. Sadly it is often the case that someone (a user) requests what they perceive as a small change to program, only to be told by the developer that it will take a long time (and cost a lot).

Degree of systematization

The data structure design method can reasonably claim to be the most systematic program design method currently available. It consists of a number of distinct steps, each of which produces a definite piece of paper. The following claims have been made of the method:

■ non-inspirational – use of the method depends little or not at all on invention or insight
■ rational – it is based on reasoned principles (structured programming and program structure based on data structure)

- teachable – people can be taught the method because it consists of well-defined steps
- consistent – given a single program specification, two different people will come up with the same program design.
- simple and easy to use
- produces designs that can be implemented in any programming language.

While these characteristics can be regarded as advantages, they can also be seen as a challenge to the traditional skills associated with programming. It is also highly contentious to say that data structure design is completely non-inspirational and rational. In particular, some of the steps arguably require a good deal of insight and creativity, for example, drawing the data structure diagram, identifying the elementary operations and placing the operations on the program structure diagram.

Applicability

Data structure design is most applicable in applications where the structure of the (input or output) data is very evident. Where there is no clear structure, the method falls down.

For example, we can assess how useful this method is for designing computational programs by considering an example. If we think about a program to calculate the square root of a number, then the input has a very simple structure, and so has the output. They are both merely single numbers. There is very little information upon which to base a program structure and no guidance for devising some iterative algorithm that calculates successively better and better approximations to the solution. Thus it is unlikely that data structure design can be used to solve problems of this type.

The role of data structure design

Data structure design's strong application area is serial file processing. Serial files are widely used. For example, graphics files (e.g. JPEG and GIF formats), sound files (e.g. MIDI), files sent to printers (e.g. PostScript format), Web pages using HTML, spreadsheet files and word processor files. Gunter Born's book (see Further Reading) lists hundreds of (serial) file types that need the programmer's attention. So, for example, if you needed to write a program to convert a file in Microsoft format to an Apple Macintosh format, data structure design would probably be of help. But perhaps the ultimate tribute to the method is the use of an approach used in compiler writing called *recursive descent*. In recursive descent the algorithm is designed so as to match the structure of the programming language and thus the structure of the input data that is being analyzed.

The main advantages of data structure design are:

- there is high "proximity" between the structure of the program and the structure of the files. Hence a minor change to a file structure will lead only to a minor change in the program
- a series of well-defined steps leads from the specification to the design. Each stage creates a well-defined product.

Summary

The basis of the data structure method is that the structure of a program can be derived from the structure of the files that the program uses. The method uses a diagrammatic notation for file and program structures. Using these diagrams, the method proceeds step by step from descriptions of the file structures to a pseudo-code design.

The steps are:

1. draw a diagram (a data structure diagram) describing the structure of each of the files that the program uses.

2. derive a single program structure diagram from the set of data structure diagrams.

3. write down the elementary operations that the program will have to carry out.

4. associate the elementary operations with their appropriate positions in the program structure diagram

5. transform the program structure diagram into pseudo-code.

In some cases, a problem exhibits an incompatibility between the structures of two of its inputs or outputs. This is known as a structure clash. The method incorporates a scheme for dealing with structure clashes.

 Exercises

10.1 Design a program to display a multiplication table such as young children use. For example, the table for numbers up to 6 is:

	1	2	3	4	5	6
1	1	2	3	4	5	6
2	2	4	6	8	10	12
3	3	6	9	12	15	18
4	4	8	12	16	20	24
5	5	10	15	20	25	30
6	6	12	18	24	30	36

The program should produce a table of any size, specified by an integer input from a text box. (The structure of the input is irrelevant to this design.)

10.2 A data transmission from a remote computer consists of a series of messages. Each message consists of:

1. a header, which is any number of **SYN** bytes

2. a control block, starting with an **F4** (hexadecimal) byte, and ending with **F5** (hexadecimal). It contains any number of bytes (which might be control information, e.g. to open an input-output device).

3. any number of data bytes, starting with **F1** (hexadecimal), and ending with **F2** (hexadecimal).

Messages must be processed in this way:

■ store any control bytes in an array. When the block is complete, call an already written method named **obeyControl**

■ every data byte should be displayed on the screen

Assume that a **readByte** operation is available to obtain a byte from the remote computer.

10.3 Compare and contrast the principles behind the following design methods:

■ functional decomposition

■ data structure design

■ data flow design

■ object oriented design.

10.4 Some proponents of the data structure design method claim that it is "non-inspirational". How much inspiration do you think is required in using the method?

10.5 Assess the advantages and disadvantages of data structure design.

10.6 Suggest facilities for a software tool that could assist in or automate using data structure design.

10.7 Evaluate data structure design under the following headings:

■ special features and strengths

■ weaknesses

■ philosophy/perspective?

■ systematic?

■ appropriate applications

■ inappropriate applications

■ is the method top-down, bottom-up or something else?

■ good for large-scale design?

■ good for small-scale design?

■ can tools assist in using the method?

Answers to self-test questions

10.1   A **new line** is needed for each occurrence of **process line.**

10.2

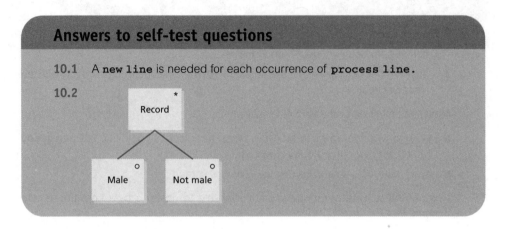

Further reading

The main reference on this method is: M.J. Jackson, *Principles of Program Design*, Academic Press, 1997.

Read all about the many serial file formats in mainstream use in: Gunter Born, *The File Formats Handbook*, International Thomson Publishing, 1995.

Object-oriented design

This chapter:

- explains how to carry out object-oriented design (OOD)
- explains how to use class–responsibility–collaborator (CRC) cards
- emphasizes the importance of using ready-made libraries.

11.1 ● Introduction

We begin this chapter by reviewing the distinctive features and principles of object-oriented programming (OOP). This sets the scene as to what an OOD seeks to exploit. Then we look at how to go about designing software. We use the Cyberspace Invaders game as the case study.

The widely agreed principles of OOP are:

- encapsulation
- inheritance
- polymorphism.

The advantages of these features is that they promote the reusability of software components. Encapsulation allows a class to be reused without knowing how it works – thus modularity and abstraction are provided. Inheritance allows a class to be reused by using some of the existing facilities, while adding new facilities in a secure manner. Polymorphism further promotes encapsulation by allowing general purpose classes to be written that will work successfully with many different types of object.

Object-oriented languages are usually accompanied by a large and comprehensive library of classes. Members of such a library can either be used directly or reused by employing inheritance. Thus the process of programming involves using existing library classes, extending the library classes, and designing brand-new classes.

During OOD, the designer must be aware of the wealth of useful classes available in the libraries. To ignore them would be to risk wasting massive design, programming and testing time. It is common experience for someone setting out to write OO software to find that nearly all of the software already exists within the library. OO development is therefore often regarded as (merely) extending library classes. This, of course, requires a discipline – the initial investment in the time to explore and learn about what might be a large library, set against the benefits that accrue later.

11.2 ● Design

One of the principles used in the design of object-oriented software is to simulate real world situations as objects. You build a software model of things in the real world. Here are some examples:

■ if we are developing an office information system, we set out to simulate users, mail, shared documents and files

■ in a factory automation system, we set out to simulate the different machines, queues of work, orders, and deliveries.

The approach is to identify the objects in the problem to be addressed and to model them as objects in the software.

One way to carry out OOD is to examine the software specification in order to extract information about the objects and methods. The approach to identifying objects and methods is:

1. look for nouns (things) in the specification – these are the objects
2. look for verbs (doing words) in the specification – these are the methods

Here is the specification for the cyberspace invaders program:

A panel (Figure 11.1) displays a defender and an alien. The alien moves sideways. When it hits a wall, it reverses its direction. The alien randomly launches a bomb that moves vertically downwards. If a bomb hits the defender, the user loses and the game is over. The defender moves left or right according to mouse movements. When the mouse is clicked, the defender launches a laser that moves upwards. If a laser hits the alien, the user wins and the game is over.

A button is provided to start a new game.

Scanning through the specification, we find the following nouns. As we might expect, some of these nouns are mentioned more than once, but the repetition does not matter for the purpose of design.

```
panel, defender, alien, wall, bomb, mouse, laser
```

These nouns correspond to potential objects, and therefore classes within the program. So we translate these nouns into the names of classes in the model. The noun **panel** translates into the **Panel** class, available in the library. The nouns **defender** and **alien** translate into the classes **Defender** and **Alien** respectively. The noun **wall**

Figure 11.1 The cyberspace invaders game

need not be implemented as a class because it can be simply accommodated as a detail within the class **Alien**. The noun **bomb** translates into class **Bomb**. The noun **mouse** need not be a class because mouse click events can be simply handled by the **Panel** class or the **Defender** class. Finally we need a class **Laser**. Thus we arrive at the following list of non-library classes:

```
Game, Defender, Alien, Laser, Bomb
```

These are shown in the class diagram (Figure 11.2). This states that the class **Game** uses the classes **Defender, Alien, Laser** and **Bomb**.

We have not yet quite completed our search for objects in the program. In order that collisions can be detected, objects need to know where other objects are and how big they are. Therefore, implicit in the specification are the ideas of the position and size of each object. These are the *x* and *y* coordinates, height and width of each object. Although these are potentially objects, they can instead be simply implemented as **int** variables within classes **Defender, Alien, Laser** and **Bomb**. These can be accessed via methods named **getX, getY, getHeight** and **getWidth**.

One object that we have so far ignored in the design is a timer from the library that is set to click at small regular time intervals, in order to implement the animation. Whenever the timer ticks, the objects are moved, the panel is cleared and all the objects

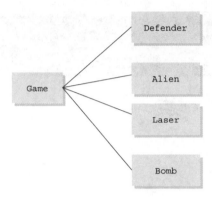

Figure 11.2 The non-library classes involved in the game program

are displayed. Another object is a random number generator, created from the library class **Random**, to control when the alien launches bombs.

We have now identified the classes that make up the game program.

We now scan the specification again, this time looking for verbs that we can attach to the above list of objects. We see:

```
display, move, hit, launch, click, win, lose
```

Again, some of these words are mentioned more than once. For example, both the alien and the defender move. Also all the objects in the game need to be displayed.

We now allocate methods to classes, with the help of the specification. This concludes the design process.

Now although we used the specification to arrive at classes and methods, we could have used an alternative formulation of the specification, use cases. Use cases were explained in Chapter 4 on requirements specification. A use case is a simple, natural language statement of a complete and useful function that a system carries out. For the game, some use cases are:

- **defender move** – when the user moves the mouse left and right, the defender object moves left and right on the screen
- **fire laser** – when the player clicks the mouse, a laser is launched upwards from the defender object
- **laser hits alien** – when a laser hits the alien, the player wins and the game is over

Notice that some of the use cases are not initiated by the user of the system. Instead they are initiated by objects within the game, such as when an alien launches a bomb.

A complete set of use cases constitutes a specification of what a system should do. We can then use them to derive classes and their methods. Again, we seek verbs (which are the classes) and verbs (which are the methods). Fortunately use cases are very suited to this process, because they emphasize actions acting on objects. So, for example, the use case **defender move** implies that there is an object **defender** that embodies methods **moveLeft** and **moveRight**.

11.1 Derive information about objects and methods from the use case:

- **laser hits alien** – when a laser hits the alien, the player wins.

While we are identifying classes and methods, we can document each class as a UML class diagram. This type of class diagram shows more detail about a class than those we have met so far. A large rectangle contains three sections. The first section simply shows the class name. The second section shows the instance variables. The third section shows the public methods provided by the class. We start with class **Game**:

```
class Game

Instance variables

panel
timer


Methods

mouseMoved
mouseClicked
actionPerformed
```

Next we consider the defender object. It has a position within the panel and a size. In response to a mouse movement, it moves. It can be displayed. Therefore its class diagram is:

```
class Defender

Instance variables

x
y
height
width


Methods

move
display
getX
getY
getHeight
getWidth
```

Next we design and document the **Alien** class. The alien has a position and a size. Whenever the clock ticks, it moves. Its direction and speed is controlled by the step size that is used when it moves. It can be created and displayed.

Class Alien
Instance variables x Y height width xStep
Methods Alien move display getX getY getHeight getWidth

SELF-TEST QUESTION

11.2 Write the class diagram for the **Bomb** class.

We now have the full list of classes, and the methods and instance variables associated with each class – we have modeled the game and designed a structure for the program.

11.3 ● Looking for reuse

The next act of design is to check to make sure that we are not reinventing the wheel. One of the main benefits of OOP is reuse of software components. At this stage we should check whether:

■ what we need might be in one of the libraries
■ we may have written a class last month that is what we need
■ we may be able to use inheritance.

We see in the cyberspace invaders software can make good use of GUI components, such as the panel, available in the library. Other library components that are useful are a timer and a random number generator.

If we find classes that are similar, we should think about using inheritance. We look at how to write the code to achieve inheritance in Chapter 15 on OOP. In Chapter 13 on refactoring, we look at identifying inheritance using the "is-a" and "has-a" tests.

We shall see how the game software can be considerably simplified by making use of inheritance.

11.4 ● Using the library

OOP is often called programming by extending the library because the libraries provided along with OO languages are so rich and so reusable. An organization will often also create its own library of classes that have been created in earlier projects. There are two distinct ways of using classes in a library:

1. creating objects from classes in the library
2. defining new classes by extending (inheriting from) classes in the library.

For example, in designing the game program, we expect the library to provide classes that implement buttons and a panel – along with classes that support the event handling associated with these widgets. For example in the Java library we can use the **Button** class directly, by creating button objects as instances of the **Button** class:

```
Button button = new Button("start");
```

The Java library also provides classes and methods that display the graphical images that the program uses.

Another way in which the library is commonly used is to form new classes by inheritance.

It is worthwhile looking in the library at the outset of design and then again at every stage of design, in case something useful can be incorporated into the design. This takes some self-discipline because it is tempting to write a method again, rather than develop an understanding of someone else's code.

11.5 ● Class–responsibility–collaborator cards

Class–responsibility–collaborator (CRC) cards are a way of helping to carry out OOD. The technique uses ordinary index cards, made out of cardboard and widely available. Each card describes an individual class as shown by the example of the **Alien** class in Figure 11.3. The designer begins by writing the class name at the head of the card. Then one area lists the methods provided by the class (its responsibilities). For the class **Alien**, these are **move**, **display**, etc. A second area lists the classes that use this class and the classes that are used by this class (the collaborators). For the class **Alien**, there is only one, the library class **Graphics** that supports displaying graphical images.

The cards representing the constituent classes are placed on a table. This way the cards can be moved around easily; their interrelationships can be visualized and adjusted as necessary.

CRC cards offer advantages as compared with a software tool. They are cheap, readily available and portable. Several people can easily collaborate, standing round the

Class name: `Alien`	
Responsibilities	Collaborators
moves	`Graphics`
displays itself	
provides its x coordinate	
provides its y coordinate	
provides its height	
provides its width	

Figure 11.3 A Sample CRC card – the class `Alien` in the cyberspace invaders game

table. It seems that the act of physically handling the cards contributes to an improved understanding of the structure of the software.

11.6 ● Iteration

Iteration is a crucial ingredient of OOD. This is because there is no guaranteed formula for finding the right set of objects to model a problem. Therefore the process is exploratory and iterative; it is common for classes to be initially proposed during a design but subsequently be discarded as the design progresses. Similarly, the need for some classes will not emerge until the implementation (coding) stage.

During each iteration, the design is refined and reanalyzed continuously. Indeed, whereas design and implementation are considered largely distinct activities in traditional software development, using the object-oriented paradigm the two activities are often indistinguishable. There are a number of reasons for this, which we will now discuss:

Prototyping is seen as an integral part of the object-oriented software design and implementation process. Prototyping recognizes that in most cases the requirements for a system are at best vague or not well understood. It is an exploratory process providing early validation (or otherwise) of analysis, design and user interface alternatives. Prototyping dictates that design and implementation proceed in at least large-grain iterative steps.

The activities which take place and the concerns which are addressed during the refinement of an OOD are identical whether it is the design or a working prototype that is being refined. Moreover, such activities as reorganizing the class to reflect some newly recognized abstraction (see Chapter 13 on refactoring) are just as likely to take place during the implementation of a prototype as during the design. The design must now be updated to reflect this change – design and implementation are now proceeding in small-grain iterative steps.

Designers must be far more aware of the implementation environment because of the impact that a large reusable class library can have on a design. Designers must not only be aware of the library classes but also design patterns (see Chapter 12).

To sum up, as noted by Meyer, one of the gurus of object-oriented development, designing is programming and programming is designing.

11.7 ● Discussion

OOD and OOP have become the dominant approach to software development. This is assisted by the availability and widespread use of programming languages that fully support OOP – such languages as C++, Ada, Smalltalk, C#, Visual Basic.Net and Java.

A number of OOD methodologies have appeared and are used. The available methodologies differ in:

■ their degree of formality

■ which features of the problem they choose to model (and not model)

■ the types of application for which they tend to be most suited (e.g. information systems versus real-time control systems).

The strengths of the object-oriented approach are:

■ the intuitive appeal of directly modeling the application as objects, classes and methods

■ the high modularity (information hiding) provided by the object and class concepts

■ the ease of reuse of software components (classes) using inheritance.

Note that OOD leads to structures that are non-hierarchical, which distinguishes it from some approaches.

Summary

OOD can be characterized as a three-stage process:

1. find the classes, i.e. determine the objects involved and their classes

2. specify what the classes are responsible for, i.e. what they do (their methods)

3. specify their collaborators, i.e. other classes they need to get their jobs done.

The following techniques and notations can be used for design:

■ identify nouns and verbs in the specification or the use cases to derive classes and methods

■ use the library – at every stage during design it is worthwhile looking in the library for classes that can either be used directly or extended by inheritance

■ use CRC cards – a means of establishing the responsibilities (methods provided) and collaborator classes of each of the classes.

Exercises

11.1 Complete the design of the game presented in the chapter. In particular, establish use cases and hence identify the methods associated with each class.

11.2 Design the software structure for each of the systems described in Appendix A.

11.3 Can OOD be characterized as a top-down, a bottom-up or some other process?

11.4 If programming and design are really two aspects of the same process (as OOD suggests), does this mean that all designers must also be programmers?

11.5 To what extent is an OOD influenced by the class library of reusable components that is available? To what extent must designers be knowledgeable about available components?

11.6 What features or indicators might you use to help identify potential flaws in an OOD? For example, what might be the problem with a class that has an excessive number of methods? What could be done about this class? Again, is there a problem with a class that only calls other classes and provides no methods that are used by other classes? What might be done about this situation?

11.7 Design a program that allows two-dimensional shapes to be drawn on the screen. A square, circle, triangle or rectangle can be selected from a list of options and positioned at a place on the screen using a mouse. A shape can be repositioned, deleted or its size changed using the usual mouse operations.

11.8 Suggest features for a software tool that would support the creation, storage and editing of class diagrams.

11.9 Suggest features for a software tool that would support the creation, storage and editing of CRC cards. Suggest features for checking the consistency of a collection of such cards.

11.10 Evaluate OOD under the following headings:

- special features and strengths.
- weaknesses
- philosophy/perspective?
- systematic?
- appropriate applications
- inappropriate applications
- is the method top-down, bottom-up or something else?
- good for large-scale design?
- good for small-scale design?
- can tools assist in using the method?

11.11 Compare and contrast the principles behind the following design methods:

- functional decomposition
- data structure design
- data flow design
- object oriented design.

Answers to self-test questions

11.1 There are objects **laser** and **alien** and therefore classes **Laser** and **Alien**. Class **Laser** has a method **checkAlienHit**.

11.2

class Bomb
Instance variables
x y height width yStep
Methods
Bomb move display getX getY getHeight getWidth

Further reading

Object-oriented design

An excellent book which presents a view of the process and notation of OOD and also contains five extensive design case studies. Widely regarded as the definitive book on OOD: G. Booch, *Object-Oriented Design with Applications*, Addison-Wesley, 2nd edn, 1993.

A wide-ranging survey of approaches and notations. Very readable. An excellent overview of the different methods and notations: Edward Yourdon, *Object-Oriented Systems Design: An Integrated Approach*, Prentice Hall, 1994.

This book provides many valuable insights into the design and implementation of object-oriented software. The early chapters provide an excellent and most readable explanation of the principles of OOP. Examples are given using the programming language Eiffel: B. Meyer, *Object-Oriented Software Construction*, Prentice Hall, 2nd edn, 1997.

This excellent book provides a coherent language independent methodology for OOD known as "responsibility-driven design": R.J. Wirfs-Brock, B. Wilkerson and L. Weiner, *Designing Object-Oriented Software*, Prentice Hall, 1990.

Unified modeling language

Two simple books that one can read and understand: Martin Fowler with Kendall Scott, *UML Distilled*, Addison-Wesley, 2000; Perdita Stevens with Rob Pooley, *Using UML*, Addison-Wesley, 2000.

Object-oriented development

Written by a consultant who has seen many successful and unsuccessful projects. He gives the results of his very practical experience. The book begins by identifying the problems of software engineering. As part of this he suggests that successful pieces of software have been written by just two people, young and without using respectable methods. He goes on to look at the expected benefits of OOD. The main part of the book is about practical OOD methods including management, "software component foundries" and how to bring about change: Tom Love, *Object Lessons: Lessons Learned in OO Development Projects*, SIGS Books, 1993.

This book complements Booch's book about the technical aspects of design. It is a companion book about the down-to-earth practical aspects of development. Very readable: Grady Booch, *Object Solutions: Managing the OO Project*, Addison-Wesley, 1996.

CHAPTER 12 | Design patterns

This chapter explains:

- how to use design patterns during development
- several major design patterns
- some valuable anti-patterns.

12.1 ● Introduction

Experienced programmers draw on half-remembered memories of software structures that they have used themselves or seen used in the past. An example of a simple programming pattern is the design of a program to find the largest number in an array of numbers. The simplest algorithm uses a variable to record the largest value that has yet been encountered. The program starts at the beginning of the array and proceeds item by item, examining each number, updating this variable as necessary:

```
largest = list[0]
index = 0
while index <= list.size() do
    if list[index] > largest then
        largest = list[index]
    end if
index = index + 1
end while
```

This is clearly a small piece of program that is easily constructed by any experienced programmer, but to novice programmers, seeing this is something of a revelation. And once seen, the programmer never forgets it. Or at least the programmer remembers the idea of what is needed, rather than the detail. This is a software pattern. Over a period of time, experienced programmers build up a large repertoire of memories of programming patterns such as this one.

A number of patterns have been identified, given names, cataloged and documented in catalogs or books. These patterns are available for off-the-shelf use, just as classes are available in class libraries. Software engineering patterns are patterns on a larger scale than the simple program seen above. The established patterns specify the structure of useful software at the architectural level. In object-oriented development, this means structures expressed in terms of classes and their interrelationships.

The strength of design patterns is that good design ideas are recorded, given a name, and explained with the aid of examples. This extends the vocabulary of software developers. It also extends the repertoire of ideas that they can use without reinventing the wheel.

To make use of patterns, the software engineer needs some recollection of the standard patterns. This is obtained by browsing a patterns catalog prior to a project. The engineer thereby retains some memory (perhaps only a partial recollection) of the patterns, then, during the early phase of software architectural design, the engineer realizes that one or more patterns may be useful. They then consult the catalog to confirm the appropriateness of the pattern and see exactly how to use it. The next step is to use the pattern as part of the design.

In summary the stages are:

1.   browse a design pattern catalog, to obtain some feel for the available patterns

2.   embark on a new design with an awareness of the patterns

3.   recognize the need for one of the established patterns

4.   consult the catalog to check the applicability of the pattern

5.   use the catalog for information on the how to use the pattern

6.   use the pattern as part of the design.

As well as architectural structure, patterns are available for such domains as user interfaces, file systems and multithreading. Patterns are also provided for activities such as testing and project management.

In order to use design patterns the programmer needs considerable experience and understanding of OOD and OOP.

Just as there are patterns (which are valuable structures) so there are anti-patterns, which are undesirable structures. The reason for identifying and cataloguing anti-patterns is to avoid them. We look at one such pattern.

In this chapter we present a number of useful patterns and use the cyberspace invaders game as an example in explaining some of the patterns.

12.2 ● Inheritance

It bears repeating that one of the major goals of the object-oriented paradigm is to produce reusable software components – components which can be reused both within the application in which they were generated but also in future applications.

The concepts of inheritance and subclassing supported by object-oriented languages allow:

- new classes of objects to be described as extensions or specializations of existing classes, i.e. a new class can be defined as a subclass of an existing class
- subclasses to inherit the behavior and state of their superclasses.

These concepts add extra dimensions to the design process. Taking into account inheritance means that a major design goal is to factor the responsibilities within a hierarchy of classes so that a responsibility attached to a superclass can be shared by all subclasses.

In Chapter 13 on refactoring we will see how the design of the cyberspace invaders program can be improved using inheritance.

12.3 ● Delegation

This is probably the simplest and most obvious pattern. It describes the situation where one class uses another. Delegation is worth emphasizing as a pattern because there is sometimes a tendency to use inheritance too enthusiastically. Delegation is, in fact, a more general way of extending the functionality of a class.

As an example, we will use another game, draughts (UK) or checkers (US). This game takes place on a chess board with a set of black pieces and a set of white pieces. Let us image a program that displays the board and the pieces on the screen as a game is played. A natural (but as we shall see later flawed) structure would be to see that black and white pieces are instances of class **Black** and **White** and that these are in turn subclasses of class **Piece**. The class diagram, showing inheritance, is shown in Figure 12.1.

However, there is a problem. When a piece reaches the end of the board, it becomes crowned and thereby gains extra powers. How do we accommodate this in the relationships between classes? The trouble is that once an object is an instance of **White**, it remains a **White**. Objects cannot change their class. So inheritance, though appealing, is inappropriate. A better relationship is shown in Figure 12.2. Here classes **Black**, **White, CrownedWhite** and **CrownedBlack** use class **Piece** in the delegation pattern. Inheritance is absent from this pattern. The class **Piece** still incorporates all the shared features of the original class **Piece** – features such as the position on the board.

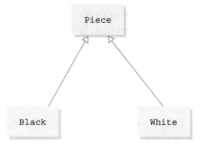

Figure 12.1 Game of draughts showing inheritance

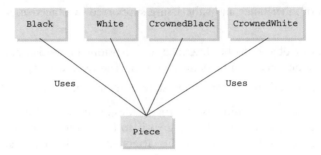

Figure 12.2 Game of draughts using delegation

But the converse is not true.
The moral is:

- anything that can be accomplished by inheritance can be achieved through delegation
- everything that can be accomplished by delegation *cannot* be achieved through inheritance. Delegation is more general mechanism than inheritance.
- inheritance can be useful for modeling static "is-a" situations
- inheritance is not appropriate for modeling "is-a-role-played-by" situations
- delegation is more widely used than inheritance.

SELF-TEST QUESTION

12.1 A soldier in the army is a private, a sergeant or a general. Do we model this as inheritance or delegation?

12.4 ● Singleton

In some systems there only needs to be one instance of a class. Normally, of course, someone writes a class so that any number of objects can be created from it. But occasionally there should only be one. An example is an object to manage the communication between a system and the database. It would be confusing if any number of classes were interacting with the database. Now it would be possible to try to achieve this affect by telling all the programmers on the team that there is one copy of the object, with such-and-such a name, written by Mo. But in a large and complex system, this could be forgotten. We can instead legislate (with the help of compiler checking) using the Singleton pattern.

Another example of the Singleton pattern is evident in the cyberspace invaders game (Appendix A), where there should only be one object representing the defender.

The following coding shows how a singleton class **Demo** can be written in Java.

```java
public class Demo {

    private static final Demo demo = new Demo();

    private Demo() {
    }

    private static Demo getInstance() {
        return demo;
    }
}
```

SELF-TEST QUESTION

12.2 Why is the constructor **Demo** labeled as **private**?

12.5 ● Factory method

Suppose that we are writing some software to handle images. An image resides in a file and there are several different common file formats – for example, jpeg and gif. We would like the facility to create an object corresponding to a graphics image, in this manner:

```java
Image image = new Image("picture.jpeg");
```

Once we have created the object, we can perform such operations as:

```java
image.rotate(90);
image.display();
image.enlarge(2, 2);
```

The problem is that all of these methods will be different for each different graphics file format. Indeed, the graphics object will be different for each file format. So one single class – **Image** – will not suffice; we need a different class for each file format. One approach would be to provide a number of classes and expect a user to call the constructor for the relevant class like this:

```java
JpegImage image = new JpegImage("fileName.jpeg");
```

But this is clumsy. The alternative is to create an abstract class **Image** that has a factory method **createImage**. Now we create an image object conveniently like this:

```java
Image image = Image.createImage("fileName.jpeg");
```

createImage is class (static) method of the class **Image**. It looks at the extension of the file name parameter and creates an appropriate object. For example, if the file type is jpeg, it creates a subclass of **Image** suitable for jpeg images. The sole purpose of this method is to create the appropriate object, making the choice at run time. So now users can treat all image file types in the same manner. The code for the factory method is:

```
class Image {

    public static Image createImage(String fileName) {
        String extension = getExtension(fileName);
        if (extension.equals("jpeg"))
            return (new JpegImage(fileName));
        if (extension.equals("gif"))
            return (new GifImage(fileName));
    }
}
```

Here we have used a method **getExtension** (not shown) that returns the extension part of a file name.

We have buried the code that creates an appropriate class within the factory method, providing a simple interface to the users.

Why could we not simply use the constructor method of class **Image**? The answer is that a constructor can only return an object of its own class. This is a limitation of constructors and, if we need to do anything different, we need to use a factory method.

12.6 ● Façade

Suppose you write a group of classes that perform some useful functions. It could be a filing system that allows other classes (users) to open a file, close a file, read and write information. One option is to tell users which classes to use and how (Figure 12.3, left-hand diagram). However, this means that a user needs to understand the structure of the subsystem to use it effectively. In addition, changes to the structure of the subsystem may require changes to its users.

A better option (Figure 12.3, right-hand diagram) is to tell users to use one class – a façade class. The façade class presents a clean and simple interface for users. It has

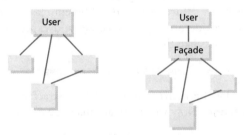

Figure 12.3 The Façade pattern

methods that provide all the functionality of the system. The detailed structure of the system is hidden from its users. The façade class knows about the structure of the group of classes and uses them as necessary. However, the classes in the group do not need to know about the façade class, so any changes to the group do not impact on the users.

12.7 ● Immutable

An immutable object is one that, once created, does not change its state. In the cyberspace invaders game, there could be objects that do not move and do not change while the game is in progress. These objects do not change their state (their internal variables). We can write an Immutable class by providing methods to access the values of the object, but none to change them. The variables within an immutable class must not be declared as constants, because they are changed (once) by the constructor method.

12.8 ● Model, view controller (observer, observable)

Many software systems have at their center a model or a simulation of the application of interest. The simulation consists of objects and a set of rules governing how they interact. In the cyberspace invaders game, the model consists of such objects as the alien, lasers and bombs that move and interact according to certain rules. The model ensures that bombs moves vertically. If a bomb strikes the defender, the user loses and the game is over.

The core model is surrounded by classes that support a user interface. The user interface consists of two parts: the elements that control the system (inputs) and the elements that allow us to view information (the outputs). In the game, the user moves the mouse to move the defender object and can fire a laser by clicking on the mouse button. These are controls. The screen shows the position of the objects, such as the alien and a laser. These are outputs (the view).

To summarize, systems often have three components:

- the model
- the view
- the controller.

The MVC pattern recognizes that many systems have this three-part structure – model, view and controller – and that the software architecture should be explicitly partitioned in the same way. This has the advantage that the view and/or the control can be changed without changing the core. For example, the user could control the defender object with a joystick instead of the mouse, or the display could be sent across the internet to the screens of multiple players. So, if the system is partitioned, we can easily change the view or the control or both.

For this pattern to work properly there has to be clear communication between the three components:

- when the user alters a control, the model must be told
- when the model changes, the view must be told.

These relationships between components are the essence of the MVC pattern. The advantages are that the model, the view or the controller can be changed without affecting any other part of the system. Furthermore, additional views and controls can be added easily.

12.9 ● Mediator

In the software for the cyberspace invaders game, there must be a method or methods that test to see whether a laser has hit an alien and whether a bomb has hit the defender. The question is: Where are these methods? One option is to place this collision detection within class **Laser** and class **Bomb**. Unfortunately this leads to a complex structure in which every bomb has to know about the defender object and every laser has to know about every alien object. This is high coupling. For example, if we introduce additional objects into the game we will need to modify class **Bomb** and class **Laser**.

A better approach is to create a mediator class. As its name suggests, this is responsible for handling relationships between objects – termed colleague objects. The essence of the mediator pattern is that colleague objects are changing (because, in this example, they are moving).

This is how the pattern is implemented. First, all the colleague objects register with the mediator object. Thereafter, when a colleague object changes its state (in this example, when it moves) it calls the mediator object. The mediator decides whether a notable event has occurred (a collision in this example) and, if necessary, notifies appropriate colleague objects (the objects involved in the collision).

The advantages are:

■ all the dependency logic is in one place

■ the colleague objects are simpler because they do not embody code to check dependencies.

SELF-TEST QUESTION

12.3 Identify differences between the Mediator pattern and the MVC pattern.

12.10 ● Pipe and Filter

This pattern describes a way of building software from a group of components that collaborate by passing a stream of information. The components behave like an assembly line. Each component inputs some information from one component, processes it and passes it on to another component, Figure 12.4. Each component is

Figure 12.4 Pipe and Filter pattern

known as a filter and the connections are known as pipes. The information flow between components is a one-way serial stream of data. Each component knows nothing about any other component. This scheme corresponds to the pipe and filter scheme that Unix provides. Many of the Unix utility programs process a stream of data and create a new output stream. Examples are given in Chapter 18 on scripting languages. Arguably, this type of connection means that the components have minimal coupling.

12.11 ● Proxy

A proxy object acts instead of some other object or objects. It fields requests, passing them on as necessary.

The classic example is that of a proxy server on the internet, which acts in place of another server because the actual server is too busy. The proxy either handles requests itself or passes a request on to an available server. A busy website, such as a successful search engine, cannot handle all the requests using a single server. Instead it uses a collection of servers, fronted by a proxy server that farms out the work to an available server.

SELF-TEST QUESTION

12.4 Compare and contrast the Proxy pattern with the Façade pattern.

12.12 ● Layers

The Layers pattern, sometimes called tiers, is a classic pattern that is used in many systems. This pattern divides a software system into hierarchical layers. In one incarnation, Figure 12.5, there are three layers. The top layer handles the user interface (sometimes called the presentation layer), the middle layer handles the application logic (sometimes called the domain logic or the business logic) and the bottom layer handles access to the database. Each layer makes requests on the services provided by the layer immediately below it, and receives replies, but there are no other dependencies in this structure.

The layers pattern can be used to structure the word processor (Appendix A). The user interface provides the display of the current document and a set of commands. The

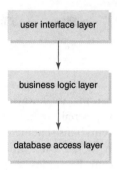

Figure 12.5 Layers

database level stores and retrieves documents. The middle layer processes commands, such as deleting text.

The strength of the Layers pattern is that it provides a large-scale structure for certain types of software. It also means that each layer of the software can be modified without affecting the other layers. For example, in the word processor, we can alter the way that commands are invoked (the presentation layer), for example, by adding menus, without changing the database access layer.

The word processor is a single-machine application. However, many current applications – such as an ATM – are network-based or internet-based. The simplest network-based architecture is the client-server architecture. This consists of two layers – the client software running on the client machine and the server software running on the server. The classic example is a web browser and a web server. The client passes a request to the server; the server responds.

A classic example of the Layers pattern is the structure of the software for internet communication, called the TCP/IP stack. Every computer that uses the internet has this software. A typical application program makes requests on the transport layer that supports the TCP protocol. This in turn makes requests of the internet layer that supports the IP protocol. This in turn calls the physical layer which actually carries out data transfers. Thus the software consists of four levels, including the application level.

Another version of the Layers pattern, with four levels, describes many networked solutions, Figure 12.6. Again, each layer uses the layer below it. The communication between presentation and server layer is carried out according to a chosen network protocol, such as HTTP.

In designing a distributed system, there are choices about which layer does what. In a thin client system, the client software does very little, while the bulk of the work is carried out on the server. In a fat client architecture, the business logic layer migrates to the client machine. The decision about where to perform processing depends on such issues as performance, maintenance and security.

Another benefit of the Layers pattern is facilitating security. The boundaries between layers serve as well-defined interfaces where security checks can be carried out. For example encryption can be used between the client and the server. Finally, Layers provide for scalability. A server acting as a proxy (see pattern above) can delegate its task to other servers as the load increases.

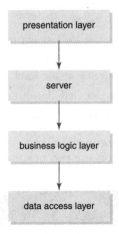

Figure 12.6 Layers in a distributed system

12.13 ● Blob – an anti-pattern

The blob is a bad structure – an anti-pattern. All the classes in the program are merged into one large class. There is structure in terms of constituent methods, but that is all. There is no large-scale structure. The blob is what someone would create if they did not really understand what OOP is about – or if they could not see how to structure the software into meaningful classes.

At one extreme the designer has the option of creating a design that consists only of one single class. This is always possible, and corresponds to a non-OOP. At the other extreme, the designer might create an unnecessarily large number of classes with many interconnections. Thus design is a matter of judgment in order to arrive at the optimal classes for the problem.

12.14 ● Discussion

Patterns represent a valuable type of reuse. You do not reuse code or classes, you reuse a design or a software structure. Such a design is probably a revelation for a novice, but is probably recognizable by experts. Giving patterns individual names means that they can be discussed easily. Cataloging patterns makes them widely available.

Some people like to distinguish types of patterns:

- architectural patterns – the highest level structures, applicable to large numbers of classes
- design patterns – patterns applicable at the level of small groups of classes
- coding patterns – applicable to detailed algorithms within methods
- anti-patterns – the opposites of patterns.

You know you understand patterns when you can see how to use two or more in your project. Many software systems use two or sometimes more patterns.

Summary

Patterns embody the experience of developers. They document useful architectural structures (Some patterns also record techniques for activities such as testing.) A pattern has a name, an application domain and a suggestion for a solution. Patterns enable novices to use the knowledge of experts. They provide a body of knowledge and a language for talking about structure. Patterns are documented in catalogs (see the reading list below) for browsing prior to and during architectural software design.

This chapter explains how to use some useful design patterns (and some anti-patterns):

- Inheritance – extending an existing class
- Delegation – using other classes to perform useful tasks
- Singleton – a class with only one instance
- Factory Method – creating the appropriate class at run time
- Façade – creating a front end to make using a collection of classes easier
- Immutable – an object that does not change
- Model-View-Controller – separating input, output and logic
- Mediator – encapsulating the interaction between classes
- Pipe and Filter – components that process a serial stream of data, passing it from one to another
- Proxy – a component that accepts requests on behalf of other components
- Layers – separating large scale architecture into levels
- Blob – an anti-pattern, a single complex class.

Exercises

12.1 Review the architectural structure of the cyberspace invaders game (Appendix A). Suggest which patterns would be useful.

12.2 In a word processor (Appendix A), how would you use the MVC pattern? Hints: what views does a word processor display? What commands does it provide?

12.3 Show how the Layers pattern can be used in the ATM software and in the library system (Appendix A).

Answers to self-test questions

12.1 If people had static roles, we could model the structures using inheritance. We could say "a private is-a soldier". But army personnel get promoted, so the best structure is delegation.

12.2 It means that it can only be called from within the class. Thus no program can call the constructor from another class. The only way to create an instance is to call **getInstance**, and this always returns the same object.

12.3 1. The MVC pattern is concerned only with the user interface, while the Mediator pattern is more general.

 2. A Mediator class is more complex because it embodies logic governing the interaction of the objects.

12.4 Both patterns act as a front end to a component or collection of components. But the motivation for Façade is to provide a clean interface. Proxy does it for performance reasons.

12.5 Both explicitly separate out the presentation software from the business logic component.

12.6 Pipe and Filter passes data in one direction only, whereas in Layers it is passed to and fro between layers. In Pipe and Filter, communication is solely by passing a stream of data, whereas in layers, some of the communication is via method calls.

Further reading

The first and most significant of the books about reusable design patterns. Written by authors now referred to as the Gang of Four (GoF). It presents a number of OO patterns, each with a name, a rationale and examples. (The examples of use are mainly in C++, but the designs are more widely applicable.) It is not an easy book and many people report that reading it is a challenge: Erich Gamma, Richard Helm, Ralph Johnson and John Vlissides, *Design Patterns: Elements of Reusable Object-Oriented Software*, Addison-Wesley, 1995.

This book is a readable catalog. Although the code examples are given in Java, you do not need to know about Java, or use Java to understand the patterns: Mark Grand, *Patterns in Java: A Catalog of Reusable Design Patterns Illustrated with UML*, 2 vols, John Wiley, 1998, 1999.

This book explores what can go wrong (calling them anti-patterns) during software development, particularly OO development, and explains how to recover from these situations. Easy to read, enjoyable and refreshing: William Brown, Raphael Malveau, Hays McCormick and Thomas Mowbray, *Anti Patterns*, John Wiley, 1998.

CHAPTER 13

Refactoring

This chapter:

- explains how to carry out refactoring
- explains several common refactorings.

13.1 ● Introduction

Refactoring is about improving an architectural design. Nowadays a design tends to be an OOD, expressed in terms of classes and their interrelationships (methods). However, design does not usually proceed in a straightforward, linear manner. Most often, design tends to be an iterative process. First, candidate classes are identified. Then some will be accepted while others will be rejected – perhaps because they have no methods or because their methods are subsumed by some other class. Methods tend to migrate from one class to another as a better understanding of the objects and their role within the problem emerges. This process is known as *refactoring*. Refactoring is the transformation of a correct program structure (e.g., a class diagram) into an improved structure.

Good ideas for refactoring are published in catalogs. Each idea has a name so that it can be referred to in conversations between developers. In this chapter we present some of the most popular refactorings. We use as an example the cyberspace invaders game (Appendix A) whose architecture is designed in the chapter on OOD.

So, the steps of refactoring are:

1. create a design
2. review the design
3. identify possible refactorings
4. carry out refactoring.

An alternative approach is to refactor periodically as design proceeds:

1. carry out some partial design
2. review the design
3. identify possible refactorings
4. carry out refactoring
5. continue from step 1.

The term coupling describes the interaction between components, while cohesion describes the interactions within a component. Many of the refactorings are aimed at minimizing coupling between components and maximizing cohesion within components. This combination promotes clarity, modularity and re-use.

13.2 ● Encapsulate Data

A variable is defined as public and it is therefore unclear who uses it and why. The remedy is to make it private and provide methods to access the data.

For example, in the game, the x coordinate of an alien could be declared (in Java) as:

```
public int x;
```

Instead, declare x as follows:

```
private int x;
```

And provide methods to read the value and change the value:

```
public void setX(int newX) {
    x = newX;
}

public int getX() {
    return x;
}
```

Encapsulating data makes it clear how data is being accessed and by whom. Data declared as public can be accessed by any part of the software in an uncontrolled fashion. Encapsulation is one of the central features of OOP.

This refactoring can always be used on any public data and its implementation is straightforward.

13.3 ● Move Method

A method is written within a class, but it uses very little of its current class. Instead it uses many of the facilities of another class. The remedy is to move the method from one class to the other.

In the game, the software needs to check whether pairs of items have collided, for example, a laser and an alien. For clarity, this collision detection is carried out by a method. This method is part of both class **Laser** and class **Alien**. This creates strong coupling between the objects. Instead move the method to a class that is responsible for checking collisions between all the objects in the game.

In general, moving a method may be necessary when:

- a class has too many methods
- a class has high coupling with another class.

Moving a method is a common refactoring situation.

13.4 ● Move Data

A variable is declared within a class, but another class uses it more. The remedy is to move the variable declaration. Clearly this also means moving the get and set methods.

13.5 ● Extract Class

A class has become too large and complex; it is doing the work of two classes. The remedy is to create a new class, extracting the appropriate variables and methods from the old class.

Ideally classes emerge from design as self-contained components that model some element of the application. In practice, as design proceeds, classes sometimes take on extra roles. Variables and methods are gradually added until the class becomes cumbersome. It becomes a candidate for fission.

13.6 ● Inline Class

A class is very small, or it does not do very much. The remedy is to incorporate it into some other class – ideally the class that uses it the most.

One way in which a class can become very small is when it has been the subject of the Move Method and the Move Variable refactorings, so that it has become sucked dry. This illustrates how many of the refactorings are interconnected – using one leads to using another, and so on.

SELF-TEST QUESTION

13.1 Compare the factoring Inline Class with the factoring Extract Class.

13.7 ● Identify composition or inheritance

Once we have identified the classes within a software system, the next step is to review the relationships between the classes. The classes that make up the software collaborate with each other to achieve the required behavior, but they use each other in different ways. There are two ways in which classes relate to each other:

1. *composition* – one object creates another object from a class using **new**. An example is a window object that creates a button object.

2. *inheritance* – one class inherits from another. An example is a class that extends the library **Frame** class.

The important task of design is to distinguish these two cases, so that inheritance can be successfully applied or avoided. One way of checking that we have correctly identified the appropriate relationships between classes is to use the "is-a" or "has-a" test:

■   the use of the phrase "is-a" in the description of an object (or class) signifies that it is probably an inheritance relationship.

■   the use of the phrase "has-a" indicates that there is no inheritance relationship. Instead the relationship is composition. (An alternative phrase that has the same meaning is "consists-of".)

We return to the cyberspace invaders game, designed in Chapter 11, seeking to find any inheritance relationships. If we can find any such relationships, we can simplify and shorten the program, making good use of reuse. In the game, several of the classes – **Defender**, **Alien**, **Laser** and **Bomb** – incorporate the same methods. These methods are: **getX**, **getY**, **getHeight** and **getWidth** that obtain the position and size of the graphical objects. We will remove these ingredients from each class and place them in a superclass. We will name this class **Sprite**, since the word sprite is a commonly used term for a moving graphical object in games programming. The UML class diagram for the **Sprite** class is:

```
class Sprite

Instance variables

x
y
height
width

Methods

getX
getY
getHeight
getWidth
```

Readers might see this more clearly if we look at the code. The Java code for the class **Sprite** is as follows:

```java
public class Sprite {

    protected int x, y, width, height;

    public int getX() {
        return x;
    }

    public int getY() {
        return y;
    }

    public int getWidth() {
        return width;
    }

    public int getHeight() {
        return height;
    }
}
```

The classes **Defender, Alien, Laser** and **Bomb** now inherit these methods from this superclass **Sprite**. Checking the validity of this design, we say "each of the classes **Defender, Alien, Laser** and **Bomb** is a **Sprite**". Figure 13.1 shows these relationships in a class diagram. Remember that an arrow points from a subclass to a superclass.

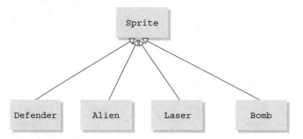

Figure 13.1 Class diagram for inherited components in the game

We have now successfully identified inheritance relationships between classes in the game program. This concludes the refactoring – we have transformed the design into a better design.

When we see common methods or variables in two or more classes, they become candidates for inheritance, but we need to be careful because delegation may be more appropriate. So we need to distinguish between the two. To sum up, the two kinds of relationship between classes are as follows.

Relationship between classes	test	Java code involves
Inheritance	is-a	extends
Composition	has-a or consists-of	new

SELF-TEST QUESTION

13.2 Analyze the relationships between the following groups of classes (are they is-a or has-a):

1. house, door, roof, dwelling
2. person, man, woman
3. car, piston, gearbox, engine
4. vehicle, car, bus.

13.8 ● Use polymorphism

Polymorphism enables objects that are similar to be treated in the same way. This means classes that share some common superclass. A section of code that uses a number of **if** statements (or a **case** statement) should be subject to scrutiny because it may be that it is making poor use of polymorphism. The purpose of the `if` statements may be to distinguish the different classes and thereby take appropriate action. But it may be simpler to refactor the class, eliminate the `if` statements and exploit polymorphism.

In the game program, we identified the commonalities in a number of classes – `Alien`, `Defender`, `Bomb` and `Laser`. We placed the common factors in a superclass called `Sprite`. Now we can treat all the objects uniformly. We place the game objects in an array list named `game` and write the following code to display them:

```
for (int s = 0; s < game.size(); s++) {
    Object item = game.get(s);
    Sprite sprite = (Sprite) item;
    sprite.display(paper);
}
```

which is much neater than a whole series of `if` statements.

13.9 ● Discussion

The idea of taking a design and changing it can be a surprise. It may seem akin to creating an ad hoc design and then experimenting with it. It has the flavor of hacking. Some people argue that a good design method should produce a good design – that it should not need improvement. Equally, many developers are reluctant to tinker with an architectural design that has been created according to sound principles. However, refactoring has a respectable pedigree. It recognizes that a perfect initial design is unlikely and it offers a number of possible strategies for improving a structure. A refactoring such as Extract Method gives the developer the green light to modify an initial design.

Note that refactoring implies that iteration is commonly used during OOD.

Summary

Refactoring means improving the architectural structure of a piece of software. This can be done at the end of design or during design.

A number of useful refactorings have been identified, given names and cataloged.

The refactorings described in this chapter are:

- Encapsulate Data
- Move Method
- Extract Class
- Inline Class
- identify composition or inheritance
- use polymorphism.

Exercises

13.1 In the cyberspace invaders game, we have already carried out a refactoring, identifying a superclass **Sprite** and applying inheritance. Some of the graphical objects in the game move vertically (bombs, lasers) while some move horizontally (alien, defender). Consider new superclasses **MovesVertically** and **MovesHorizontally** and draw the class diagrams for this new inheritance structure. Assess whether this refactoring is useful.

13.2 At what stage do you stop the process of refactoring?

13.3 Examine your architectural designs for the software case studies (Appendix A) and see if refactoring is achievable and desirable.

Answers to self-test questions

13.1 Inline Class is the opposite of the Extract Class.

13.2 **1.** a house has-a roof and a door. A house is-a dwelling

   2. a man (and a woman) is-a person

   3. an engine has-a piston and a gearbox and an engine

   4. a car and a bus is-a vehicle.

The basics

This chapter reviews the basic features of a programming language suitable for software engineering, including:

- design principles
- syntax
- control structures
- methods and parameters
- data typing
- simple data structures.

14.1 ● Introduction

Everyone involved in programming has their favorite programming language, or language feature they would like to have available. There are many languages, each with their proponents. So this chapter is probably the most controversial in this book. This chapter is not a survey of programming languages, nor is it an attempt to recommend one language over another. Rather, we wish to discuss the features that a good programming language should have from the viewpoint of the software engineer. We limit our discussion to "traditional" procedural languages, such as Fortran, Cobol, Ada, C++, Visual Basic, C# and Java. (Other approaches to programming languages are functional programming and logic programming.)

The main theme of this chapter is a discussion of the basic features a language should provide to assist the software development process. That is, what features encourage the development of software which is reliable and maintainable?

A significant part of the software engineer's task is concerned with how to model, within a program, objects from some problem domain. Programming, after all, is largely the manipulation of data. In the words of Niklaus Wirth, the designer of Pascal, "Algorithms + Data Structures = Programs" – which asserts the symbiosis between data and actions. The data description and manipulation facilities of a programming language should therefore allow the programmer to represent "real-world" objects easily and faithfully. In recent years, increasing attention has been given to the problem of providing improved data abstraction facilities for programmers. We discuss this in Chapter 15 on programming language features for OOP.

As we shall see, most mainstream programming languages have a small core and all the functionality of the language is provided by libraries. This chapter addresses this core. Facilities for programming in the large are reviewed in Chapter 16. Other features of languages – exceptions and assertions – are dealt with in Chapter 17.

14.2 ● Classifying programming languages and features

It is important to realize that programming languages are very difficult animals to evaluate and compare. For example, although it is often claimed that language X is a general purpose language, in practice languages tend to be used within particular communities. Thus, Cobol has been the preferred language of the information systems community, Fortran, the language of the scientist and engineer, C, the language of the systems programmer and Ada, the language for developing real-time or embedded computer systems. Cobol is not equipped for applications requiring complex numerical computation, just as the data description facilities in Fortran are poor and ill suited to information systems applications.

Programming languages are classified in many ways. For example, "high-level" or "low-level". A high-level language, such as Cobol, Visual Basic or C#, is said to be problem-oriented and to reduce software production and maintenance costs. A low-level language, such as assembler, is said to be machine-oriented, facilitating the programmer's complete control over the efficiency of their programs. Between high- and low-level languages, another category, the systems implementation language or high-level assembler, has emerged. Languages such as C attempt to bind into a single language the expressive power of a high-level language and the ultimate control which only a language that provides access at the register and primitive machine instruction level can provide. Languages may also be classified using other concepts, such as whether they are weakly or strongly typed. This is discussed below.

14.3 ● Design principles

Simplicity, clarity and orthogonality

One school of thought argues that the only way to ensure that programmers will consistently produce reliable programs is to make the programming language simple. For programmers to become truly proficient in a language, the language must be small and simple enough that it can be understood in its entirety. The programmer can then use the language with confidence, probably without recourse to a language manual.

Cobol and PL/1 are examples of languages which are large and unwieldy. For example, Cobol currently contains about 300 reserved words. Not surprisingly, it is a common programming error mistakenly to choose a reserved word as a user-defined identifier. What are the problems of large languages? Because they contain so many features, some are seldom used and, consequently, rarely fully understood. Also, since language features must not only be understood independently, but also in terms of their interaction with each other, the larger the number of features, the more complex it will be and the harder to understand their interactions. Although smaller, simpler languages are clearly desirable, the software engineer of the near future will often have to wrestle with existing large, complex languages. For example, to meet the requirements laid down by its sponsors, the US Department of Defense, the programming language Ada is a large and complex language requiring a 300-page reference manual to describe it.

The clarity of a language is also an important factor. In recent years, there has been a marked and welcome trend to design languages for the programmers who program in them rather than for the machines the programs are to run on. Many older languages incorporate features that reflect the instruction sets of the computers they were originally designed to be executed on. As one example, consider the Fortran arithmetic **if** statement, which has the following form:

```
if (expression) label1,label2,label3
```

This statement evaluates **expression** and then branches to one of the statements labeled **label1**, **label2**, or **label3** depending on whether the result is positive, zero, or negative. The reason for the existence of this peculiar statement is that early IBM machines had a machine instruction which compared the value of a register to a value in memory and branched to one of three locations. The language designers of the 1960s were motivated to prove that high-level languages could generate efficient code. Although we will be forever grateful to them for succeeding in proving this point, they introduced features into languages, such as Cobol and Fortran, which are clumsy and error-prone from the programmer's viewpoint. Moreover, even though the languages have subsequently been enhanced with features reflecting modern programming ideas, the original features still remain.

A programming language is the tool that programmers use to communicate their intentions. It should therefore be a language which accords with what people find natural, unambiguous and meaningful – in other words, clear. Perhaps language designers are not the best judges of the clarity of a new language feature. A better approach to testing a language feature may be to set up controlled experiments in which subjects are asked to answer questions about fragments of program code. This experimental psychology approach is gaining some acceptance and some results are discussed in the section on control abstractions.

A programmer can only write reliable programs if he or she understands precisely what every language construct does. The quality of the language definition and supporting documentation are critical. Ambiguity or vagueness in the language definition erodes a programmer's confidence in the language. It should not be necessary to have to write and run a program fragment to confirm the semantics of some language feature.

Programming languages should also display a high degree of orthogonality. This means that it should be possible to combine language features freely; special cases and restrictions should not be prevalent. Java and similar languages distinguish between two types of variables – built-in primitive types and proper objects. This means that these two groups must be treated differently, for example, when they are inserted into a data structure. A lack of orthogonality in a language has an unsettling effect on programmers; they no longer have the confidence to make generalizations and inferences about the language.

It is no easy matter to design a language that is simple, clear and orthogonal. Indeed, in some cases these goals would seem to be incompatible with one another. A language designer could, for the sake of orthogonality, allow combinations of features that are not very useful. Simplicity would be sacrificed for increased orthogonality! While we await the simple, clear, orthogonal programming language of the future, these concepts remain good measures with which the software engineer can evaluate the programming languages of today.

14.4 ● Language syntax

The syntax of a programming language should be consistent, natural and promote the readability of programs. Syntactic flaws in a language can have a serious effect on program development.

One syntactic flaw found in languages is the use of **begin-end** pairs or bracketing conventions, {}, for grouping statements together. Omitting an **end** or closing bracket is a very common programming error. The use of explicit keywords, such as **endif** and **endwhile**, leads to fewer errors and more readily understandable programs. Programs are also easier to maintain. For example, consider adding a second statement with the Java **if** statement shown below.

```
if (integerValue > 0)
    numberOfPositiveValues = numberOfPositiveValues + 1;
```

We now have to group the two statements together into a compound statement using a pair of braces.

```
if (integerValue > 0) {
    numberOfPositiveValues = numberOfPositiveValues + 1;
    numberOfNonZeroValues = numberOfNonZeroValues + 1;
}
```

Some editing is required here. Compare this with the explicit keyword approach in the style of Visual Basic. Here the only editing required would be the insertion of the new statement.

```
if (integerValue > 0)
    numberOfPositiveValues = numberOfPositiveValues + 1;
endif
```

In addition, explicit keywords eliminate the classic "dangling else" problem prevalent in many languages – see the discussion of selection statements below

Ideally the static, physical layout of a program should reflect as far as is possible the dynamic algorithm which the program describes. There are a number of syntactic concepts which can help achieve this goal. The ability to format a program freely allows the programmer the freedom to use such techniques as indentation and blank lines to highlight the structure and improve the readability of a program. For example, prudent indentation can help convey to the programmer that a loop is nested within another loop. Such indentation is strictly redundant, but assists considerably in promoting readability. Older languages, such as Fortran and Cobol, impose a fixed formatting style on the programmer. Components of statements are constrained to lie within certain columns on each input source line. For example, Fortran reserves columns 1 through 5 for statement labels and columns 7 through 72 for program statements. These constraints are not intuitive to the programmer. Rather they date back to the time when programs were normally presented to the computer in the form of decks of 80-column punched cards and a program statement was normally expected to be contained on a single card.

The readability of a program can also be improved by the use of *meaningful identifiers* to name program objects. Limitations on the length of names, as found in early versions of Basic (two characters) and Fortran (six characters), force the programmer to use unnatural, cryptic and error-prone abbreviations. These restrictions were dictated by the need for efficient programming language compilers. Arguably, programming languages should be designed to be convenient for the programmer rather than the compiler, and the ability to use meaningful names, irrespective of their length, enhances the self-documenting properties of a program. More recent languages allow the programmer to use names of unrestricted length, so that program objects can be named appropriately.

Another factor which affects the readability of a program is the consistency of the syntax of a language. For example, operators should not have different meanings in different contexts. The operator "=" should not double as both the assignment operator and the equality operator. Similarly, it should not be possible for the meaning of language keywords to change under programmer control. The keyword `if`, for example, should be used solely for expressing conditional statements. If the programmer is able to define an array with the identifier `if`, the time required to read and understand the program will be increased as we must now examine the context in which the identifier `if` is used to determine its meaning.

14.5 ● Control structures

A programming language for software engineering must provide a small but powerful set of control structures to describe the flow of execution within a program unit. In the late 1960s and 1970s there was considerable debate as to what control structures were required. The advocates of structured programming have largely won the day and there is now a reasonable consensus of opinion as to what kind of primitive control structures are essential. A language must provide primitives for the three basic structured programming constructs; sequence, selection and repetition. There are, however, considerable variations both in the syntax and the semantics of the control structures found in modern programming languages.

Early programming languages, such as Fortran, did not provide a rich set of control structures. The programmer used a set of low-level control structures, such as the unconditional branch or **goto** statement and the logical **if** to express the control flow within a program. For example, the following Fortran program fragment illustrates the use of these low-level control structures to simulate a condition controlled loop.

```
        n = 10
10      if (n .eq. 0) goto 20
        write (6,*) n
        n = n - 1
        goto 10
20      continue
```

These low-level control structures provide the programmer with too much freedom to construct poorly structured programs. In particular, uncontrolled use of the **goto** statement for controlling program flow leads to programs which are, in general, hard to read and unreliable.

There is now general agreement that higher level control abstractions must be provided and should consist of:

- **sequence** – to group together a related set of program statements
- **selection** – to select whether a group of statements should be executed or not based on the value of some condition
- **repetition** – to execute repeatedly a group of statements.

This basic set of primitives fits in well with the top-down philosophy of program design; each primitive has a single entry point and a single exit point. These primitives are realized in similar ways in most programming languages. For brevity, we will look in detail only at representative examples from common programming languages. For further details on this subject refer to Chapter 7 on structured programming.

14.6 ● Selection

Java, in common with most modern languages, provides two basic selection constructs The first, the **if** statement, provides one or two-way selection and the second, the **case** statement provides a convenient multiway selection structure.

Dangling else

Does the language use explicit closing symbols, such as **endif**, thus avoiding the "dangling else" problem? Nested **if** structures of the form shown below raise the question of how **if**s and **else**s are to be matched. Is the "dangling" **else** associated with the outer or inner **if**? Remember that the indentation structure is of no consequence.

```
if (condition)
    if (condition)
        statement1
else
    statement2
```

Java resolves this dilemma by applying the rule that an **else** is associated with the most recent non-terminated **if** lacking an **else**. Thus, the **else** is associated with the inner **if**. If, as the indentation suggests, we had intended the **else** to be associated with the outer **if**, we have to resort to clumsy fixes. But the clearest and cleanest solution is afforded by the provision of explicit braces (or key words) as follows.

```
if (condition) {
    if (condition) {
        statement1
    }
}
else {
    statement2
}
```

Nesting

Nested **if** statements can quite easily become unreadable. Does the language provide any help? For example, the readability of "chained" **if** statements can be improved by the introduction of an **elsif** clause. In particular, this eliminates the need for multiple **endif**s to close a series of nested **if**s. Consider the following example, with and without the **elsif** form. Java does not provide an **elsif** facility, but some languages do, for example, Visual Basic.Net.

```
if condition1 then                      if condition1 then
    statement1                              statement1
else if condition2 then                 elsif condition2 then
    statement2                              statement2
    else if condition3 then             elsif condition3 then
        statement3                          statement3
        else if condition4 then         elsif condition4 then
            statement4                      statement4
            else                        else
                statement5                  statement5
            endif                       endif
        endif
    endif
endif
```

Case

Like other languages, Java provides a **case** or **switch** statement. Here is used to find the number of days in each month:

```
switch (month) {

    case 1:
    case 3:
    case 5:
    case 8:
    case 10:
    case 12:
        days = 31;
        break;

    case 4:
    case 6:
    case 9:
    case 11:
        days = 30;
        break;

    case 2:
        days = 28;
        break;

    default:
        days = 0;
        break;

}
```

The **break** statement causes control to be transferred to the end of the **switch** statement. If a **break** statement is omitted, execution continues onto the next case and generally this is not what you would want to happen. So inadvertently omitting a **break** statement creates an error that might be difficult to locate. If the **default** option is omitted, and no case matches, nothing is done.

The expressiveness of the **case** statement is impaired if the type of the case selector is restricted. It should not have to be an integer (as above), but in most languages it is. Similarly, it should be easy to specify multiple alternative case choices (e.g. **1 | 5 | 7** meaning 1 or 5 or 7) and a range of values as a case choice (e.g. **1 .. 99**). But Java does not allow this.

The reliability of the **case** statement is enhanced if the case choices must specify actions for *all* the possible values of the case selector. If not, the semantics should, at least, clearly state what will happen if the case expression evaluates to an unspecified choice. The ability to specify an action for all unspecified choices through a **default** or similar clause is appealing.

There is something of a controversy here. Some people argue that when a **case** statement is executed, the programmer should be completely aware of all the possibilities that can occur. So the **default** statement is redundant and just an invitation to be lazy and sloppy. Where necessary, the argument goes, a **case** statement should be preceded by **if** statements that ensure that only valid values are supplied to the case statement.

if-not

It would be reasonable to think that there would no longer be any controversy over language structures for selection. The **if-else** is apparently well established. However, the lack of symmetry in the **if** statement is open to criticism. While it is clear that the **then** part is carried out if the condition is true, the **else** part is rather tagged on at the end to cater for all other situations. Experimental evidence suggests that significantly fewer bugs arise if the programmer is required to restate the condition (in its negative form) prior to the **else** as shown below:

```
if condition
      statement1
not condition else
      statement2
endif
```

14.7 ● Repetition

Control structures for repetition traditionally fall into two classes. There are loop structures where the number of iterations is fixed, and those where the number of iterations is controlled by the evaluation of some condition. Fixed length iteration is often implemented using a form similar to that shown below:

```
for control_variable =
      initial_expression to final_expression step step_expression
do
      statement(s)
endfor
```

The usefulness and reliability of the **for** statement can be affected by a number of issues as now discussed

Should the type of the loop control variable be limited to integers? Perhaps any ordinal type should be allowed. However, reals (floats) should not be allowed. For example, consider how many iterations are specified by the following:

```
for x = 0.0 to 1.0 step 0.33 do
```

Here it is not at all obvious exactly how many repetitions will be performed, and things are made worse by the fact that computers represent real values only approximately.

(Note how disallowing the use of reals as loop control variables conflicts with the aim of orthogonality).

The semantics of the **for** is greatly affected by the answers to the following questions. When and how many times are the initial expression, final expression and step expressions evaluated? Can any of these expressions be modified within the loop? What is of concern here is whether or not it is clear how many iterations of the loop will be performed. If the expressions can be modified and the expressions are recomputed on each iteration, then there is a distinct possibility of producing an infinite loop. Similar problems arise if the loop control variable can be modified within the loop.

The scope of the loop control variable is best limited to the **for** statement, as in Java. If it is not, then what should its value be on exit from the loop, or should it be undefined?

Condition-controlled loops are simpler in form. Almost all modern languages provide a leading decision repetition structure (**while-do**) and some, for convenience, also provide a trailing decision form (**repeat-until**).

```
while condition do              repeat
    statement(s)                    statement(s)
endwhile                        until condition
```

The **while** form continues to iterate while a condition evaluates to true. Since the test appears at the head of the form, the **while** performs zero or many iterations of the loop body. The **repeat**, on the other hand, iterates until a condition is true. The test appears following the body of the loop, ensuring that the **repeat** performs at least one iteration. Thus the **while** statement is the more general looping mechanism of the two, so if a language provides only one looping mechanism, it should therefore be the **while**. However the **repeat** is sometimes more appropriate in some programming situations.

SELF-TEST QUESTION

14.1 Identify a situation where **repeat** is more appropriate than **while**.

Some languages provide the opposites of these two loops:

```
do
    statement(s)
while condition
```

and:

```
until condition do
    statement(s)
end until
```

C, C++, C# and Java all provide **while-do** and **do-while** structures. They also provide a type of **for** statement that combines together several commonly used ingredients. An example of this loop structure is:

```
for (i = 0; i < 10; i++) {
    statement(s)
}
```

in which:

■ the first statement within the brackets is done once, before the loop is executed
■ the second item, a condition, determines whether the loop will continue
■ the third statement is executed at the end of each repetition.

We will meet yet another construct for repetition – the **foreach** statement – in the chapter on object-oriented programming language features (Chapter 15). This is convenient for processing all the elements of a data structure.

The **while** and **repeat** structures are satisfactory for the vast majority of iterations we wish to specify. For the most part, loops which terminate at either their beginning or end are sufficient. However, there are situations, notably when encountering some exceptional condition, where it is appropriate to be able to branch out of a repetition structure at an arbitrary point within the loop. Sometimes it is necessary to break out of a series of nested loops rather than a single loop. In many languages, the programmer is limited to two options. The terminating conditions of each loop can be enhanced to accommodate the "exceptional" exit, and **if** statements can be used within the loop to transfer control to the end of the loop should the exceptional condition occur. This solution is clumsy at best and considerably decreases the readability of the code. A second, and arguably better, solution is to use the much-maligned **goto** statement to branch directly out of the loops. Ideally, however, since there is a recognized need for n and a half times loops, the language should provide a controlled way of exiting from one or more loops. Java provides the following facility where an orderly **break** may be made but only to the statement following the loop(s).

```
while (condition) {
    statement(s)
    if (condition) break;
    statement(s)
}
```

In the example above, control will be transferred to the statement following the loop when **condition** is true. This may be the only way of exiting from this loop.

```
here:
    while (condition) {
        while (condition) {
```

```
            statement(s)
            if (exitCondition) break here;
            statement(s)
        }
    }
```

In the second example above, control will be transferred out of both **while** loops when **exitCondition** is true. Note how the outer **while** loop is labeled **here:** and how this label is used by the **if** statement to specify that control is to be transferred to the end of the **while** loop (not the beginning) when **exitCondition** is satisfied.

SELF-TEST QUESTION

14.2 Sketch out the code for a method to search an array of integers to find some desired integer. Write two versions – one using the **break** mechanism and one without **break**.

The languages C, C++, Ada and Java provide a mechanism such as the above for breaking out in the middle of loops.

There is some controversy about using **break** statements. Some people argue that it is simply too much like the notorious **goto** statement. There is a difference, however, because **break** can only be used to break out of a loop, not enter into a loop. Neither can **break** be used to break out of an **if** statement. Thus it might be argued that **break** is a **goto** that is under control.

Handling errors or exceptional situations is a common programming situation. In the past, such an eventuality was handled using the **goto** statement. Nowadays features are built in to programming languages to facilitate the more elegant handling of such situations. We discuss the handling of exceptions in Chapter 17.

14.8 ● Methods

Procedural or algorithmic abstraction is one of the most powerful tools in the programmer's arsenal. When designing a program, we abstract *what* should be done before we specify *how* it should be done. Before OOP, program designs evolved as layers of procedural abstractions, each layer specifying more detail than the layer above. Procedural abstractions in programming languages, such as procedures and functions, allow the layered design of a program to be accurately reflected in the structure of the program text. Even in relatively small programs, the ability to factor a program into small, functional modules is essential; factoring increases the readability and maintainability of programs. What does the software engineer require from a language in terms of support for procedural abstraction? We suggest the following list of requirements:

- an adequate set of primitives for defining procedural abstractions
- safe and efficient mechanisms for controlling communication between program units
- simple, clearly defined mechanisms for controlling access to data objects defined within program units.

Procedures and functions

The basic procedural abstraction primitives provided in programming languages are procedures and functions. Procedures can be thought of as extending the statements of the language, while functions can be thought of as extending the operators of the language. A procedure call looks like a distinct statement, whereas a function call appears as or within an expression.

The power of procedural abstraction is that it allows the programmer to consider the method as an independent entity performing a well-described task largely independent of the rest of the program. When a procedure is called, it achieves its effect by modifying the data in the program which called it. Ideally, this effect is communicated to the calling program unit in a controlled fashion by the modification of the parameters passed to the procedure. Functions, like their mathematical counterparts, return only a single value and must therefore be embedded within expressions. A typical syntax for writing procedures and functions is shown below:

```
void procedureName(parameters) {
    declarations
    procedure body
}

resultType functionName(parameters) {
    declarations
    function body
    return value;
}
```

It is critical that the interface between program units be small and well defined if we are to achieve independence between units. Ideally both procedures and functions should only accept but not return information through their parameters. A single result should be returned as the result of calling a function.

For example, to place text in a text box, use a procedure call as illustrated by the following code:

```
setText("your message here");
```

and a function call to obtain a value:

```
String text = getText();
```

Unfortunately, most programming languages do not enforce even these simple, logical rules. Thus it is largely the responsibility of the programmer to ensure that procedures and functions do not have *side effects*. A side effect is any change to information outside a method caused by a call – other than the parameters to a procedure. Most programming languages do not prevent programmers from directly accessing and modifying data objects (global data) defined outside of the local environment of the method.

Along with pointers and the `goto` statement, global data has come to be regarded as a major source of programming problems. We shall see in Chapter 15? (on object-oriented features of programming languages) how, in classes, access to global data is controlled.

Many abstractions, particularly those which manipulate recursive data structures such as lists, graphs, and trees, are more concisely described recursively. Some languages, for example Cobol and Fortran, do not support recursion.

14.9 ● Parameter-passing mechanisms

We have seen that, ideally:

- parameters are passed to a procedure so that the procedure will accomplish some task. There is no need for information to be passed back to the caller. So there is no need for parameter values to change.

- functions communicate a value back to the caller as the return value. So again there is no need for parameter values to be changed.

Two major schemes for parameters have emerged:

- **call by value** (termed value parameters) – this means that a copy of the information is passed as the parameter. Therefore the method can use the information but cannot change it.

- **call by reference** (termed reference parameters) – this means that a pointer to the information is passed as the parameter. Therefore the method can both access and change the information.

These pointers are not a problem because the pointers are not themselves accessible to the programmer. (The programmer cannot access or change the pointer, merely the information pointed to.) The pointer is simply the mechanism for communicating the information. We discuss programming using pointers in Chapter 15 on object-oriented programming.

The programming language *could* enforce a discipline where procedures and functions can only be supplied with value parameters, but most do not. A number of parameter-passing schemes are employed in programming languages but no language provides a completely safe and secure parameter-passing mechanism.

There is a performance consideration for value parameters. Passing by value is inefficient for passing large, aggregate data structures such as an array, as a copy must be made. In such situations, it is commonplace to pass the data structure by reference even if the parameter should not be modified by the method.

Java provides the following scheme. All primitive data terms are passed by value, which is most commendable, but all proper objects are passed by reference. No distinction is made between procedures and functions. Thus a method of either type (procedure or function) can modify any non-primitive parameter and it is left to the programmer to enforce a discipline over changing parameters. A small concession is that the pointer to an object cannot be changed, for example to point to another object.

Fortran employs only a single parameter passing mode: call by reference. Thus, undesirably, all actual parameters in Fortran may potentially be changed by any sub-routine or function. The programmer is responsible for ensuring the safe implementation of input and output parameters. Using call by reference, the location of the actual parameter is bound to the formal parameter. The formal and actual parameter names are thus *aliases*; modification of the formal parameter automatically modifies the actual parameter. This is what you might expect of a language where arrays are often used, and the performance hit of copying arrays is unacceptable. Fortran also, unfortunately, restricts the type of result that may be returned from functions to scalar types only (i.e. not arrays etc.).

Visual Basic.Net provides the choice of value or reference parameters, described by the key words **ByVal** (the default) and **ByRef** in the method header. But when objects are passed, they are always passed by reference.

In C#, by default, primitive data items are passed by value, objects are passed by reference. But you can pass a primitive data item by reference if the parameter is preceded by the key word **ref** in both the method header and the method call. You can also precede an object name by **ref**, in which case you are passing a pointer to a pointer. This means that the method can return an entirely different object.

Call by value-result is often used as an alternative to call by reference for input-output parameters. It avoids the use of aliases at the expense of copying. Parameters passed by value-result are initially treated as in call by value; a copy of the value of the actual parameter is passed to the formal parameter, which again acts as a local variable. Manipulation of the formal parameter does not immediately affect the actual parameter. On exit from the procedure, the final value of the formal parameter is assigned into the actual parameter. *Call by result* may be used as an alternative to call by reference for output parameters. Parameters passed by value are treated exactly as those passed by value-result except that no initial value is assigned to the local formal parameter.

Ada identifies three types of parameter:

- input parameters to allow a method read-only access to an actual parameter. The actual parameter is purely an input parameter; the method should not be able to modify the value of the actual parameter

- output parameters to allow a procedure write-only access to an actual parameter. The actual parameter is purely an output parameter; the procedure should not be able to read the value of the actual parameter

- input-output parameters to allow a procedure read-and-write access to an actual parameter. The value of the actual parameter may be modified by the procedure.

Ada only allows input variables to functions. The parameter-passing mechanisms used in Ada (described as **in, out** and **in out**) would therefore seem to be ideal. However,

Ada does not specify whether they are to be implemented using sharing or copying. Though beneficial to the language implementer, since the space requirements of the parameter can be used to determine whether sharing or copying should be used, this decision can be troublesome to the programmer. In the presence of aliases, call by value-result and call by reference may return different results.

14.10 ● Primitive data types

Programmers are accustomed to being provided with a rudimentary set of primitive data types. These are provided built in and ready made by the programming language. They usually include:

■ Boolean

■ char

■ integer

■ real or floating point.

These data types are accompanied by a supporting cast of operations (relational, arithmetic, etc.). For each type, it should be possible to clearly define the form of the literals or constants which make up the type. For example, the constants `true` and `false` make up the set of constants for the type Boolean. Similarly, we should be able to define the operations for each type. For the type Boolean, these might include the operations =, <>, **not, and,** and **or**.

In most languages the primitive data types are not true objects (in the sense of objects created from classes). But in Eiffel and Smalltalk, every data type is a proper object and can be treated just like any other object.

For certain application domains, advanced computation facilities, such as extended precision real numbers or long integers, are essential. The ability to specify the range of integers and reals and the precision to which reals are represented reduces the dependence on the physical characteristics, such as the word size, of a particular machine. This increases the portability of programs. However, some languages (for example C and C++) leave the issue of the precision and range of numbers to the compiler writer for the particular target machine. Java gets around this sloppiness by precisely defining the representation of all its built-in data types. Whatever machine a program is executed on, the expectation is that data is represented in exactly the same manner. Thus the program will produce exactly the same behavior, whatever the machine.

14.11 ● Data typing

A data type is a set of data objects and a set of operations applicable to all objects of that type. Almost all languages can be thought of as supporting this concept to some extent. Many languages require the programmer to define explicitly the type (e.g. integer or character) of all objects to be used in a program, and, to some extent or another, depending on the individual language, this information prescribes the operations that can be applied to the objects. Thus, we could state, for example, that Fortran, Cobol, C, C++, Ada, C#, Visual Basic.Net and Java are all typed languages. However, only Ada, C#, Visual Basic.Net and Java would be considered strongly typed languages.

A language is said to be *strongly typed* if it can be determined at compile-time whether or not each operation performed on an object is consistent with the type of that object. Operations inconsistent with the type of an object are considered illegal. A strongly typed language therefore forces the programmer to consider more closely how objects are to be defined and used within a program. The additional information provided to the compiler by the programmer allows the compiler to perform automatic type checking operations and discover type inconsistencies. Studies have shown that programs written in strongly typed languages are clearer, more reliable, and more portable. Strong typing necessarily places some restrictions on what a programmer may do with data objects. However, this apparent decrease in flexibility is more than compensated for by the increased security and reliability of the ensuing programs.

Languages such as Lisp, APL, and POP-2 allow a variable to change its type at run-time. This is known as *dynamic typing* as opposed to the *static typing* found in languages where the type of an object is permanently fixed. Where dynamic typing is employed, type checking must occur at run-time rather than compile-time. Dynamic typing provides additional freedom and flexibility but at a cost. More discipline is required on the part of the programmer so that the freedom provided by dynamic typing is not abused. That freedom is often very useful, even necessary, in some applications, for example, problem-solving programs which use sophisticated artificial intelligence techniques for searching complex data structures would be very difficult to write in languages without dynamic typing.

What issues need to be considered when evaluating the data type facilities provided by a programming language? We suggest the following list:

- does the language provide an adequate set of primitive data types?
- can these primitives be combined in useful ways to form aggregate or structured data types?
- does the language allow the programmer to define new data types? How well do such new data types integrate with the rest of the language?
- to what extent does the language support the notion of strong typing?
- when are data types considered equivalent?
- are type conversions handled in a safe and secure manner?
- is it possible for the programmer to circumvent automatic type checking operations?

14.12 ● Strong versus weak typing

The debate as to whether strongly typed languages are preferable to weakly typed languages closely mirrors the earlier debate among programming language aficionados about the virtues of the `goto` statement. The pro-`goto` group argued that the construct was required and its absence would restrict programmers. The anti-`goto` group contended that indiscriminate use of the construct encouraged the production of "spaghetti-like" code.

The weakly typed languages group similarly argue that some types of programs are very difficult, if not impossible, to write in strongly typed languages. For example, a program that manipulates graphical images will sometimes need to perform arithmetic on the image and at other times examine the data bit-by-bit.

The strongly typed languages group argue that the increased reliability and security outweigh these disadvantages. A compromise has been struck; strong typing is generally seen as highly desirable but languages provide well-defined escape mechanisms to circumvent type checking for those instances where it is truly required.

Weakly typed languages such as Fortran and C provide little compile-time type checking support. However, they do provide the ability to view the representation of information as different types. For example, using the **equivalence** statement in Fortran, a programmer is able to subvert typing:

```
integer a
logical b
equivalence a, b
```

The variable b is a **logical**, which is the Fortran term for Boolean. The **equivalence** declaration states that the variables **a** and **b** share the same memory. While economy of storage is the primary use of the **equivalence** statement, it also allows the same storage to be interpreted as representing an integer in one case and a logical (Boolean) in the second. The programmer can now apply both arithmetic operations and logical operations on the same storage simply by choosing the appropriate alias (**a** or **b**) to reference it.

This incredible language feature is dangerous because programs using it are unclear. Moreover such programs are not portable because the representations used for integers and Booleans are usually machine dependent.

To a small number of programming applications, the ability to circumvent typing to gain access to the underlying physical representation of data is essential. How can this be provided in a language that is strongly typed? The best solution is probably to force the programmer to state *explicitly* in the code that they wish to violate the type checking operations of the language. This approach is taken by Ada, where an object may be reinterpreted as being of a different type only by using the unchecked conversion facility.

The question of conversion between types is inextricably linked with the strength of typing in a language. Fortran, being weakly typed, performs many conversions (or coercions) implicitly during the evaluation of arithmetic expressions. These implicit conversions may result in a loss of information and can be dangerous to the programmer. As we saw earlier, Fortran allows mixed mode arithmetic and freely converts reals to integers on assignment.

Java and other strongly typed languages perform implicit conversions *only* when there will be no accompanying loss of information. Thus, an assignment of an integer to a real variable results in implicit conversion of the integer to a real – the programmer does nothing. However, an attempt to assign a real value to an integer variable will result in a type incompatibility error. Such an assignment must be carried out using an explicit conversion function. That is, the programmer is forced by the language to explicitly consider the loss of information implied by the use of the conversion function. In Java, for example, a real can be converted to an integer, but only by using an explicit casting operator:

```
float f = 1.2345;
int i = (int) f;
```

The casting operator is the name of the destination type, enclosed in brackets – in this case (int). When this is used, the compiler accepts that the programmer is truly asking for a conversion and is responsibly aware of the possible consequences.

SELF-TEST QUESTION

14.3 Java provides shift and Boolean operations for integers and reals. Does this violate strong typing?

14.13 ● User-defined data types (enumerations)

The readability, reliability, and data abstraction capabilities of a language are enhanced if the programmer can extend the primitive data types provided by the language. The ability to define user-defined types separates the languages C, C++ and Ada from their predecessors. For example, consider the following definition of a C++ enumerated type which is introduced by the key word **enum**:

```
enum Day {Monday, Tuesday, Wednesday, Thursday, Friday, Saturday,
          Sunday};
```

The type **Day** is a new type. Variables of this type may *only* take on values that are the literals of that type (that is **Monday, Tuesday**, etc). Now we can declare a variable of this type, as follows:

```
Day today;
```

And we can perform such operations as

```
today = Monday;
if (today == Saturday) etc
```

We also get some type checking carried out by the compiler. Assignments such as the following will be flagged as type errors by the compiler.

```
today = January;
today = 7;
```

In a language without this facility, we are forced to map the days of the week onto integers, so that 1 means Monday etc. But then we get no help from the compiler when we write (correct) statements, such as:

```
int today;
today = 2;
```

or even the "illegal"

```
today = 0;
```

since **today** is an integer variable and therefore may be assigned any integer value.

SELF-TEST QUESTION

14.4 Make the case for user-defined types.

Enumerated types, such as the C++ facility described above, have their limitations. An enumerated type can be declared, variables created, assignments and comparisons carried out, but these are the only operations and we cannot create any more. For example, in the above example one cannot write a method **nextDay**. Moreover different **enums** cannot contain identical names. For example, we are prevented from writing:

```
enum Weekend {Saturday, Sunday};
```

because the names clash with those already in **enum Day**.

Arguably, if the language provides classes (Chapter 15) it does not need **enums**. In fact the Java **enum** facility is almost a class.

14.14 ● Arrays

Composite data types allow the programmer to model structured data objects. The most common aggregate data abstraction provided by programming languages is the *array*: a collection of homogeneous elements (all elements of the same type) which may be referenced through their positions (usually an integer) within the collection. Arrays are characterized by the type of their elements and by the index or subscript range or ranges which specify the size, number of dimensions and how individual elements of the array may be referenced.

For example, the Java array definition shown below defines an array named **table**. It is a one-dimensional array of integers with the subscript varying from 0 through 9. In Java, subscripts always start at 0, betraying the C origins of the language as a language close to machine instructions.

```
int table[] = new int[10];
```

Individual elements of the array are referenced by specifying the array name and an expression for each subscript, for example, `table[2]`.

The implementation of arrays in programming languages raises the following considerations:

- what restrictions are placed on the element type? For complete freedom of expression there should be no restrictions.
- valid indices should be any subrange of numbers (e.g. 2010 to 2020)
- at what time must the size of an array be known? The utility of arrays in a programming language is governed by the time (compile-time or run-time) at which the size of the array must be known.
- what operations may be applied to complete arrays? For example, it is very convenient to be able to carry out array assignment or comparison between compatible arrays using a single concise statement.
- are convenient techniques available for the initialization of arrays?

The time at which a size must be specified for an array has implications on how the array may be used. In Java, as in most languages, the size of an array must be defined statically – the size and subscript ranges are required to be known at compile-time. This has the advantage of allowing the compiler to generate code automatically to check for out-of-range subscripts. However, the disadvantage of this simple scheme is that, to allow the program to accommodate data sets of differing sizes, we would like to delay deciding the size of the array until run-time. Most languages provide arrays whose size is fixed at compile-time, so if variable size is needed, a dynamic data structure is the answer (see Chapter 15).

SELF-TEST QUESTION

14.5 Argue for and against the language making array subscripts start at 0.

14.15 ● Records (structures)

Data objects in problem domains are not always simply collections of homogeneous objects (same types). Rather, they are often collections of heterogeneous objects (different types). Although such collections can be represented using arrays, many programming languages provide a *record* data aggregate. Records (or structures as they are termed in C and C++) are generalizations of arrays where the elements (or fields) may be of different types and where individual components are referenced by (field) name rather than by position.

For example, the C++ `struct` definition shown below describes information relating to a time. Each object of type `Time` has three components named `hour`, `minute` and `second`.

```
struct Time {
    int hour;
    int minute;
    int second;
}
```

We can now declare a variable of this type:

```
Time time;
```

Components of records are selected by name. The method used by Ada, PL/1 and C++ first specifies the variable and then the component. For example,

```
time.minute = 46;
```

Each component of a record may be of any type – including aggregate types, such as arrays and records. Similarly, the element type of an array might be a record type. Programming languages which provide such data abstractions as arrays and records and allow them to be combined orthogonally in this fashion allow a wide range of real data objects to be modeled in a natural fashion.

The languages Cobol, PL/1, C, C++, C# and Ada support records. (In C, C++ and C# a record is termed a **struct**.) The Java language does not provide records as described above because this facility can simply be implemented as a class, using the object-oriented features of the language (see Chapter 15). Simply declare a class, with the requisite fields within it.

SELF-TEST QUESTION

14.6   Make the case for arrays and records.

Summary

In this chapter we have surveyed the basic characteristics that a programming language should have from the viewpoint of the software engineer. It seems that small things – like syntax – can affect software reliability and maintenance.

Some people think that a language should be rich in features – and therefore powerful. Other people think that a language should be small but elegant so that it can be mastered completely by the programmer.

The following issues are considered to be important:

- matching the language to the application area of the project
- clarity, simplicity, and orthogonality
- syntax
- control abstractions
- primitive data types
- data typing
- enumerations
- arrays
- records (structures).

● Exercises

14.1 Suppose that you were asked to design a new programming language for software engineering.

- select and justify a set of control structures
- select and justify a set of primitive data types.

14.2 Argue either for or against strong typing in a programming language.

14.3 How many kinds of looping structure do we need in a programming language? Make suggestions.

14.4 From the discussion in this chapter, list the possible problem features with either programming languages in general or a programming language of your choice.

14.5 "In language design, small is beautiful." Discuss.

14.6 Argue for or against the inclusion of the **break** statement in a programming language

14.7 The language LISP has the ultimate simple syntax. Every statement is a list. For example:

```
(+ 1 2)
```

returns the sum of the parameters.

Investigate the syntax of Lisp and discuss whether every language could and should have syntax that is as simple.

Answers to self-test questions

14.1 When some input from the user's keyboard is required. It must be checked and, if necessary, new input solicited until the input is correct.

14.2
```
int[] table;

boolean search(int wanted) {
    boolean found = false;
    int i = 0;

    endSearch:
        while (i < table.length) {
            if (table[i] == wanted) {
                found = true;
                break endSearch;
            }
            i++;
        }
    return found;
}
```

Without using **break**:

```
int[] table;

boolean search(int wanted) {
    boolean found = false;
    int i = 0;

    while (i < table.length and found == false) {
        if (table[i] == wanted)
            found = true;
        else
            i++;
    }
    return found;
}
```

14.3 Yes and no.

Clearly these operations are not something that should be allowed with integers and reals.

But in Java the bit structure of these data types is precisely defined. Also the effects of these operations are precisely defined. So these particular data types have an extended set of valid operations.

14.4 The benefits are program clarity, better modeling of the problem, compile-time checking and run-time checking.

14.5 This is a case of expressive power and convenience versus fast performance.

14.6 Arrays and records allow the programmer to create and use data structures that match the problem to be solved in a convenient and natural fashion. This fosters fast development, reliability and maintainability.

Further reading

See the references at the end of Chapter 16.

CHAPTER 15

Object-oriented programming

This chapter:

- explains how encapsulation, inheritance and polymorphism are provided in a programming language
- explains the role of libraries in object-oriented programming
- explains the idea of generics or templates
- explains provision for dynamic data structures and garbage collection.

15.1 ● Introduction

Most current mainstream languages embody OOP. The three pillars of OOP are encapsulation, inheritance and polymorphism. This chapter explains how the programming language can support these concepts. The language used for illustration is Java, and the case study is the cyberspace invaders game (Appendix A).

We go on to explain how classes can be made more general using the concept of generics, sometimes termed templates.

Next we discuss approaches to creating dynamic data structure – structures that expand and contract as necessary. In particular, we look at using pointers.

Finally we explore the challenge of garbage collection – what happens to computer memory after it has been used as part of a dynamic data structure.

15.2 ● Encapsulation

Encapsulation means bringing together data and actions that are related. In OOP such a collection is called a class. It consists of some related variable declarations and some methods. A class is a template or blueprint for any number of objects that can be created from it. In many programming languages, including Java, this is accomplished using the key word **new**. Creating an object is also known as instantiating an object.

We will use the example of the cyberspace invaders game, Figure 15.1, to illustrate encapsulation. The program displays a number of graphical objects at various times on

Figure 15.1 Cyberspace invaders

the screen – an alien, a laser, a bomb and the user. We will represent each of these as
an object.

We will represent the alien as an object, but to create an object, we have to write a
class (a blueprint for any number of aliens). In Java, we write the class as follows:

```java
class Alien {

    private int x, y;
    private int size;
    private ImageIcon alienImage;

    public Alien(int newX, int newY, int newSize) {
        x = newX;
        y = newY;
        size = newSize:
        alienImage = new ImageIcon("c:/alien.jpg");
    }

    public void display(JPanel panel) {
        Graphics paper = panel.getGraphics();
        alienImage.paintIcon(panel, paper, x, y);
    }
```

```
        public void moveLeft(int amount) {
            x = x - amount;
        }
        public void moveRight(int amount) {
            x = x + amount;
        }
    }
```

As you can see, the class consists of a grouping of variable declarations, at the top, followed by methods. The **public** methods act as the outward appearance of the class, acting upon the **private** variables within it.

The method **Alien** is termed a constructor method or simply a constructor. (In Java a constructor method has the same name as the class name.) It is called when an object is created from the class to initialize variables within the object. A class can have any number (including zero) constructors.

We can now create an object named **alien** from the class **Alien** as follows:

```
    Alien alien = new Alien(100, 100, 10);
```

And then we can use it:

```
    alien.moveLeft(100);
    alien.display(paper);
```

Here we see the classic notation **object.method** which is so characteristic of OOP.

SELF-TEST QUESTION

15.1 Add a method named **moveDown** to the class **Alien**.

OOP supports the concept of information hiding, that is, users should be provided with sufficient information to use the data type but nothing more. Users of a class should be provided with a specification of the effect of each of the operations provided and a description of how to use each operation. They should not be required to know the representation of the class nor be able to access the implementation other than indirectly through a method provided.

The class **Alien** encapsulates and hides all the information about an alien and how it is to be used. The interior of the class is inaccessible from outside the class; this is enforced by the compiler. So no one can tamper – by mistake or malice – with the data that represents an alien. The only way that an alien object can be accessed is via the methods such as **display** and **moveLeft** that are provided. Thus access to an alien object is carefully controlled. This constitutes the best form of modularity – access is via method calls, rather than by direct access to data. Good style means that only in rare cases will a class permit direct access to data within itself.

Often (though not in the **Alien** example shown above) there will need to be additional methods that the class needs in order to carry out its tasks. These are **private** methods that need not and therefore should not be accessible from outside the class.

A class represents a real fusion of data and actions. A class extends the built-in data types provided by the language, so that the programmer can invent data suitable for the problem being solved. The programmer specifies how the data can be manipulated and thus creates truly abstract data.

The advantages of encapsulation are:

- to make useful classes generally available
- to use a class without the need to know how it works
- to have the flexibility to modify a class without affecting its users.

Properties

We have seen that it is very bad practice to make **public** any of the instance variables of a class. Some languages, for example, C# and Visual Basic, provide a mechanism that simulates accessing variables directly. This feature, called properties, enables users to have convenient but controlled access to the data associated with an object. In general there are two distinct kinds of access to data:

1. reading a value – called *get* access
2. writing the value – called *set* access.

For example, suppose we want to allow a user of an alien object to refer to (get) the *x* coordinate of the alien and display its value in a text field. The value is held in the **private** variable named **x** at the top of the class. Using a property named **xCoord**, we can write:

```
textField.setText(Integer.toString(alien.xCoord));
```

Suppose also that we want the user to be able to change (set) the value of the *x* coordinate. Using the property facility we can write:

```
alien.xCoord = 56;
```

The way to provide these facilities is to write a property. Here is the revised class that includes the property code:

```
public class AlienWithProperties {

        private int x;
        private int y;
        private int size;
        private ImageIcon alienImage;
```

```
public Alien(int newX, int newY, int newSize) {
    x = newX;
    y = newY;
    size = newSize;
    alienImage = new ImageIcon("c:/alien.jpg");
}

public void moveLeft(int amount) {
    x = x - amount;
}

public void moveRight(int amount) {
    x = x + amount;
}

public void display(JPanel panel) {
    Graphics paper = panel.getGraphics();
    alienImage.paintIcon(panel, paper, x, y);
}

public int xCoord {
    get {
        return x;
    }
    set {
        x = value;
    }
}

}
```

The header for a property looks similar to a method header, except that there are no brackets to specify parameters. The property consists of two complementary components – one has **get** as the heading and the other has **set** as the heading. The **get** part is like a function method – it returns the desired value. The **set** part is like a method – it assigns the value using the special keyword **value** as shown. Note that this code is in the style of Java, but it is not Java, since Java does not support a property mechanism.

If we only need a way of viewing a property (but not changing its value), we write the property declaration like this:

```
public int xCoord {
    get {
        return x;
    }
}
```

If, on the other hand we need to change a value, but do not need the facility to view it, we write:

```
public int xCoord {
    set {
        x = value;
    }
}
```

When you see properties for the first time, you may be tempted to wonder why such a long-winded mechanism is needed. Surely it would be easier simply to declare the value **x** as **public**? Then the user of the object could simply refer to the value as **alien.x**. This is possible, but it is very bad practice – for the reasons discussed above to do with encapsulation. What the property feature gives is the *appearance* of direct access to data, with all the security of access via methods.

SELF-TEST QUESTION

15.2 Write a property to allow a user only **get** access to the *y* coordinate of an alien.

Method or property?

Some programming languages provide both methods and properties as mechanisms for accessing an object. So how do we choose which to use? The answer is to use methods when you want an object to carry out some action. (A method usually has a name that is a verb.) Use properties when you want to refer to some information associated with an object. (A property usually has a name that is a noun.)

Examples of methods associated with an alien, discussed above, are: **display**, **moveUp**, **moveDown**, **moveLeft**, and **moveRight**. Examples of alien properties are: **xCoord**, **yCoord**, and **size**.

Sometimes there is a choice over whether to make something a property or a method, and the choice is a matter of style. For example, to change the color of a component we could have a method **changeColor**; alternatively we could provide a property named **color**.

Some people argue that the only proper access to objects is via method calls and that therefore properties are superfluous.

SELF-TEST QUESTION

15.3 In designing a class **Account** to represent a bank account, which of the following should be methods and which should be properties?

```
creditAccount, debitAccount, currentBalance,
calculateInterest, name
```

15.3 ● Library classes

Most modern languages are small – they provide a few simple facilities, such as control structures and the ability to write classes. The power of the language is provided by the libraries of ready-made classes that are supplied alongside the language.

For example, most modern languages (including Java) provide a class **ArrayList**, which is like an array, but better. An array list is similar to an array in that it stores a collection of items, each of which is referred to using an integer subscript (index). But, in contrast to an array, items can be added or removed from anywhere within an array list. Also an array list grows and shrinks as necessary to accommodate the required data. An array list holds strings, integers, GUI components or any other type of data.

To use an array list, you create an instance (an object) like this:

```
ArrayList arrayList = new ArrayList();
```

Then you can add items to it, as shown in the example:

```
arrayList.add(alien);
```

which inserts the item at the end of the data.

In common with other library classes, an array list comes with a useful set of methods. Here are some of the methods for array lists.

`add(int index, Object item)`	inserts the specified item at the specified position
`add(Object item)`	appends the item to the end of the array list
`clear()`	removes all the items from the array list
`contains(Object item)`	returns **true** if the object is in the array list
`get(int index)`	returns the element at the specified position
`remove(int index)`	removes the element at the specified position
`set(int index, Object item)`	replaces the item at the specified position with the item
`size()`	returns the number of elements in the array list.

So, facilities such as array lists are not part of the language but are provided as part of the library. Libraries typically provide a massive range of classes, so that the activity of programming becomes a search for useful classes. This is a view of programming in which the programmer writes very little code, instead making reuse of a vast repository of ready-made components.

> ## SELF-TEST QUESTION
>
> **15.4** Write a class **Stack** that implements a first-in, last-out structure. Use an array list to hold items of type **String**. Provide **public** operations **pop** and **push**. **push** adds an item to the top of the stack. **push** removes an item from the top of the stack. The class could be used like this:
>
> ```
> Stack stack = new Stack();
> stack.push("Mary");
> ```

15.4 ● Inheritance

Real-world systems depend on our ability to classify and categorize. Elephants, tigers, polar bears, horses and cows are all mammals; lead, silver and platinum are metals; savings, current and term deposits are types of bank accounts, and so on. Through classification, we are able to associate characteristics common to all members of a class. All mammals are vertebrates (have backbones), are warm-blooded and have hair on their bodies; all metals have atomic weights; and all bank accounts have balances.

We often think of objects as specializations of other objects. Precious metals are specializations of metals, sports cars are specializations of cars, romance novels are specializations of books, and so on. All precious metals are metals but not all metals are precious metals. Similarly, all sports cars are cars and all romance novels are books, but the reverse is not true. Similarly, quadrilaterals and triangles are polygons, and squares and rectangles are special kinds of quadrilaterals. Furthermore, a square is a special kind of rectangle. Extending this notion, we can view one class of objects as a *subclass* of another. We can also talk about one class being a superclass of another.

What does it mean to say that one class is a subclass of another? Intuitively, we mean that the subclass has all the characteristics of the more general class but extends it in some way. Precious metals have all the characteristics of metals but, in addition, they can be distinguished from some metals on the basis of monetary value. Similarly, quadrilaterals are specializations of polygons with four sides. Polygons can have any number of sides. Squares are specializations of quadrilaterals where all four sides have equal length, and adjacent sides are perpendicular to one another. Applying these arguments in reverse, we can describe the superclass of a class as being a generalization of the class.

One of the best ways to describe something new to someone else is to describe it in terms of something that is similar, that is, by describing how it differs from something known. An example is that a zebra is a horse with stripes! This concise definition conveys a substantial amount of information to someone familiar with horses but not with zebras.

We now extend the cyberspace invaders program so that we can create and display the other objects – the bomb, the laser and the user. We already have a class **Alien** that describes aliens. We now consider writing a class **Bomb** to describe bombs. But we soon realize that aliens and bombs have things in common, for example, their *x, y* coordinates and their size, so although we could write completely separate classes, we can exploit the common features of the classes. We do this by writing a class **Sprite** that embodies the commonality. This name is chosen because, in computer games programs, a sprite is the term for a graphical object. Here it is:

```
class Sprite {

    protected int x, y;
    protected size;

    public void moveLeft(int amount) {
        x = x - amount;
    }

    public void moveRight(int amount) {
        x = x + amount;
    }
}
```

You can see that the variables and methods within this class are relevant to all the game objects. You will also notice that the variables declared at the head of the class that were described as **public**, are now described as **protected**. This means that they are accessible from any subclasses, as we shall see in a moment.

We can now write class **Alien** so as to exploit the class **Sprite** as follows:

```
class Alien extends Sprite {

    private ImageIcon alienImage;

    public Alien(int newX, int newY, int newSize) {
        x = newX;
        y = newY;
        size = newSize;
        alienImage = new ImageIcon("c:/alien.jpg");
    }

    public void display(JPanel panel) {
        Graphics paper = panel.getGraphics();
        alienImage.paintIcon(panel, paper, x, y);
    }
}
```

and you can see that this is now shorter than it was. The operative word in this code is **extends**. This is the Java keyword stating that class **Alien** inherits the features of class **Sprite**. All the **public** variables and methods become part of class **Alien**. The terminology is that **Alien** is a subclass of **Sprite**, **Sprite** is the superclass of **Alien**, **Alien** extends **Sprite**, **Sprite** is the base class of **Alien**.

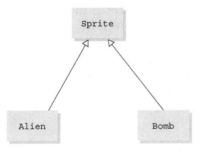

Figure 15.2 Class diagram showing inheritance

The relationships between classes are often shown in a UML class diagram, such as Figure 15.2. Each class is shown as a rectangle. An arrow points from a subclass to a superclass. This diagram says that both **Alien** and **Bomb** are subclasses of **Sprite**.

The variables **x**, **y**, and **size** are labeled **protected** rather than **private**. This means that they can be used within the subclass. But they are still inaccessible from anywhere else.

SELF-TEST QUESTION

15.5 Write class **Bomb**.

Inheritance is a way of exploiting commonality between classes. Another view is that it is a mechanism for making use of an existing class, inheriting its useful features and adding new features. So it is a scheme for software reuse. Inheriting means that an existing class is retained intact. To use it we do not need to make changes, which might disrupt the existing class. So we can safely reuse classes.

When you start to write a new program, you look for useful classes in the library and you look at any classes you have written in the past. This object-oriented approach to programming means that, instead of starting programs from scratch, you build on earlier work. It's not uncommon to find a class that looks useful, and does nearly what you want, but not exactly what you want. Inheritance is a way of resolving this problem. With inheritance, you use an existing class as the basis for creating a modified class.

15.5 ● Polymorphism

We again use as an example the cyberspace invaders program that displays graphical images on the screen – an alien, a bomb and similar. The program uses a class named **Sprite**, which describes all the shared attributes of these images, including where they are in the window. Here is a program fragment that uses the classes **Sprite**, **Alien** and

Bomb to create two objects, storing them in an array list named **game**, and displaying them. The display is shown in Figure 15.1.

```
Alien alien = new Alien(20, 20, 100);
Bomb bomb = new Bomb(80, 80, 10);
ArrayList game = new ArrayList();
game.add(alien);
game.add(bomb);

for (int s = 0; s < game.size(); s++) {
    Object item = game.get(s);
    Sprite sprite = (Sprite) item;
    sprite.display(paper);
}
```

Polymorphism is in use here – the method **display** is called on two occasions with different results according to which object is in use. You can see that the two calls of **display** within the **for** loop:

```
sprite.display(paper);
```

give two different outputs. Two different outputs are displayed because the Java system automatically selects the version of **display** associated with the class of the object. When method **display** is first called, the variable **sprite** contains the object **alien** and so the version of **display** in the class **Alien** is called. Then the corresponding thing happens with **bomb**. This is the essence of polymorphism.

The class of an object is determined when the object is created using new classes, and stays the same whatever happens to the object. Whatever you do to an object in a program, it always retains the features it had when it was created. An object can be assigned to a variable of another class and passed around the program as a parameter, but it never loses its true identity.

Polymorphism allows us to write a single concise statement, such as:

```
sprite.display(paper);
```

instead of a series of **if** statements like this:

```
if (sprite instanceof Alien) {
    Alien alien = (Alien) sprite;
    alien.display(paper);
}
if (sprite instanceof Bomb) {
    Bomb bomb = (Bomb) sprite;
    bomb.display(paper);
}
```

which is clumsy and long-winded. This uses the keyword `instanceof` to ask if an object is a member of a named class. If there are a large number of graphical objects, there are a correspondingly large number of `if` statements. Avoiding this complexity demonstrates how powerful and concise polymorphism is.

As we have seen in this small example, polymorphism often makes a segment of program smaller and neater through the elimination of a series of `if` statements. But this achievement is much more significant than it may seem. It means that such statements as:

```
sprite.display(paper);
```

know nothing about the possible variety of objects that may be used as the value of `sprite`. So information hiding (already present in large measure in an OOP) is extended. We can check this by assessing how much we would need to change this program to accommodate some new type of graphical object (some additional subclass of `Sprite`), say a laser. The answer is that we would not need to modify it at all – we could simply add the new object. This means that the program is enormously flexible. Thus polymorphism enhances modularity, reusability and maintainability.

Polymorphism helps construct programs that are:

- concise (shorter than they might otherwise be)
- modular (unrelated parts are kept separate)
- easy to change and adapt (for example, introducing new objects).

In general, the approach to exploiting polymorphism within a particular program is as follows:

1. identify any similarities (common methods and variables) between any objects or classes in the program
2. design a superclass that embodies the common features of the classes
3. design the subclasses that describe the distinctive features of each of the classes, whilst inheriting the common features from the superclass
4. identify any place in the program where the same operation must be applied to any of the similar objects. It may be tempting to use `if` statements at this location. Instead, this is the place to use polymorphism.
5. make sure that the superclass contains an abstract method corresponding to the method that is to be used polymorphically.

The code fragment shown above, with an array list and a `for` loop, is an example of a commonly occurring situation in software, where the entire contents of a collection are processed. It is so common that some languages provide a `foreach` control structure. In Java, the above `for` loop can be rewritten more concisely as:

```
for (Object item : game) {
    ((Sprite) item).display(paper);
}
```

Each time that the **for** statement repeats, it obtains the next element from the array list **game**.

15.6 ● Single versus multiple inheritance

As we have seen, Java supports single inheritance – a class can inherit from only one immediate superclass. Seen as a class diagram, the relationships between classes appear as a tree (a computer science tree, with the root at the top). Smalltalk, Ada, C# and Visual Basic.Net also provide single inheritance.

However, the widely used language C++ provides multiple inheritance, as does Eiffel. In such a language, a class can inherit from not just one but several superclasses. In life we are not just a person, we also belong to other categories, such as brothers, daughters, soccer lovers, carnivores. So a class representing a person is a subclass of all these superclasses, inheriting variables and methods from them all.

There is no doubt that multiple inheritance is more complicated – both to provide in the language and to use. C++ was widely seen as an overcomplicated language and subsequent languages, such as Java and C#, have seen simplifications in many areas, including abandoning multiple inheritance in favor of single. In some languages, including Java and C#, one role of multiple inheritance has been replaced by the interface facility described in Chapter 16 on programming in the large.

15.7 ● Generics

The strong typing philosophy of programming languages like Java and Ada can have a detrimental effect on programming efficiency. For example, suppose we defined a stack of strings class with the normal stack operations of **push** and **pop**, as posed in the self-test question above. If we subsequently needed another stack type but one in which the elements were Booleans rather than strings then clearly the specification and implementation would be identical apart from the different stack element types. In some languages, our only recourse would be to duplicate the stack code, but with minor differences. A more powerful stack abstraction is required which allows the stack element type to be parameterized.

We will use the Java cyberspace invaders game discussed above to see how generics can be used. An array list named **game** contains objects representing various items (alien, bomb, laser) at various positions within a panel. To display all the shapes, we execute a loop:

```
for (int s = 0, s < game.size(); s++) {
    sprite sprite = (Sprite) game.get(s);
    sprite.display(paper);
}
```

Notice that the objects retrieved from the array list need to be casted into **Sprite** objects using a casting operator, **(Sprite)** in this case. This is because an array list holds only objects of the class **Object**. We can avoid this if we create an array list that can only contain **Sprite** objects, as follows:

```
ArrayList <Sprite> shapes = new ArrayList();
```

The declaration, with the class **Sprite** enclosed in diamond brackets, says that this new array list is to contain only **Sprite** objects. Remember that **ArrayList** is a Java library class. We have qualified it by saying it must contain only **Sprite** objects. So now we can avoid the casting operation, rewriting the above as follows:

```
for (int s = 0, s < game.size(); s++) {
    Sprite sprite = game.get(s);
    sprite.display(paper);
}
```

But there is much more to be gained than brevity. The compiler can check that only objects of the class **Sprite** (or its subclasses) are added to the array list in statements such as:

```
game.add(alien);
```

Thus errors can be caught at compile time, rather than at (more embarrassingly) run time. The run-time error would be an **InvalidCastException** when an object copied from the array list is casted.

In summary, generics allow more concise programming (by avoiding casting) and better compile-time checking.

SELF-TEST QUESTIONS

15.6 Write a method that accepts as a parameter an array list of **String** objects. Each string is an integer number. Return the sum of the numbers.

15.7 Suggest a drawback of generics.

Generics are provided in Ada, Java and C++ but are not provided in C.

15.8 ● Dynamic data structures and pointers

Many programs need to acquire temporary memory to carry out their task. Examples are a graphics program that needs to acquire sufficient memory to represent an image in memory, and a word processor that needs memory to hold the text of a document. In the cyberspace invaders game, objects representing lasers and bombs are created and destroyed.

In an object-oriented language, memory is required each time a new object is created (instantiated) to provide space for the data associated with the object. This space can be released when the object is no longer required. Similarly, if a non-object-oriented language is used, a program will often need temporary workspace in which to build a data structure that grows and shrinks according to the demand. These are sometimes termed *dynamic data structures*, and clearly it requires dynamic memory management.

SELF-TEST QUESTION

15.8 Think of an example of a program that needs to acquire memory dynamically.

In C or C++, the programmer can explicitly issue a request (using the function `malloc`) to the memory manager component of the operating system to obtain a region of memory. Subsequently a call to function `free` returns the space to the memory manager.

The *pointer* data type is provided by such modern languages as Ada and C++ but not by older languages, such as Fortran and Cobol. More recently, the Java language does not provide pointers accessible to the programmer. Pointers provide the programmer with the ability to refer to a data object indirectly. We can manipulate the object "pointed" to or referenced by the pointer. Pointers are particularly useful in conjunction with dynamic data structures – situations where the size of a data collection cannot be predicted in advance or where the structure of the collection is dynamically varying. Typically pointers are used to link one record to another in what is called a linked data structure.

In some languages, recursive data structures, such as lists and trees, are more easily described using pointers. Similarly, such operations as deleting an element from a linked list or inserting a new element into a balanced binary tree are more easily accomplished using pointers. Although such data types can be implemented using arrays, the mapping is less clear and certainly less flexible. Also performance is often faster when a dynamic structure is used.

SELF-TEST QUESTION

15.9 Compare inserting a new item into a structure implemented as:

■ an array
■ a dynamic linked data structure.

The use of pointers brings considerable power and flexibility, but with the consequent responsibility. It is well recognized that the explicit use of pointers is extremely dangerous because it can lead to major errors (or subtle but dangerous errors). The pointer is often mentioned in the same sentence as the infamous `goto` statement as a potential source for obtuse and error-prone code. A number of issues should be considered when evaluating a language's implementation of pointers.

Since the same data object may be referenced through more than one pointer variable, care must be taken not to create a "dangling" pointer. That is, a pointer which references a location that is no longer in use. Does the language provide any assistance in reducing the opportunities for such errors?

The security of pointers is enhanced in such languages as Ada and Java, which require the programmer to bind a pointer variable to reference only objects of a particular type. Programs written in such languages as C and C++, which allow pointers to dynamically reference different types of object, are notoriously awkward to debug.

What provisions (e.g. scoping mechanisms, explicit programmer action or garbage collection procedures) does the language provide for the reclamation of space which is no longer referenced by any pointer variable? This issue is discussed below.

In Java, the program has no explicit access to memory addresses and it is therefore impossible for such a program to make the kind of mistake possible in C++. When a Java program needs memory, it creates a new object. For example, a program can instantiate an object of type **Button** by:

```
Button aButton = new Button("Press here");
```

This creates a pointer to the new object **aButton**. In Java this pointer is termed a *reference*, but there is no way in which the Java program can misuse this pointer. For example, arithmetic is not permitted on a reference, nor can the pointer be used to refer to an object of another class. (Both these operations are allowed in a C++ program.) Thus the Java program is prevented from causing a whole class of subtle and dangerous errors.

15.9 ● Garbage collection

A subtle source of errors can arise when memory is freed (or not) after being allocated to hold some dynamic data structure. In C++, the programmer explicitly issues a function call to free memory. The memory manager then adds the retrieved memory to its pool of available memory; this process is termed *garbage collection*. When used incorrectly, two types of errors can arise:

1. *memory leaks* – memory is no longer in use, but has not been reclaimed by the memory manager
2. *memory corruption* (dangling pointer) – memory has been returned from use, but is still in use.

In a memory leak, a program acquires some memory, uses it, but then fails to return it for garbage collection. This memory is thereby rendered useless. In a program that only runs for a short time, the memory is reclaimed when the program terminates, so that there is no great problem. However, if the program is a component in a real-time system, it may have an effectively infinite lifetime, in which case memory loss is serious.

In memory corruption, a program acquires some memory, uses it, returns it for garbage collection, but then continues to use it. This is, of course, a programming error, but in large complex programs such a mistake is not unusual. The memory management system may now allocate this same memory area to some other program (or to the same program). The consequence is that two programs are now using the same area of memory unknown to each other. This tends to result either in a program crash – if we are lucky – but often the result is some subtle error, which manifests itself in some strange manner, some time after the crime has been committed. For example, some data has become mysteriously corrupted. In such a situation, debugging becomes a nightmare.

In Java, the garbage collection system periodically and automatically checks for objects that are no longer in use. It then frees any available memory. Thus the programmer is freed from the task of keeping track of what memory is in use and many potential errors are therefore avoided. The disadvantage is that the programmer has limited control over when the garbage collector does its work. This might be done in a variety of ways, depending on the implementation:

- at periodic time intervals
- when available memory is exhausted
- never (planning that demand will not exceed supply)
- when a program explicitly requests it.

The garbage collector needs a stable situation in order to analyze and collect unused memory and therefore an implementation will normally freeze all running programs when the garbage collector goes into action. This means that programs may be suspended at unpredictable times. For some applications this is probably acceptable. However, for real-time programs, sudden unpredictable stops are unacceptable and a special attention to scheduling the garbage collection is required.

In summary, C++ supports explicit allocation and deallocation of memory, with explicit access to memory pointers. This is power with considerable responsibility. In Java, allocation and deallocation is implicit and automatic, with no access to memory pointers. This avoids a notorious class of programming bugs.

SELF-TEST QUESTION

15.10 Draw up a table that compares the memory allocation scheme of C++ with that of Java according to the criteria software reliability, development effort and performance (run-time speed).

Summary

Writing a class means that strongly related elements of data and actions are grouped together. A class presents an interface to its users and hides information about its internal workings. It means that the user of a class need not worry about its implementation. This promotes abstraction in thinking about the structure of software. It also means that a class can be changed without any effect on the rest of the program (provided that it continues to present the same interface). Thus classes promote modularity.

Extending (inheriting from) a class is another way of making use of existing components (classes). A subclass inherits the facilities of its immediate superclass and all the superclasses. Most languages support *single inheritance*. A class can extend the facilities of an existing class by providing one or more of:

- additional methods
- additional variables
- methods that override (act instead of) methods in the superclass.

Polymorphism means that similarities between objects can be exploited in the code that uses objects. This means that software is more concise and more easily adapted.

Altogether encapsulation, inheritance and polymorphism mean that software is modular, concise and adaptable. It also means that greater use can be made of libraries of useful components. The programming language must explicitly support these features for OOP to be viable.

Generics enable tailor-made collections to be constructed. This makes programs more concise and assists with compile-time type checking, and consequently software reliability.

There are a number of approaches to garbage collection for software that uses dynamic allocation of memory. Some schemes are automatic but may create timing problems. Some schemes rely on the programmer to make explicit requests, but this can lead to subtle memory problems.

Exercises

15.1 Explain how classes, inheritance and polymorphism support software development.

15.2 Explain how classes, inheritance and polymorphism promote reusable software.

15.3 Suppose that you were asked to design a new programming language for software engineering:

- select and justify a mechanism for encapsulation
- select and justify a mechanism for modularity.

15.4 Explain what the term modularity means. Assess how well the following features of programming languages contribute to modularity:

- methods
- classes.

15.5 Assess the generics feature.

15.6 Argue for and against pointers in a programming language.

15.7 Argue for and against automatic garbage collection.

Answers to self-test questions

15.1
```
public void moveDown(int amount) {

    y = y + amount;
}
```

15.2
```
public int yCoord {
    get {
        return y;
    }
}
```

15.3   Methods: `creditAccount`, `debitAccount`, `calculateInterest`
       Properties: `currentBalance`, `name`

15.4
```
class Stack {

    private Arraylist s = new Arraylist();

    public void push(String item) {
        s.add(0, item);
    }

    public String pop() {
        String item = (String) s.get(0);
        s.remove(0);
        return item;
    }
}
```

```
15.5    class Bomb extends Sprite {

            private ImageIcon bombImage;

            public Bomb(int newX, int newY, int newSize) {
                x = newX;
                y = newY;
                size = newSize;
                bombImage = new ImageIcon("c:/bomb.jpg");
            }

            public void display(Jpanel panel) {
                Graphics paper = panel.getGraphics();
                bombImage.paintIcon(panel, paper, x, y);
            }

            public void move() {
                y = y - 20;
            }
        }

15.6    public int sum(ArrayList <String> list) {
            int total = 0;
            for (int i = 0; i < list.size(); i++) {
                total = total + Integer.parseInt(list.get(i));
            }
            return total;
        }
```

15.7   Generics complicate the language.

15.8   There are many possible answers. Here are just two:

1. a file sort program, because you never know how long the file will be

2. A web browser program, because you do not know in advance how big a web page will be.

15.9   In an array, all items after the insertion point have to be moved down the array, a time-consuming process. In a dynamic structure, only the pointer in the immediately preceding item needs to be updated – a very fast operation.

15.10

Factor	C++	Java
reliability	poor	good
development effort	greater	smaller
performance	faster	unpredictable

Further reading

Smalltalk-80 is the Rolls Royce of object-oriented language. It is completely object-oriented – even control structures like repetition and **if** statements are objects. Like Java it supports single inheritance. Like Java it provides a large and comprehensive library that the programmer uses and inherits from to provide facilities including windowing, graphics and data structures. The definitive book on Smalltalk-80: Adele Goldberg and David Robson, *Smalltalk 80, the Language*, Addison-Wesley, 1989.

The definitive book on the Eiffel language. The first few chapters are a wonderfully clear exposition of the principles of OOP: Bertrand Meyer, *Object-Oriented Software Construction*, Prentice Hall, New York, 2000.

CHAPTER

16 Programming in the large

This chapter:

- reviews the facilities needed for large programs
- explains the ideas of packages and their scopes
- explains scopes for large software
- explains using interfaces to describe the structure of software
- explains using interfaces for interoperability
- discusses separate compilation.

16.1 ● Introduction

The programming of very large, complex software projects, or programming in the large, introduces many new problems for the software engineer. First, what are the characteristics of such software systems? The size of the code is an obvious factor. Large systems consist of tens of thousands of lines of source code; systems with hundreds of thousands of lines are not uncommon. Projects of this size must be developed by teams of programmers; for very large projects the programming team may consist of hundreds of programmers. Such systems are implemented over a long period of time and when completed are expected to undergo continual maintenance and enhancement over an extended lifetime.

Many of the problems associated with such large projects are logistical, caused by the sheer size of the task and the number of personnel involved. Methodologies for managing such projects have been developed and are discussed in other sections of this book. Clearly, many software tools, other than the programming language being used, are required to assist and control the development of such large systems. A recent trend has been to integrate these software tools with a particular programming language to form an integrated software development environment. In this section we concentrate on support for programming in the large at the programming language level.

It is useful to divide up the discussion into those features required to support *programming in the small* and those required to support *programming in the large*.

By *programming in the small*, we mean those features of the language required to support the coding of individual program modules or small programs. In this category, we include the simplicity, clarity and orthogonality of the language, the language syntax and facilities for control and data abstraction. We reviewed these features in Chapters 14 and 15.

By *programming in the large*, we mean those features of the language which support the development of large programs. Here, we define a "large" program as one whose size or complexity dictates that it be developed by a number of programmers and which consists of a collection of individually developed program modules. In this category we include facilities for the separate compilation of program modules, features for controlling the interaction between program modules, high-level functional and data abstraction tools and programming environments or support tools associated with the language.

What support can we expect from a programming language? The programmer's chief tool in managing complexity is abstraction. Abstraction allows the programmer to keep a problem intellectually manageable. The programming language must therefore provide mechanisms which can be used to encapsulate the most common abstractions used by programmers: functional (or procedural) abstraction and data abstraction. The simplest mechanism, provided by nearly all programming languages, is the method, a program unit which allows the encapsulation of a functional abstraction. Programming in the large requires that higher-level abstraction primitives than the method be provided. We have already met one such structure – the class. This helps considerably, but we need still higher-level structuring mechanisms.

The use of abstractions promotes modularity which itself encourages the production of reusable code and promotes the notion of information hiding. Modularity and module independence are essential in an environment where individual modules will most often be developed by different programmers. The programming language can support development in multiprogrammer environments by providing mechanisms for hiding from a user irrelevant detail concerning the implementation of a module. Additionally, the interface between modules must be carefully controlled. It is essential to eliminate the possibility that the implementation of one module may affect another module in some unanticipated manner. This is also important when a system is being maintained or enhanced in some way. It must be possible to localize the effect of some system enhancement or error fix to specific modules of the system; side effects of changes should not propagate throughout the complete system. Clearly, many of these issues are as much system design issues as they are programming language issues. No programming language will solve the problems of a poor system design. On the other hand, the implementation of a good system design can be hampered if the implementation language is of limited expressive power.

If components are to be developed independently, the programming language must also provide facilities for independent compilation. In addition, the language should provide strong type checking across component boundaries to ensure the consistency of calls to externally defined components. All the major modern programming languages for software engineering (C++, Ada, C# and Java) carry out such checks. Another acute problem in large programs concerns the handling of unexpected events during the execution of a program. Programming language features for exception handling are discussed in Chapter 17.

In summary we can identify several needs for programming in the large:

- to be able to see the overall structure of the system
- to compile separately and link program modules
- to be able to access software libraries, e.g. graphics or mathematical methods
- to be able to reuse software components that have been created for one system as part of a new system – in order to reduce development costs
- to provide facilities that support the construction of a large piece of software by a team.

16.2 ● Packages

The idea of a class is to group together a set of methods and data that are related in some way. This then constitutes a programming unit that is bigger than a single method or data item. So instead of describing a large program as consisting of 50 methods and 10 data items, we can view it as a collection of, say, 10 classes. This is potentially easier to understand, design, code, debug, test and maintain. (Even worse, we could think of a program in terms of 10,000 lines of coding.)

The next stage is to group classes into packages. Again, instead of thinking of a program as 100 classes, we can see it as a collection of 10 packages. The Java libraries provide thousands of useful classes. For convenience, the classes are grouped into packages. Here, for example, are some of the Java library packages with an outline of their contents:

java.lang	*contains the classes that support the main features of the language like* `Object`, `String`, *number, exception and threads*
java.util	*these are useful utility classes, such as* `Random` *and* `ArrayList`
java.io	*text input and output streams for characters and numbers*
java.net	*classes that carry out networking functions, socket programming, interacting with the internet*
javax.swing	*this includes the classes to provide GUI components, such as buttons* (`JButton`), *labels* (`JLabel`) *and sliders* (`JSlider`).
java.awt	*awt stands for Abstract Window Toolkit. The graphics methods, such as* `drawLine`, *are here.*
java.applet	*the classes provide support for Java applets (programs run from a web browser).*

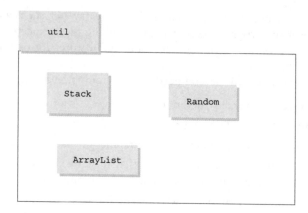

Figure 16.1 A package diagram

UML provides a graphical notation for describing packages. Figure 16.1 shows a package named **util** which consists of three classes **Random, ArrayList** and **Stack**. Showing the contents of a package is optional. This notation is useful for visualizing the large-scale architectural structure of software.

Packages represent the highest-level programming units, which ranges from the small size to the large, as follows:

■ statements

■ methods

■ classes

■ packages.

The languages C++ and C# provide a mechanism termed *namespaces* that is similar to packages.

We will now see how packages are used within a programming language.

16.3 ● Using packages

Java programs typically start with **import** statements, such as:

```
import java.awt.*;
import java.awt.event.*;
import javax.swing.*;
```

java.awt, java.awt.event and **javax.swing** are the names of packages. Each of these packages contains a number of useful classes. For example, the class **JButton** is in the package **javax.swing**.

The **import** statements enable a program conveniently to use the classes provided by the packages. Because the **import** statement is present, we can simply refer to **JButton** without difficulty. For example:

```
JButton button = new JButton("go");
```

If the **import** statement was omitted, we could still use the class **JButton**, but we would need to refer to it by its full name – **javax.swing.JButton**. This would be inconvenient and cumbersome. Hence we see the value of the **import** statement.

If we only need to import an individual class, say **JButton**, from within a package, we can spell it out:

```
import javax.swing.JButton;
```

Using * means that we want to import all the classes within the named package. So if we need to use more than one from a package, it is simpler to use the * notation.

SELF-TEST QUESTION

16.1 Classes called **Monday**, **Tuesday**, **Wednesday**, **Thursday**, **Friday**, **Saturday** and **Sunday** are grouped in a package called **week**. Write down the Java **import** statement that will be needed to use the class **Friday**. Write the statement to create an object **friday** of the class **Friday**. Write down the **import** statement that will be needed to use all the classes in the package.

In C and C++, a program almost always begins with an **include** declaration. For a system package the declaration is typically:

```
#include <stdio.h>
```

or, for a programmer's own package:

```
#include "myFile.h"
```

The **include** statement is a directive to the compiler to include within the current source file a copy of the named file. A file with the suffix **.h** is, by convention, a header file and it is files of this type that normally appear in the **include** statement. A header file is a source code file that contains the declaration of the methods to be found within a package. These declarations are, in C terminology, the prototypes of the available methods – their names and parameters. The C and C++ languages have a rule that a method has to be declared (textually) before it can be used. When a declaration like this is present, the program can refer to the methods within the package described and it will compile successfully. Subsequently the object code of the packages is linked.

16.4 ● Creating packages

Suppose a system consists of three groups of classes:

1. classes that handle the user interface
2. classes that access the database
3. classes that handle the central logic of the program.

We create three packages, named **gui**, **database** and **logic**. Next we need to ensure that individual classes are in the correct package. In Java this is accomplished using the **package** statement written at the head of the class. So, if we have a class named **Login** that handles the login part of the GUI, we write the following at the head of the class:

```
package gui;
public class Login
```

If you omit a **package** statement, it means that the class is placed, by default, in a package with no name.

SELF-TEST QUESTION

16.2 A class named **Backup** is to be placed in a package named **database**. Write the **package** statement and the class heading.

16.5 ● Scoping in large programs

We have already seen how a program can access other packages using **import** or **include** statements. The issue is: What packages, methods and (rarely) variables are accessible to any given package? When you create and use packages, some new scope rules come into play. The essence is that classes within the same package can access each other very easily.

When you write a method in Java, you specify that it is **private, public, protected** or simply give it no prefix. The prefix determines who can access the method: **public** means that the method is available to all. **private** means that it is accessible only within the class. **protected** means that the method can be used by any subclass.

If you give a method no prefix, it means that the method is accessible from anywhere within the same package, but inaccessible from outside. This is also true of classes, constructors and variables. This means that the programmer can establish a close relationship between methods in the same package. This accords with the idea that classes in the same package are related to each other.

16.6 ● Interfaces

The structure of a large program is often derived by using some design method, as described in other chapters in this book. Typically the structure is described in a graphical notation, such as a class diagram. However, some programming languages enable this large-scale, or architectural, structure to be expressed within the programming language itself. In Java, for example, the specification of each class can be written in the programming language. The collection of specifications then constitutes a description of the architecture of the software. The notation used to describe these components is termed an *interface* or a *module interconnection language*.

We will use the Java notation to illustrate how classes can be described. First, here is the description of a stack class.

```
interface StackInterface {
    void push(int item);
    int pop();
}
```

A user of the stack class does not need to know how it works, but knows how to call it. The stack might be represented as an array, a linked list or even (if it was large enough) as a file. This is abstraction at work. It frees the programmer from thinking about detail in order that they can concentrate on the bigger picture. The implementation of the stack could be changed (because of performance improvement or the elimination of bugs), but any packages that use it would not be affected. The stack class could easily be reused in some other program because the interface to it is clean.

SELF-TEST QUESTION

16.3 Suggest one drawback to this kind of specification.

An interface can be compiled along with any other classes, but clearly cannot be executed. However, someone who is planning to *use* a class can compile the program along with the interface and thereby check that it is being used correctly.

Once the classes that comprise a new software project have been identified and specified, the classes can then either be written from scratch or retrieved from an existing library. A person who is implementing an interface can specify in the heading of the class that a particular interface is being implemented. For example, in Java:

```
class Stack implements StackInterface
```

Notice that the class as a whole is described as implementing the **StackInterface** interface. The compiler will then check that this class has been written to comply with the interface declaration, that is, it provides the methods **push** and **pop** together with their appropriate parameters. The rule is that if you implement an interface, you must

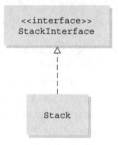

Figure 16.2 A class and its interface

implement *every* method described in the interface. Any deviation results in compiler errors.

We can describe the relationship between a class and its interface using a UML class diagram. See for example Figure 16.2. In a UML class diagram, an interface is shown as a rectangle. The interface name is preceded by the word `<<interface>>`. The `implements` relationship is shown as a dotted arrow.

Interfaces can also be used to describe an inheritance structure. For example, suppose we wanted to describe an interface for a `BetterStack` that is a subclass of the `Stack` interface described above. We can write in Java:

```
public interface BetterStackInterface
                  extends StackInterface {
    boolean empty();
}
```

which inherits the interface `StackInterface` and states that the interface `BetterStackInterface` has an additional method, named `empty`, to test whether the stack is empty. We could similarly describe a whole tree structure of classes as interfaces, describing purely their outward appearance and their subclass–superclass relationships.

In summary, the characteristics of an interface facility (module description language) are:

■ it is textual (though we could think of tools to convert the text into graphics)
■ it is an extension of the programming language (therefore consistent, easy to learn and checkable by the compiler)
■ it allows specification of the external appearance of classes – their names, their visible methods, the parameters required.

The advantages of being able to write descriptions like this are:

■ during design, we can describe the grand structure of a piece of software in a fairly formal way. The description can be checked by a language processor.

- during coding, the description can be used as part of the class specification. The compiler can also check for consistency between the description and the class coding.

- during maintenance, the description can be used as documentation in order to learn about the overall structure of the system. It can be used as input to a tool that creates various reports on the structure – e.g., a class diagram. Finally, following update of the software, consistency checking can be reapplied using the compiler.

What interfaces *cannot* describe are:

- the implementations of methods (but that is the whole point of interfaces)
- which classes use which other classes, the has-a relationships (this needs some other notation).

SELF-TEST QUESTION

16.4 Write specifications (interfaces) for the classes in the following software system.

A patient monitoring system (Appendix A) monitors the vital signs of a single hospital patient and delivers messages to the nurses' station. It consists of the following classes, each followed by their methods. Make assumptions about the parameters associated with the methods.

- class `Clock` provides methods `init`, `waitSeconds`, `getHours`, `getMinutes`, `getSeconds`
- class `Display` provides methods `init`, `flashLight`, `unflashLight`, `soundKlaxon`, `unsoundKlaxon`, `displayMessage` and `clearScreen`
- class `Heart` provides methods `readRate` and `readPressure`
- class `Lungs` provides method `readRate`
- class `Temp` provides method `readTemp`

16.7 ● Interfaces and interoperability

Household appliances, such as toasters and electric kettles, come with a power cord with a plug on the end of it. The design of the plug is standard (throughout a country) and ensures that an appliance can be used anywhere (within the country). Thus the adoption of a common interface ensures interoperability. In Java, interfaces can be used in a similar fashion to ensure that objects exhibit a common interface. When such an object is passed around a program, we can be sure that it supports all the methods specified by the interface description.

As an example, we declare an interface named **Displayable**. Any class complying with this interface must include a method named **display** which displays the object. The interface declaration in Java is:

```
public interface Displayable {
    void display(Graphics paper);
}
```

Now we write a new class, named **Square**, which represents square graphical objects. We say in the header of the class that it implements **Displayable**. We include within the body of the class the method **display**:

```
public class Square implements Displayable {

    private int x, y, size;

    public void display(Graphics paper) {
        paper.setColor(Color.black);
        paper.drawRectangle(x, y, size, size);
    }

    // other methods of the class Square

}
```

As the heading states, this class (and any object created from it) conforms to the **Displayable** interface. It means that any object of this class can be passed around a program and we are confident that, when necessary, it can be displayed by calling its method **display**.

SELF-TEST QUESTION

16.5 We wish to write a new class **Circle** that implements the **Displayable** interface. Write the header for the class.

16.8 ● Multiple interfaces

Just as a TV has interfaces both to a power source and to a signal source, so can we specify that a class implements a number of interfaces.

Java, for example, is a language that provides single inheritance – a class can inherit from (or be the subclass of) only one class. The class structure is a tree, with the root at the top, in which a class can have many subclasses but only one superclass. Figure 16.3 shows illustrative classes **Circle** and **Game** as subclasses of superclass **JFrame**. Each class appears only within a single tree and each class has only a single superclass.

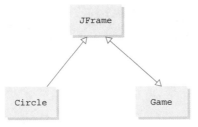

Figure 16.3 Single inheritance

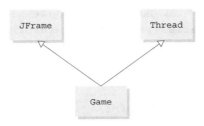

Figure 16.4 Multiple inheritance (supported in C++ but not in Java)

Sometimes we would like a class to inherit from more than one superclass as described in the following class header and shown in Figure 16.4.

```
public class Game extends JFrame, Thread  //  error
```

But this heading is wrong because it attempts to extend two classes. This would be called *multiple inheritance*. Some languages, such as C++, permit multiple inheritance while Java does not. Multiple inheritance allows a class to inherit sets of methods from a number of classes, and it is therefore potentially very powerful.

If we think about classification systems in science and nature, it is often the case that objects belong to more than one class. We humans, for example, belong to one gender class, but also to a class that likes a particular type of music. So we all belong in one inheritance tree for gender, another for musical taste, another for mother tongue, and so on.

Interfaces provide a way of emulating a facility similar to multiple inheritance. This is because, while a class can only extend a single class, it can implement any number of interfaces.

Multiple interfaces are illustrated in Figure 16.5. This example is coded in Java as follows:

```
public class Game extends JFrame implements InterfaceA, InterfaceB
```

If **Game** inherited from **InterfaceA** and **InterfaceB**, it would inherit a set of methods from **InterfaceA** and **InterfaceB**. But instead **Game** is implementing interfaces **InterfaceA** and **InterfaceB**, and these interfaces have no methods on offer.

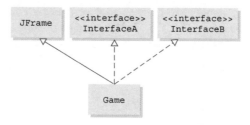

Figure 16.5 Multiple interfaces

What this means is that class **Game** agrees to provide the methods described in **InterfaceA** and **InterfaceB** – that **Game** has agreed to conform to certain behavior. The code for implementing **InterfaceA** and **InterfaceB** has to be written as part of the class **Game**.

16.9 ● Separate compilation

A programming language is ill suited for the development of large, complex programs if it does not provide facilities for the separate compilation of program modules. Large programs must necessarily be developed by teams of programmers; individual pro-grammers must be able to work independently and at the same time be able to access programs written by other members of the team. Programming language support is required for the integration of routines that have been developed separately. Additional sup-port in this area is often provided by environmental tools, such as linkers, cross-reference generators, file librarians and source code control systems. What support should the programming language itself provide? We suggest the following:

■ independent compilation of program modules
■ easy access to libraries of precompiled software
■ the ability to integrate together components written in different languages
■ strong type checking across module boundaries
■ the ability to avoid the unnecessary recompilation of precompiled modules.

One of the foremost reasons for the continued popularity of Fortran is the tremen-dous resource of reusable software available to scientists and engineers through the readily accessible libraries of scientific and engineering subroutines. Fortran provides independent compilation of modules at the subroutine level and easy access to library routines but performs no run-time checking of calls to external routines. It is the responsibility of the programmer to check that the correct number and type of param-eters are used in the calling program.

Java and similar languages provide far greater support for separate compilation than Fortran. Classes may be compiled as separate modules with strong type checking across module boundaries to ensure that they are used in accordance with their specifications. The specification and implementation of a class may be compiled in two separate parts.

This has a number of advantages for the software engineer. The strong type checking ensures that all specifications stay in line with their implementations. Also, it means that once the specification for a class has been compiled, modules which use that class may also be compiled (even before the implementation of the class has been completed).

C, C++, C# and Java are all (fairly) small languages and most of their functionality is provided by large and comprehensive libraries. These libraries are separately compiled.

Summary

It is often convenient to group the classes of a large program into packages. Each package is given a name. Classes within a package can be used by giving the full name of the package and class. A more convenient alternative is to use a statement such as the Java **import** statement. The classes can be placed in the appropriate package by employing the Java **package** statement.

Scope rules mean that classes within the same package have special access rights to each other.

Interfaces are used to describe the services provided by a class. Interfaces are useful for describing the structure of software. This description can be checked by the compiler. Interfaces can also be used to ensure that a class conforms to a particular interface. This supports interoperability. Most modern languages support multiple interfaces, but only support single inheritance.

For large software, separate compilation is a vital facility.

Exercises

16.1 Assess the difficulties of developing large-scale software and suggest programming language features to help solve the problems that you have identified.

16.2 The facility to describe interfaces as seen in modern languages enables specification of the services provided by a class. Consider extending such a language so that it also describes:

- the classes that each class uses
- the classes that use each class.

What would be the advantages and disadvantages of this notation?

16.3 Assess whether and how it would be possible to extend the interface notation to packages.

16.4 The design goals of Ada were readability, strong typing, programming in the large, exception handling data abstraction, and generic units. Explain the meanings of these objectives and comment on their validity. Assess whether they are complementary or contradictory. If you are familiar with Ada, assess it against these aims.

16.5 Some of the stated design aims for Java are that it should be simple, object-oriented, network-savvy, interpreted, robust, secure, architecture neutral, portable, high-performance and dynamic.

Explain the meanings of these objectives. Assess whether they are complementary or contradictory. If you are familiar with Java, assess it against these aims.

16.6 Take a language of your choice. Search out the design aims and explain their meaning. Assess how well the language matches the design aims. Assess the language against the criteria developed in this chapter.

16.7 What aims and what language features would you expect to find in a language designed for each of the following application domains?

- information systems
- scientific programming
- systems programming
- real-time embedded systems.

How suitable is your favorite language for each of these application domains?

16.8 Compare and contrast Ada with C++.

16.9 Compare and contrast C++ with Java.

16.10 Cobol (or Fortran) is an outdated language. Discuss.

Answers to self-test questions

16.1 To use class **Friday** put:

```
import week.Friday;
```

To create an object of the class **Friday** put:

```
Friday friday = new Friday();
```

To use all the classes in the package put:

```
import week.*;
```

16.2
```
package database;

public class Backup
```

16.3 A specification of this kind only specifies the method names and their parameters. It does not specify any more closely what a method does – other than via any comments.

16.4
```
interface Clock {
      void init();
      void waitSeconds(int seconds);
      int getHours();
      int getMinutes();
      int getSeconds();
}

interface Display {
      void init();
      void flashLight();
      void unflashLight();
      void soundKlaxon();
      void unsoundKlaxon();
      void displayMessage(String message);
      void clearScreen();
}

interface Heart {
      int readRate();
      int readPressure();
}

interface Lungs {
      int readRate();
}

interface Temp {
      int readTemp();
}
```

16.5 `public class Circle implements Displayable`

Further reading

A good collection of papers from the computer science literature which critically evaluate and compare these three programming languages: A. Feuer and N. Gehani, *Comparing and Assessing Programming Languages, Ada, Pascal and C*, Prentice Hall, 1984.

An excellent text for students wishing to explore further the fundamental principles underlying programming languages: B.J. Maclennan, *Principles of Programming Languages: Design, Evaluation and Implementation*, Dryden Press, 1987.

An authoritative account of the ANSI standard version of the language in a classic book. Ritchie was the designer of C, a language originally closely associated with the UNIX operating system: Brian W. Kernighan and Dennis Ritchie, *The C Programming Language*, Prentice Hall, 2nd edn, 1988.

The definitive source on C++, but not an easy read: Bjarne Stroustrup, *The C++ Programming Language*, Addison-Wesley, 2nd edn, 1991.

This is a selection of books that look at programming languages in general:

Carlo Ghezzi and Mehdi Jazayeri, *Programming Language Concepts*, John Wiley, 1997.

Terence Pratt, *Programming languages: Design and Implementation*, Prentice Hall, 1995.

Michael L. Scott, *Programming Language Pragmatics*, Morgan Kaufman, 1998.

Mark Woodman (ed.), *Programming languages*, International Thomson Computer Press, 1996.

CHAPTER

17 | Software robustness

This chapter explains:

- how to categorize faults
- how faults can be detected
- how recovery can be made from faults
- exception handling
- recovery blocks
- how to use n-version programming
- how to use assertions.

17.1 ● Introduction

Robust software is software that tolerates faults. Computer faults are often classified according to who or what causes them:

- user errors
- software faults (bugs)
- hardware faults.

An example of a user error is entering alphabetic data when numeric data is expected. An example of a software fault is any of the many bugs that inhabit most software systems. An example of a hardware fault is a disk failure or a telecommunication line that fails to respond.

In fault tolerance, the hardware and software collaborate in a kind of symbiosis. Sometimes the hardware detects a software fault; sometimes the software detects a hardware fault. In some designs, when a hardware fault occurs, the hardware copes with the situation, but often it is the role of the software to deal with the problem. When a software fault occurs, it is usually the job of the software to deal with the problem. In some systems, when a user error arises, again it is the role of the software to cope. In many situations, of course, when a fault arises nothing is done to cope with it and the system crashes. This chapter explores measures that can be taken to detect and deal with all types of computer fault, with emphasis on remedial measures that are implemented by software.

We will see in Chapter 19 on testing that eradicating every bug from a program is almost impossible. Even when formal mathematical methods for program development are used to improve the reliability of software, human error creeps in so that even mathematical proofs can contain errors. As we have seen, in striving to make a piece of software as reliable as possible, we have to use a whole range of techniques

Software fault tolerance is concerned with trying to keep a system going in the face of faults. The term *intolerance* is sometimes used to describe software that is written with the assumption that the system will always work correctly. By contrast, fault *tolerance* recognizes that faults are inevitable and that therefore it is necessary to cope with them. Moreover, in a well-designed system, we strive to cope with faults in an organized, systematic manner.

We will distinguish between two types of faults – *anticipated* and *unanticipated*. Anticipated faults are unusual situations, but we can fairly easily foresee that they will occasionally arise. Examples are:

■ division by zero

■ floating point overflow

■ numeric data that contains letters

■ attempting to open a file that does not exist.

What are *unanticipated faults*? The name suggests that we cannot even identify, predict or give a name to any of them. (Logically, if we can identify them, they are anticipated faults.) In reality this category is used to describe very unusual situations. Examples are:

■ hardware faults (e.g. an input-output device error or a main memory fault)

■ a software design fault (i.e. a bug)

■ an array subscript that is outside its allowed range

■ the detection of a violation by the computer's memory protection mechanism.

Take the last example of a memory protection fault. Languages like C++ allow the programmer to use memory addresses to refer to parameters and to data structures. Access to pointers is very free and the programmer can, for example, actually carry out arithmetic on pointers. This sort of freedom is a common source of errors in C++ programs. Worse still, errors of this type can be very difficult to eradicate (debug) and may persist unseen until the software has been in use for some time. Of course this type of error is a mistake made by a programmer, designer or tester – a type of error sometimes known as a logic error. The hardware memory protection system can help with the detection of errors of this type because often the erroneous use of a pointer will eventually often lead to an attempt to use an illegal address.

Clearly, the difference between anticipated and unanticipated faults is a rather arbitrary distinction. A better terminology might be the words "exceptional circumstances" and "catastrophic failures". Whatever jargon we use, we shall see that the two categories of failure are best dealt with by two different mechanisms.

Having identified the different types of faults, let us now look at what has to be done when a fault occurs. In general, we have to do some or all of the following:

- detect that a fault has occurred
- assess the extent of the damage that has been caused
- repair the damage
- treat the cause of the fault.

As we shall see, different mechanisms deal with these tasks in different ways.

How serious a problem may become depends on the type of the computer application. For example power failure may not be serious (though annoying) to the user of a personal computer. But a power failure in a safety critical system is serious.

SELF-TEST QUESTION

17.1 Categorize the following eventualities:

1. the system stack (used to hold temporary variables and method return addresses) overflows
2. the system heap (used to store dynamic objects and data structures) overflows
3. a program tries to refer to an object using the null pointer (a pointer that points to no object)
4. the computer power fails
5. the user types a URL that does not obey the rules for valid URLs.

17.2 ● Fault detection by software

Faults can be prevented and detected during software development using the following techniques:

- good design
- using structured walkthroughs
- employing a compiler with good compile-time checking
- testing systematically
- run-time checking.

Techniques for software design, structured walkthroughs and testing are discussed elsewhere in this book. So now we consider the other two techniques from this list – compile-time checking and run-time checking. Later we go on to discuss the details of automatic mechanisms for run-time checking.

Compile-time checking

The types of errors that can be detected by a compiler are:

■ a type inconsistency, e.g. an attempt to perform an addition on data that has been declared with the type string.

■ a misspelled name for a variable or method

■ an attempt by an instruction to access a variable outside its legal scope.

These checks may seem routine and trivial, but remember the enormous cost of the NASA probe sent to Venus which veered off course because of the erroneous Fortran repetition statement:

```
DO 3 I = 1.3
```

This was interpreted by the compiler as an assignment statement, giving the value 1.3 to the variable DO 3 I. In the Fortran language, variables do not have to be declared before they are used and if Fortran was more vigilant, the compiler would have signaled that a variable DO 3 I was undeclared.

Run-time checking

Errors that can be automatically detected at run-time include:

■ division by zero

■ an array subscript outside the range of the array.

In some systems these are carried by the software and in others by hardware.

There is something of a controversy about the relative merits of compile-time and run-time checking. The compile-time people scoff at the run-time people. They compare the situation to that of an aircraft with its "black box" flight recorder. The black box is completely impotent in the sense that it is unable to prevent the aircraft from crashing. Its only ability is in helping diagnose what happened after the event. In terms of software, compile-time checking can *prevent* a program from crashing, but run-time checking can only detect faults. Compile-time checking is very cheap and it needs to be done only once. Unfortunately, it imposes constraints on the language – like strong typing – which limits the freedom of the programmer (see Chapter 14 for a discussion of this issue). On the other hand run-time checking is a continual overhead. It has to be done whenever the program is running and it is therefore expensive. Often, in order to maintain good performance, it is done by hardware rather than software.

In general, it seems that compile-time checking is better than run-time checking. However, run-time checking has the last word. It is vital because not everything can be checked at compile time.

SELF-TEST QUESTION

17.2 Add to the list above checks that can only be done at run-time and therefore, by implication, cannot be done at compile-time.

Incidentally, it is common practice to switch on all sorts of automatic checking for the duration of program testing, but then to switch off the checking when development is complete – because of concern about performance overheads. For example, some C++ compilers allow the programmer to switch on array subscript checking (during debugging and testing), but also allow the checking to be removed (when the program is put into productive use). C.A.R Hoare, the eminent computer scientist, has compared this approach to that of testing a ship with the lifeboats on board but then discarding them when the ship starts to carry passengers.

We have looked at automatic checking for general types of fault. Another way of detecting faults is to write additional software to carry out checks at strategic times during the execution of a program. Such software is sometimes called an *audit module*, because of the analogy with accounting practices. In an organization that handles money, auditing is carried out at different times in order to detect any fraud. An example of a simple audit module is a method to check that a square root has been correctly calculated. Because all it has to do is to multiply the answer by itself, such a module is very fast. This example illustrates that the process of checking for faults by software need not be costly – either in programming effort or in run-time performance.

SELF-TEST QUESTION

17.3 Devise an audit module that checks whether an array has been sorted correctly.

Another term used to describe software that attempts to detect faults is *defensive programming*. It is normal to check (validate) data when it enters a computer system – for example, numbers are commonly scrupulously checked to see that they only contain digits. But within software it is unusual to carry out checks on data because it is normally assumed that the software works correctly. In defensive programming the programmer inserts checks at strategic places throughout the program to provide detection of design errors. A natural place to do this is to check the parameters are valid at the entry to a method and then again when a method has completed its work. This approach has been formalized in the idea of assertions, explained below.

17.3 ● Fault detection by hardware

We have already seen how software checks can reveal faults. Hardware also can be vital in detecting consequences of such software errors as:

- division by zero, more generally arithmetic overflow
- an array subscript outside the range of the array
- a program which tries to access a region of memory that it is denied access to, e.g. the operating system.

Of course hardware also detects hardware faults, which the hardware often passes on to the software for action. These include:

- memory parity checks
- device time-outs
- communication line faults.

Memory protection systems

One major technique for detecting faults in software is to use hardware protection mechanisms that separate one software component from another. (Protection mechanisms have a different and important role in connection with data security and privacy, which we are not considering here.) A good protection mechanism can make an important contribution to the detection and localization of bugs. A violation detected by the memory protection mechanism means that a program has gone berserk – usually because of a design flaw.

To introduce the topic we will use the analogy of a large office block where many people work. Along with many other provisions for safety, there will usually be a number of fire walls and fire doors. What exactly is their purpose? People were once allowed to smoke in offices and public buildings. If someone in one office dropped a cigarette into a waste paper basket and caused a fire, the fire walls helped to save those in other offices. In other words, the walls limited the spread of damage. In computing terms, does it matter how much the software is damaged by a fault? – after all it is merely code in a memory that can easily be re-loaded. The answer is "yes" for two reasons. First, the damage caused by a software fault might damage vital information held in files, damage other programs running in the system or crash the complete system. Second, the better the spread of damage is limited, the easier it will be to attempt some repair and recovery. Later, when the cause of the fire is being investigated, the walls help to pinpoint its source (and identify the culprit). In software terminology, the walls help find the cause of the fault – the bug.

One of the problems in designing buildings is the question of where to place the firewalls. How many of them should there be, and where should they be placed? In software language, this is called the issue of *granularity*. The greater the number of walls, the more any damage will be limited and the easier it will be to find the cause. But walls are expensive and they also constrain normal movement within the building.

Let us analyze what sort of protection we need within programs. At a minimum we do not want a fault in one program to affect other programs or the operating system. We therefore want protection against programs accessing each other's main memory space. Next it would help if a program could not change its own instructions, although this would not necessarily be true in functional or logic programming. This idea prompts us to consider whether we should have firewalls *within* programs to protect programs against themselves. Many computer systems provide no such facility – when a program goes berserk, it can overwrite anything within the memory available to it. But if we examine a typical program, it consists of fixed code (instructions), data items that do not change (constants) and data items that are updated. So, at a minimum, we should expect these to be protected in different ways. But of course, there is more structure to a program than this. If we look at any program, it consists of methods, each with its own data. Methods share data. One method updates a piece of data, while another merely references it. The ways in which methods access variables can be complex.

In many programs, the pattern of access to data is not hierarchical, nor does it fit into any other regular framework. We need a matrix in order to describe the situation. Each row of the matrix corresponds to method. Each column corresponds to a data item. Looking at a particular place in the table gives the allowed access of a method to a piece of data.

To summarize the requirements we might expect of a protection mechanism, we need the access rights of software to *change* as it enters and leaves methods. An individual method may need:

- execute access to its code
- read access to parameters
- read access to local data
- write access to local data
- read access to constants
- read or write access to a file or i/o device
- read or write access to some data shared with another program
- execute access to other methods.

Different computer architectures provide a range of mechanisms, ranging from the absence of any protection in most early microcomputers, to sophisticated segmentation systems in the modern machines. They include the following systems:

■ base and limit registers

■ lock and key

■ mode switch

■ segmentation

■ capabilities.

A discussion of these topics is outside the scope of this book, but is to be found in books on computer architecture and on operating systems.

This completes a brief overview of the mechanisms that can be provided by the hardware of the computer to assist in fault tolerance. The beauty of hardware mechanisms is that they can be mass-produced and therefore can be made cheaply, whereas software checks are tailor-made and may be expensive to develop. Additionally, checks carried out by hardware may not affect performance as badly as checks carried by software.

17.4 ● Dealing with damage

Dealing with the damage caused by a fault encompasses two activities:

1. assessing the extent of the damage
2. repairing the damage.

In most systems, both of these ends are achieved by the same mechanism. There are two alternative strategies for dealing with the situation:

1. forward error recovery
2. backward error recovery.

In *forward error recovery*, the attempt is made to continue processing, repairing any damaged data and resuming normal processing. This is perhaps more easily understood when placed in contrast with the second technique. In *backward error recovery*, periodic dumps (or snapshots) of the state of the system are taken at appropriate *recovery points*. These dumps must include information about any data (in main memory or in files) that is being changed by the system. When a fault occurs, the system is "rolled back" to the most recent recovery point. The state of the system is then restored from the dump and processing is resumed. This type of error recovery is common practice in information systems because of the importance of protecting valuable data.

If you are cooking a meal and burn the pan, you can do one of two things. You can scrape off the burnt food and serve the unblemished food (pretending to your family or friends that nothing happened). This is forward error recovery. Alternatively, you can start the preparation of the damaged dish again. This is backward error recovery.

SELF-TEST QUESTION

17.6 You are driving in your car when you get a flat tire. You change the tire and continue. What strategy are you adopting – forward or backward error recovery?

Now that we have identified two strategies for error recovery, we return to our analysis of the two main types of error. Anticipated faults can be analyzed and predicted. Their effects are known and treatment can be planned in detail. Therefore forward error recovery is not only possible but most appropriate. On the other hand, the effects of unanticipated faults are largely unpredictable and therefore backward error recovery is probably the only possible technique. But we shall also see how a forward error recovery scheme can be used to cope with design faults.

17.5 ● Exceptions and exception handlers

We have already seen that we can define a class of faults that arise only occasionally, but are easily predicted. The trouble with occasional error situations is that, once detected, it is sometimes difficult to cope with them in an organized way. Suppose, for example, we want a user to enter a number, an integer, into a text field, see Figure 17.1.

The number represents an age, which the program uses to see whether the person can vote or note. First, we look at a fragment of this Java program without exception handling. When a number has been entered into the text field, the event causes a method called **actionPerformed** to be called. This method extracts the text from the text field called **ageField** by calling the library method **getText**. It then calls the library function **parseInt** to convert the text into an integer and places it in the integer variable **age**. Finally the value of age is tested and the appropriate message displayed:

Figure 17.1 Program showing normal behavior

```
public void actionPerformed(ActionEvent event) {
    String string = ageField.getText();
    age = Integer.parseInt(string);
    if (age > 18)
        response.setText("you can vote");
    else
        response.setText("you cannot vote");
}
```

This piece of program, as written, provides no exception handling. It assumes that nothing will go wrong. So if the user enters something that is not a valid integer, method **parseInt** will fail. In this eventuality, the program needs to display an error message and solicit new data, (see Figure 17.2).

To the programmer, checking for erroneous data is additional work, a nuisance, that detracts from the central purpose of the program. For the user of the program, however, it is important that the program carries out vigilant checking of the data and when appropriate displays an informative error message and clear instructions as to how to proceed. What exception handling allows the programmer to do is to show clearly what is normal processing and what is exceptional processing.

Here is the same piece of program, but now written using exception handling. In the terminology of exception handling, the program first makes a *try* to carry out some action. If something goes wrong, an exception is *thrown* by a piece of program that detects an error. Next the program *catches* the exception and deals with it.

```
public void actionPerformed(ActionEvent event) {
    String string = ageField.getText();
    try {
        age = Integer.parseInt(string);
    }
    catch (NumberFormatException e){
        response.setText("error. Please re-enter number");
        return;
    }
    if (age > 18)
        response.setText("you can vote");
    else
        response.setText("you cannot vote");
}
```

In the example, the program carries out a **try** operation, enclosing the section of program that is being attempted. Should the method **parseInt** detect an error, it throws a **NumberFormatException** exception. When this happens, the section of program enclosed by the **catch** keyword is executed. As shown, this displays an error message to the user of the program.

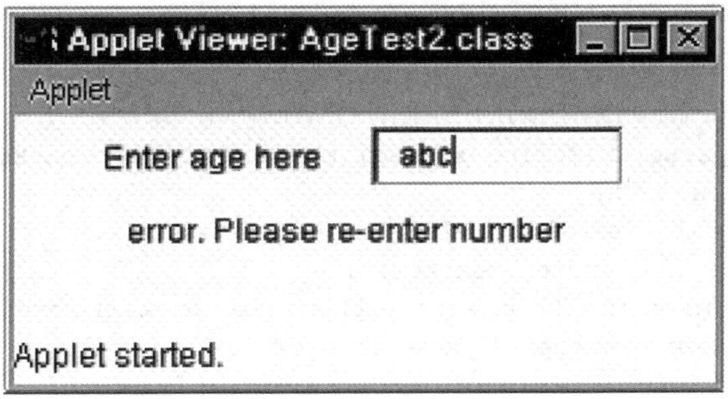

Figure 17.2 Program showing exceptional behavior

The addition of the exception-handling code does not cause a great disturbance to this program, but it does highlight what checking is being carried out and what action will be taken in the event of an exception. The possibility of the method **parseInt** throwing an exception must be regarded as part of the specification of **parseInt**. The contract for using **parseInt** is:

1. it is provided with one parameter (a string)

2. it returns an integer (the equivalent of the string)

3. it throws a **NumberFormatException** if the string contains illegal characters.

There are, of course, other ways of dealing with exceptions, but arguably they are less elegant. For example, the **parseInt** method could be written so that it returns a special value for the integer (say -999) if something has gone wrong. The call on **parseInt** would look like this:

```
age = Integer.parseInt(string);
if (age == -999)
    response.setText("error. Please re-enter number");
else
    if (age > 18)
        response.setText("you can vote");
    else
        response.setText("you cannot vote");
```

You can see that this is inferior to the **try-catch** program. It is more complex and intermixes the normal case with the exceptional case. Another serious problem with this approach is that we have had to identify a special case of the data value – a value that might be needed at some time.

Yet another strategy is to include in every call an additional parameter to convey error information. The problem with this solution is, again, that the program becomes encumbered with the additional parameter and additional testing associated with every method call, like this:

```
age = Integer.parseInt(string, error);
if (error) etc
```

Let us turn to examining how an exception is thrown, using the same example. In Java, the method **parseInt** can be written as follows:

```
public int parseInt(String string) throws NumberFormatException {
    int number = 0;
    for (int i = 0; i < string.length(); i++) {
        char c = string.charAt(i);
        if (c < '0' || c > '9') throw new NumberFormatException();
        number = number * 10 + (c - '0');
    }
    return number;
}
```

You can see that in the heading of the method the exception that may be thrown is declared, along with the specification of any parameters and return value. If this method detects that any of the characters within the string are illegal, it executes a **throw** instruction. This immediately terminates the method and transfers control to a **catch** block designed to handle the exception. In our example, the **catch** block is within the method that calls **parseInt**. Alternatively the **try-catch** combination can be written within the same method as the **throw** statement. Or it can be written within any of the methods in the calling chain that led to calling **parseInt**. Thus the designer can choose an appropriate place in the software structure at which to carry exception handling. The position in which the exception handler is written helps both to determine the action to be taken and what happens after it has dealt with the situation.

SELF-TEST QUESTION

17.7 The method **parseInt** does not throw an exception if the string is of zero length. Amend it so that it throws the same exception in this situation.

What happens after an exception has been handled? In the above example, the **catch** block ends with a **return** statement, which exits from the current method, **actionPerformed** and returns control to its caller. This is the appropriate action in this case – the program is able to recover and continue in a useful way. In general the options are either to recover from the exception and continue or to allow the program to gracefully degrade. The Java language mechanism supports various actions:

■ handle the exception. Control flow then either continues on down the program or the method can be exited using a **return** statement.

■ ignore the exception. This is highly dangerous and always leads to tears, probably after the software has been put into use.

■ throw another exception. This passes the buck to another exception handler further up the call chain, which the designer considers to be a more appropriate place to handle the exception.

> **SELF-TEST QUESTION**
>
> 17.8 What happens if the `return` statement is omitted in the above example of the exception handler?

In the above example, the application program itself detected the exception. Sometimes, however, it is the operating system or the hardware that detects an exception. An example is an attempt to divide by zero, which would typically be detected by the hardware. The hardware would alert the run-time system or operating system, which in turn would enter any exception handler associated with this exception.

The mechanism described above is the exception handling facility provided in Java. Similar mechanisms are provided in Ada and C++.

In old software systems the simplest solution to handling exceptions was to resort to the use of a `goto` statement to transfer control out of the immediate locality and into a piece of coding designed to handle the situation. The use of a `goto` was particularly appealing when the unusual situation occurred deep within a set of method calls. The `throw` statement has been criticized as being a `goto` statement in disguise. The response is that `throw` is indeed a "structured `goto`", but that its use is restricted to dealing with errors and therefore it cannot be used in an undisciplined way.

In summary, exception handlers allow software to cope with unusual, but anticipated, events. The software can take appropriate remedial action and continue with its tasks. Exception handlers therefore provide a mechanism for forward error recovery. In Java, the mechanism consists of three ingredients:

1. a `try` block, in which the program attempts to behave normally
2. the program `throws` an exception
3. a `catch` block handles the exceptional situation.

17.6 ● Recovery blocks

Recovery blocks are a way of structuring backward error recovery to cope with unanticipated faults. In backward error recovery, periodic dumps of the state of the system are made at recovery points. When a fault is detected, the system is restored to its state at the most recent recovery point. (The assumption is that this is a correct state of the system.)

The system now continues on from the recovery point, using some alternative course of action so as to avoid the original problem.

An analogy: if you trip on a banana skin and spill your coffee, you can make a fresh cup (restore the state of the system) and carry on (carefully avoiding the banana skin).

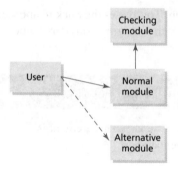

Figure 17.3 Components in a recovery block scheme

As shown in Figure 17.3, backward error recovery needs:

1. the primary software component that is normally expected to work
2. a check that it has worked correctly
3. an alternative piece of software that can be used in the event of the failure of the primary module.

We also need, of course, a mechanism for taking dumps of the system state and for restoring the system state. The recovery block notation embodies all of these features. Taking as an example a program that uses a method to sort some information, a fault tolerant fragment of program looks like this:

```
ensure dataStillValid
by
     superSort
  else by
     quickSort
  else by
     slowButSureSort
  else error
```

Here **supersort** is the primary component. When it has tried to sort the information, the method **dataStillValid** tests to see whether a failure occurred. If there was a fault, the state of the program is restored to what it was before the sort method was executed. The alternative method **quickSort** is then executed. Should this now fail, a third alternative is provided. If this fails, there is no other alternative available, and the whole component has failed. This does not necessarily mean that the whole program will fail, as there may be other recovery blocks programmed by the user of this sort module.

What kinds of fault is this scheme designed to cope with? The recovery block mechanism is designed primarily to deal with unanticipated faults that arise from bugs (design faults) in the software. When a piece of software is complete, it is to be expected that there will be residual faults in it, but what cannot be anticipated is the whereabouts of the bugs.

Recovery blocks will, however, also cope with hardware faults. For example, suppose that a fault develops in the region of main memory containing the primary sort method. The recovery block mechanism can then recover by switching over to an alternative method. There are stories that the developers of the recovery block mechanism at Newcastle University, England, used to invite visitors to remove memory boards from a live computer and observe that the computer continued apparently unaffected.

We now examine some of the other aspects of recovery blocks.

The acceptance test

You might think that acceptance tests would be cumbersome methods, incurring high overheads, but this need not be so. Consider for example a method to calculate a square root. A method to check the outcome, simply by multiplying the answer by itself, is short and fast. Often, however, an acceptance test cannot be completely foolproof – because of the performance overhead. Take the example of the sort method. The acceptance test could check that the information had been sorted, that is, is in sequence. However, this does not guarantee that items have not been lost or created. An acceptance test, therefore, does not normally attempt to ensure the correctness of the software, but instead carries out a check to see whether the results are acceptably good.

Note that if a fault like division by zero, a protection violation, an array subscript out of range occurs while one of the sort methods is being executed, then these also constitute the result of checks on the behavior of the software. (These are checks carried out by the hardware or the run-time system.) Thus either software acceptance tests or hardware checks can trigger fault tolerance.

The alternatives

The software components provided as backups must accomplish the same end as the primary module. But they should achieve this by means of a different algorithm so that the same problem doesn't arise. Ideally the alternatives should be developed by different programmers, so that they are not unwittingly sharing assumptions. The alternatives should also be less complex than the primary, so that they will be less likely to fail. For this reason they will probably be poorer in their performance (speed).

Another approach is to create alternatives that provide an increasingly degraded service. This allows the system to exhibit what is termed *graceful degradation*. As an example of graceful degradation, consider a steel rolling mill in which a computer controls a machine that chops off the required lengths of steel. Normally the computer employs a sophisticated algorithm to make optimum use of the steel, while satisfying customers' orders. Should this algorithm fail, a simpler algorithm can be used that processes the orders strictly sequentially. This means that the system will keep going, albeit less efficiently.

Implementation

The language constructs of the recovery block mechanism hide the preservation of variables. The programmer does not need to explicitly declare which variables should be stored and when. The system must save values before any of the alternatives is executed, and restore them should any of the alternatives fail. Although this may seem a formidable task, only the values of variables that are changed need to be preserved, and the notation highlights which ones these are. Variables local to the alternatives need not be stored, nor need parameters passed by value. Only global variables that are changed need to be preserved. Nonetheless, storing data in this manner probably incurs too high an overhead if it is carried out solely by software. Studies indicate that, suitably implemented with hardware assistance, the speed overhead might be no more than about 15%.

No programming language has yet incorporated the recovery block notation. Even so, the idea provides a framework which can be used, in conjunction with any programming language, to structure fault tolerant software.

17.7 ● n-version programming

This form of programming means developing n versions of the same software component. For example, suppose a fly-by-wire airplane has a software component that decides how much the rudder should be moved in response to information about speed, pitch, throttle setting, etc. Three or more version of the component are implemented and run concurrently. The outputs are compared by a voting module, the majority vote wins and is used to control the rudder (see Figure 17.4).

It is important that the different versions of the component are developed by different teams, using different methods and (preferably) at different locations, so that a minimum of assumptions are shared by the developers. By this means, the modules will use different algorithms, have different mistakes and produce different outputs (if they do) under different circumstances. Thus the chances are that when one of the components fails and produces an incorrect result, the others will perform correctly and the faulty component will be outvoted by the majority.

Clearly the success of an n-programming scheme depends on the degree of independence of the different components. If the majority embody a similar design fault, they will fail together and the wrong decision will be the outcome. This is a bold assumption, and some studies have shown a tendency for different developers to commit the same mistakes, probably because of shared misunderstandings of the (same) specification.

The expense of n-programming is in the effort to develop n versions, plus the processing overhead of running the multiple versions. If hardware reliability is also an issue,

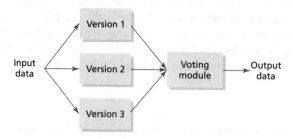

Figure 17.4 Triple modular redundancy

as in fly-by-wire airplanes, each version runs on a separate (but identical) processor. The voting module is small and simple, consuming minimal developer and processor time.

For obvious reasons, an even number of versions is not appropriate.

The main difference between the recovery block and the n-version schemes is that in the former the different versions are executed sequentially (if need be).

Is n-programming forward error recovery or is it backward error recovery? The answer is that, once an error is revealed, the correct behavior is immediately available and the system can continue forwards. So it is forward error recovery.

17.8 ● Assertions

Assertions are statements written into software that say what should be true of the data. Assertions have been used since the early days of programming as an aid to verifying the correctness of software. An assertion states what should always be true at a particular point in a program. Assertions are usually placed:

- at the entry to a method – called a *precondition*, it states what the relationship between the parameters should be
- at the end of a method – called a *postcondition*, it states what the relationship between the parameters should be
- within a loop – called a *loop invariant*, it states what is always true, before and after each loop iteration, however many iterations the loop has performed.
- at the head of a class – called a *class invariant*, it states what is always true before and after a call on any of the class's public methods. The assertion states a relationship between the variables of an instance of the class.

An example should help see how assertions can be used. Take the example of a class that implements a data structure called a stack. Items can be placed in the data structure by calling the public method **push** and removed by calling **pop**. Let us assume that the stack has a fixed length, described by a variable called **capacity**. Suppose the class uses a variable called **count** to record how many items are currently in the stack. Then we can make the following assertions at the level of the class. These class invariant is:

```
assert count >= 0;
assert capacity >= count;
```

These are statements which must always be true for the entire class, before or after any use is made of the class. We can also make assertions for the individual methods. Thus for method **push**, we can say as a postcondition:

```
assert newCount = oldCount + 1;
```

For the method **push**, we can also state the following precondition:

```
assert oldCount < capacity;
```

> **SELF-TEST QUESTION**
>
> 17.9 Write pre- and post-conditions for method **pop**.

Note that truth of assertions does not guarantee that the software is working correctly. However, if the value of an assertion is false, then there certainly is a fault in the software. Note also that violation of a precondition means that there is a fault in the user of the method; a violation of a postcondition means a fault in the method itself.

There are two main ways to make use of assertions. One way is to write assertions as comments in a program, to assist in manual verification. On the other hand, as indicated by the notation used above, some programming languages (including Java) allow assertions to be written as part of the language – and their correctness is checked at run-time. If an assertion is found to be false, an exception is thrown.

There is something of an argument about whether assertions should be used only during development, or whether they should also be enabled when the software is put into productive use.

17.9 ● Discussion

Fault tolerance in hardware has long been recognized – and accommodated. Electronic engineers have frequently incorporated redundancy, such as triple modular redundancy, within the design of circuits to provide for hardware failure. Fault tolerance in software has become more widely addressed in the design of computer systems as it has become recognized that it is almost impossible to produce correct software. Exception handling is now supported by all the mainstream software engineering languages – Ada, C++, Visual Basic, C# and Java. This means that designers can provide for failure in an organized manner, rather than in an ad hoc fashion. Particularly in safety-critical systems, either recovery blocks or *n*-programming is used to cope with design faults and enhance reliability.

Fault tolerance does, of course, cost money. It requires extra design and programming effort, extra memory and extra processing time to check for and handle exceptions. Some applications need greater attention to fault tolerance than others, and safety-critical systems are more likely to merit the extra attention of fault tolerance. However, even software packages that have no safety requirements often need fault tolerance of some kind. For example, we now expect a word processor to perform periodic and automatic saving of the current document, so that recovery can be performed in the event of power failure or software crash. End users are increasingly demanding that the software cleans up properly after failures, rather than leave them with a mess that they cannot salvage. Thus it is likely that ever-increasing attention will be paid to improving the fault tolerance of software.

Summary

Faults in computer systems are caused by hardware failure, software bugs and user error. Software fault tolerance is concerned with:

- detecting faults
- assessing damage
- repairing the damage
- continuing.

Of these, faults can be detected by both hardware and software.

One hardware mechanism for fault detection is protection mechanisms, which have two roles:

1. they limit the spread of damage, thus easing the job of fault tolerance

2. they help find the cause of faults.

Faults can be classified in two categories – anticipated and unanticipated.

Recovery mechanisms are of two types:

- backward – the system returns to an earlier, safe state
- forward – the system continues onwards from the error.

Anticipated faults can be dealt with by means of forward error recovery. Exception handlers are a convenient programming language facility for coping with these faults.

Unanticipated faults – such as software design faults – can be handled using either of:

- recovery blocks, a backward error recovery mechanism
- *n*-programming, a forward error recovery mechanism.

Assertions are a way of stating assumptions that should be valid when software executes. Automatic checking of assertions can assist debugging.

Exercises

17.1 For each of the computer systems detailed in Appendix A, list the faults that can arise, categorizing them into user errors, hardware faults and software faults. Decide whether each of the faults is anticipated or unanticipated. Suggest how the faults could be dealt with.

17.2 Explain the following terms, giving an example of each to illustrate your answer: fault tolerance, software fault tolerance, reliability, robustness, graceful degradation.

17.3 Consider a programming language with which you are familiar. In what ways can you deliberately (or inadvertently) write a program that will:

1. crash
2. access main memory in an undisciplined way
3. access a file protected from you.

What damage is caused by these actions? How much damage is possible? Assuming you didn't already know it, is it easy to diagnose the cause of the problem? Contemplate that if it is possible *deliberately* to penetrate a system, then it is certainly possible to do it by accident, thus jeopardizing the reliability and security of the system.

17.4 "Compile-time checking is better than run-time checking." Discuss.

17.5 Compare and contrast exception handling with assertions.

17.6 The Java system throws an **IndexOutOfBoundsException** exception if a program attempts to access elements of an array that lie outside the valid range of subscripts. Write a method that calculates the total weekly rainfall, given an array of floating point numbers (values of the rainfall for each of seven days of the week) as its single parameter. The method should throw an exception of the same type if an array is too short. Write code to catch the exception.

17.7 Outline the structure of recovery block software to cope with the following situation. A fly-by-wire aircraft is controlled by software. A normal algorithm calculates the optimal speed and the appropriate control surface and engine settings. A safety module checks that the calculated values are within safe limits. If they are not, it invokes an alternative module that calculates some safe values for the settings. If, again, this module fails to suggest safe values, the pilots are alerted and the aircraft reverts to manual control.

17.8 Compare and contrast the recovery block scheme with the *n*-programming scheme for fault tolerance. Include in your review an assessment of the development times and performance overheads associated with each scheme.

17.9 Searching a table for a desired object is a simple example of a situation in which it can be tempting to use a **goto** to escape from an unusual situation. Write a piece of program to search a table three ways:

1. using **goto**
2. using exceptions
3. avoiding both of these.

Compare and contrast the three solutions.

17.10 Consider a program to make a copy of a disk file. Devise a structure for the program that uses exception handlers so that it copes with the following error situations:

1. the file doesn't exist (there is no file with the stated name)

2. there is a hardware fault when reading information from the old file

3. there is a hardware fault when writing to the new file.

Include in your considerations actions that the filing system (or operating system) needs to take.

17.11 Explain the difference between using a **goto** statement and using a **throw** statement. Discuss their relative advantages for dealing with exceptions.

17.12 "There is no such thing as an exceptional situation. The software should explicitly deal with all possible situations." Discuss.

17.13 Some word processors provide an undo command. Suppose we interpret a user wanting to undo what they have done as a fault, what form of error recovery does the software provide and how is it implemented?

17.14 Examine the architecture and operating system of a computer for which you have documentation. Investigate what facilities are provided for detecting software and hardware faults.

17.15 Compare and contrast approaches to fault tolerance in software with approaches for hardware.

Answers to self-test questions

17.1 **1.** unanticipated

2. unanticipated

3. unanticipated

4. anticipated

5. anticipated

17.2 stack overflow
use of a null pointer

17.3 The module could check that all the items in the new array are in order. (This is not foolproof because the new array could contain different data to the old.)

17.4 Pro: prevent the spread of damage, assist in diagnosing the cause.
Cons: expensive hardware and software, reduction in performance (speed).

→

17.5 The answer depends on the particular software

17.6 Forward, because you continued your journey. It was an anticipated fault. However, as far as the tire is concerned, it is backward error recovery, because it is replaced by some other component.

17.7 Add the line:

```
if (string.length() == 0) throw new
    NumberFormatException();
```

at the start of the method.

17.8 Control continues down the program, which dangerously tests the value of the information returned by `parseInt`.

17.9 The precondition is `assert oldCount > 0;`
The postcondition is `assert newCount = oldCount - 1;`

Further reading

The programming language Pascal has a strong reputation for being a secure language, with extensive compile-time checking to prevent software faults. But these three authors set out to show how vulnerable it actually is. It is a study in paranoia: J. Walsh, W.J. Sneeringer and C.A.R. Hoare, Ambiguities and insecurities in Pascal, *Software – Practice and Experience*, 7 (1977), pp. 685–96.

For a more detailed treatment of some of the topics described in this chapter, see: Hoang Pham (ed.), *Fault-Tolerant Software Systems: Techniques and Applications*, IEEE Computer Society Press, 1992.

The following book has a chapter that explains how software errors can be quantified: M.L. Shooman, *Software Engineering*, McGraw-Hill International, 1986.

CHAPTER 18

Scripting

This chapter:

- explains the principles of scripting languages
- gives examples of using scripting languages.

18.1 ● Introduction

Scripting is the duct tape or glue of computing. It is a means of constructing software quickly, usually by combining existing components and programs. The product may not be elegant, but it works. For example, suppose we write an e-mail program. We would like the user to be able to click on a URL within an e-mail and get taken immediately into a web browser that displays the page. So we need the e-mail program to be able to invoke the web browser. This is the kind of interoperability that can be provided by a scripting language.

A scripting language is a particular kind of programming language. Examples include the Unix shell scripting language, Perl and Python. However, general-purpose languages, such as Visual Basic and C, can also be used for scripting.

Traditionally scripting languages have been interpreted, but this is no longer an identifying feature.

In this chapter, we use the Unix shell language as the example to expose the scripting approach.

18.2 ● Unix

Unix is a general-purpose operating system available widely on personal computers, servers and mainframe computers. Two workers at Bell telephones reputedly developed it in an attic. This pedigree explains its conceptual simplicity and beauty. From such small beginnings, Unix has become widely popular and has spawned such derivatives as

GNU/Linux. For reasons that we shall shortly see, Unix can act as an excellent basis for scripting.

Unix provides:

- a textual command language, based on command verbs followed by parameters
- the facility to write programs in the command language
- a filing system, with tree-structured directories (folders)
- a set of useful utility programs, called filters, e.g. a file copy tool
- a facility, called pipes, for joining filters together.

These facilities are now commonly found in many operating systems, but Unix was the first system to provide them.

Unix consists of a small kernel, augmented by a rich set of small utility programs, the filters. An example of a filter is a program to display a list of the files within a particular directory. Perhaps because only two people designed it, Unix is built around a few simple concepts. One of the fundamental ideas of Unix is the notion that software (including Unix itself) should be built from small general-purpose components that are developed individually. These components can be used individually but also can be combined as necessary in order to satisfy a new requirement. A filter is a program that inputs a serial stream of information, processes it and outputs a second serial stream. Other examples of Unix-provided filters:

- count the number of lines or characters in a file
- a file copy program
- print a file with specified formatting
- spool a file to the printer
- print all lines in a file that contain a specified textual pattern
- a lexical analyzer.

Filters are combined by taking the output from one and feeding it as input to another. The stream of data that flows from one filter to another is known as a pipe. This combination of filters and pipes is carried out by Unix under the control of the command language.

An example of using a filter is the command:

```
ls
```

When you type a Unix command such as this, you invoke the filter with the same name. The filter named **ls** displays on the screen the names of all the files in the current directory, one per line. Another tool, named **wc**, inputs a file and gives a line, word and character count for that file. The output of **wc** can be controlled by providing parameters, and the parameter **-l** specifies that lines should be counted, so that the command:

```
wc -l file
```

tells us how many lines the file `file` contains. (The majority of Unix commands offer a choice of parameters to modify their output). Putting these two tools together, the Unix command:

```
ls | wc -l
```

pipes the output from the filter `ls` into the input for the filter `wc`. The final output is therefore the number of files in the current directory.

SELF-TEST QUESTION

18.1 The command:

```
grep "Alice" < file
```

outputs those lines in the file `file` that contain the string `Alice`. Write a pipelined command to count how many lines in the file contain the string `Alice`.

The vertical bar symbol in a Unix command signifies that the output stream from one filter is to be directed not to its default file, but to the input of another filter.

We have seen that Unix provides a useful but limited number of facilities as filters, plus a facility to combine filters. Thus when some new software is required, there are three options:

1. use an existing filter
2. combine the existing filters using pipes
3. write a new filter and combine it with existing filters using pipes.

Combining filters is rather like writing programs, but at a higher level – the Unix filters are the language primitives, and pipes provide the mechanism for combining them to produce more powerful facilities. The command language describes the interactions.

Filters tend to be short and simple – 90 of the standard Unix filters (other than compilers) are less than 1,200 lines (about 20 pages) of high-level programming language statements. An individual filter is usually written in the programming language C, which is the core language of Unix. A filter reads from an input pipe and outputs to an output pipe. It opens an input pipe just as if it was opening a file, then it reads data serially from the pipe (or file) until the end of data (file) is encountered. The filter sends its output to an output stream by writing data as if to a serial file.

All the Unix tools are designed to do a specific single task well, rather than supporting many, optional features. However, any options are specified using parameters.

In summary, the main virtues of Unix as a basis for scripting are:

- a number of small, highly modular, general-purpose components called filters are provided
- under the control of the command language, software is constructed by combining filters with other filters using pipes.

The Unix approach is based on the assumption that connecting programs via serial streams is modular and flexible.

SELF-TEST QUESTION

18.2 Name another mechanism for connecting components.

18.3 ● Discussion

A successful scripting language needs to provide the following features:

- easy manipulation of file and folder (directory) names. The user needs to be able to change file names, create files, create folders, move files and copy files with ease.
- good string manipulation. The user needs to be able to analyze strings, such as an HTML file, and create files of new strings.
- calling other programs and components. The user needs a convenient facility to call programs and components written in other languages. This includes accessing a large and comprehensive library of classes and methods.
- combining programs and components. This is the facility to combine existing components or programs. In Unix, this is accomplished using the pipe mechanism.
- weak data typing. A scripting language is often used to read data from a file (or an internet connection), analyze it and convert it into some other form. An example is a file in a particular graphics file format which needs to be rendered or converted into some other file format. Thus the program needs to be relaxed about the exact type of the data it is processing. In contrast, a strongly typed data language insists on the clear separation of data types.

What is the essential difference between a scripting language and a programming language? In a programming language, a typical operation is adding two numbers; in a scripting language a typical operation is invoking a program (perhaps to add two numbers).

Summary

A scripting language is a language that glues existing programs together. It allows us to combine existing programs in useful ways. It is a means of reusing software.

The key characteristic of a scripting language is that it provides a facility to invoke other programs. The programs can be passed information as parameters or alternatively the programs can pass information as data streams.

In addition scripting languages typically provide comprehensive facilities for manipulating strings, files and directories.

Exercises

18.1 Compare and contrast the facilities of a language for scripting with those required of a conventional programming language.

18.2 Review the features of the Unix scripting language.

18.3 Compare and contrast the Unix pipes and filters approach to constructing software with an approach that makes the maximum reuse of libraries, as in Java and C#.

18.4 Assess Perl or Python as a scripting language.

Answers to self-test questions

18.1 `grep "Alice" < file | wc -l`

18.2 Method calls

Further reading

There are lots of good books on Unix. But if you want to read the original classic paper, it is: B.W. Kernighan and J.R. Mashey, The Unix programming environment, *IEEE Computer*, April 1981, pp. 12–24.

PART

D

VERIFICATION

Testing

This chapter:

- identifies the problem of effective testing
- explains how to carry out black box (functional) testing
- explains how to carry out white box (structural) testing
- explains the principles behind these approaches to testing
- introduces some other testing techniques
- explains how to carry out unit testing
- explains how to carry out system (integration) testing.

19.1 ● Introduction

Verification is the general term for techniques that aim to produce fault-free software. Testing is a widely used technique for verification, but note that testing is just one technique amongst several others. This chapter explains several approaches to testing.

Remember that there is a separate collection of techniques for carrying out *validation* – which are techniques which strive to make sure that software meets its users needs

Software is complex and it is difficult to make it work correctly. Currently the dominant technique used for verification is testing. And testing typically consumes an enormous proportion (sometimes as much as 50%) of the effort of developing a system. Microsoft employ teams of programmers (who write programs) and completely separate teams of testers (who test them). At Microsoft there are as many people involved in testing as there are in programming.

Arguably, verification is a major problem and we need good techniques to tackle it. Often, towards the end of a project, the difficult decision has to be made between continuing the testing or delivering the software to its customers or clients.

We begin this chapter by discussing the general problem of testing – and discover that there is a significant problem. We consider approaches called black box and white box testing.

There are a whole number of associated testing techniques, which we outline.

The problems of testing large pieces of software that consist of many components are severe – particularly if all the components are combined at one and the same time.

19.2 ● The nature of errors

It would be convenient to know how errors arise, because then we could try to avoid them during all the stages of development. Similarly, it would be useful to know the most commonly occurring faults, because then we could look for them during verification. Regrettably, the data is inconclusive and it is only possible to make vague statements about these things.

Specifications are a common source of faults. A software system has an overall specification, derived from requirements analysis. In addition, each component of the software ideally has an individual specification that is derived from architectural design. The specification for a component can be:

■ ambiguous (unclear)

■ incomplete

■ faulty.

Any such problems should, of course, be detected and remedied by verification of the specification prior to development of the component, but, of course, this verification cannot and will not be totally effective. So there are often problems with a component specification.

This is not all – there are other problems with specifications. During programming, the developer of a component may misunderstand the component specification.

The next type of error is where a component contain faults so that it does not meet its specification. This may be due to two kinds of problem:

1. errors in the logic of the code – an error of commission

2. code that fails to meet all aspects of the specification – an error of omission.

This second type of error is where the programmer has failed to appreciate and correctly understand all the detail of the specification and has therefore omitted some necessary code.

Finally, the kinds of errors that can arise in the coding of a component are:

■ data not initialized

■ loops repeated an incorrect number of times.

■ boundary value errors.

Boundary values are values of the data at or near critical values. For example, suppose a component has to decide whether a person can vote or not, depending on their age. The voting age is 18. Then boundary values, near the critical value, are 17, 18 and 19.

As we have seen, there are many things that can go wrong and perhaps therefore it is no surprise that verification is such a time-consuming activity.

19.3 ● The problem of testing

We now explore the limitations of testing. Consider as an illustration a method to calculate the product of its two integer parameters. First, we might think of devising a *selection* of test data values and comparing the actual with the expected outcome. So we might choose the values 21 and 568 as sample values. Remembering negative numbers, we might also choose −456 and −78. If we now look at possible coding for the procedure, we can immediately see the drawback with this approach:

```
public int product(int x, int y) {
    int p;
    p = x * y;
    if (p == 42) p = 0;
    return p;
}
```

The problem is that, for some reason – error or malice – the programmer has chosen to include an **if** statement, which leads to an incorrect value in certain cases. The test data that was chosen above would not reveal this error, nor, almost certainly, would any other selection of test data. Thus use of selective test data cannot guarantee to expose bugs. Now it could be argued that the bug is obvious in this example – simply by looking at the program. But looking at a program is not testing – it is a technique called inspection that is discussed later in this chapter.

A second method of testing, called exhaustive testing, would be to use all possible data values, in each case checking the correctness of the outcome. But even for the method to multiply two 32-bit integers would take 100 years (assuming a 1 millisecond integer multiply instruction is provided by the hardware of the computer). So exhaustive testing is almost always impracticable.

These considerations lead us to the unpalatable conclusion that it is impossible to test any program exhaustively. Thus any program of significant size is likely to contain bugs.

19.4 ● Black box (functional) testing

Knowing that exhaustive testing is infeasible, the *black box* approach to testing is to devise sample data that is representative of all possible data. We then run the program, input the data and see what happens. This type of testing is termed black box testing because no knowledge of the workings of the program is used as part of the testing – we only consider inputs and outputs. The program is thought of as being enclosed within a black box. Black box testing is also known as functional testing because it uses only knowledge of the function of the program (not how it works).

Ideally, testing proceeds by writing down the test data and the expected outcome of the test before testing takes place. This is called a test specification or schedule. Then you run the program, input the data and examine the outputs for discrepancies between the predicted outcome and the actual outcome. Test data should also check whether exceptions are handled by the program in accordance with its specification.

Consider a program that decides whether a person can vote, depending on their age (Figure 19.1). The minimum voting age is 18.

We know that we cannot realistically test this program with all possible values, but instead we need some typical values. The approach to devising test data for black box testing is to use *equivalence partitioning*. This means looking at the nature of the input data to identify common features. Such a common feature is called a partition. In the voting program, we recognize that the input data falls into two partitions:

1. the numbers less than 18

2. the numbers greater than or equal to 18

This can be diagrammed as follows:

0	17	18	infinity

There are two partitions, one including the age range 0–17 and the other partition with numbers 18 to infinity. We then take the step of asserting that every number within a partition is equivalent to any other, for the purpose of testing this program. (Hence the term equivalence partitioning.) So we argue that the number 12 is equivalent to any other in the first partition and the number 21 is equivalent to any number in the

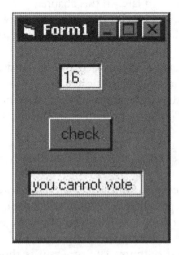

Figure 19.1 The voting checker program

second. So we devise two tests:

Test number	Data	Outcome
1	12	cannot vote
2	21	can vote

We have reasoned that we need two sets of test data to test this program. These two sets, together with a statement of the expected outcomes from testing, constitute a test specification. We run the program with the two sets of data and note any discrepancies between predicted and actual outcome.

Unfortunately we can see that these tests have not investigated the important distinction between someone aged 17 and someone aged 18. Anyone who has ever written a program knows that using **if** statements is error prone, so it is advisable to investigate this particular region of the data. This is the same as recognizing that data values at the edges of the partitions are worthy of inclusion in the testing. Therefore we create two additional tests:

Test number	Data	Outcome
3	17	cannot vote
4	18	can vote

In summary, the rules for selecting test data for black box testing using equivalence partitioning are:

1. partition the input data values
2. select representative data from each partition (equivalent data)
3. select data at the boundaries of partitions.

In the last program, there is a single input; there are four data values and therefore four tests. However, most programs process a number of inputs. Suppose we wish to test a program that displays the larger of two numbers, each in the range 0–10,000, entered into a pair of text boxes. If the values are equal, the program displays either value.

Each input is within a partition that runs from 0 to 10,000. We choose values at each end of the partitions and sample values somewhere in the middle:

first number:	0	54	10,000
second number:	0	142	10,000

Now that we have selected representative values, we need to consider what combinations of values we should use. Exhaustive testing would mean using every possible combination of every possible data value, but this is, of course, infeasible. Instead, we use every combination of the representative values. So the tests are:

Test number	1st number	2nd number	Outcome
1	0	0	0
2	0	142	142
3	0	10,000	10,000
4	54	0	54
5	54	142	142
6	54	10,000	10,000
7	10,000	0	10,000
8	10,000	142	10,000
9	10,000	10,000	10,000

Thus the additional step in testing is to use every combination of the (limited) representative data values.

SELF-TEST QUESTION

19.1 In a program to play the game of chess, the player specifies the destination for a move as a pair of indices, the row and column number. The program checks that the destination square is valid, that it is not outside the board. Devise black box test data to check that this part of the program is working correctly.

19.5 ● White box (structural) testing

This form of testing makes use of knowledge of how the program works – the structure of the program – as the basis for devising test data. In white box testing every statement in the program is executed at some time during the testing. This is equivalent to ensuring that every path (every sequence of instructions) through the program is executed at some time during testing. This includes null paths, so an **if** statement without an **else** has two paths and every loop has two paths. Testing should also include any exception handling carried out by the program.

Here is the Java code for the voting checker program we are using as a case study:

```java
public void actionPerformed(ActionEvent event) {
    int age;
    age = Integer.parseInt(textField.getText());
    if (age >= 18) {
        result.setText("you can vote");
    }
```

```
    else {
        result.setText("you cannot vote");
    }
}
```

In this program, there are two paths (because the **if** has two branches) and therefore two sets of data will serve to ensure that all statements are executed at some time during the testing:

Test number	Data	Expected outcome
1	12	cannot vote
2	21	can vote

If we are cautious, we realize that errors in programming are often made within the conditions of **if** and **while** statements. So we add a further two tests to ensure that the **if** statement is working correctly:

Test number	Data	Expected outcome
3	17	cannot vote
4	18	can vote

Thus we need four sets of data to test this program in a white box fashion. This happens to be the same data that we devised for black box testing. But the reasoning that led to the two sets of data is different. Had the program been written differently, the white box test data would be different. Suppose, for example, the program used an array, named **table**, with one element for each age specifying whether someone of that age can vote. Then the program is simply the following statement to look up eligibility:

```
result.setText(table[age]);
```

and the white box testing data is different.

SELF-TEST QUESTION

19.2 A program's function is to find the largest of three numbers. Devise white box test data for this section of program. The code is:

```
int a, b, c;
int largest;
```

```
if (a >= b) {
    if (a >= c) {
        largest = a;
    }
    else {
        largest = c;
    }
}
else {
    if (b >= c) {
        largest = b;
    }
    else {
        largest = c;
    }
}
```

19.3   In a program to play the game of chess, the player specifies the destination for a move as a pair of integer indices, the row and column number. The program checks that the destination square is valid, that is, not outside the board. Devise white box test data to check that this part of the program is working correctly.

The code for this part of the program is:

```
if ((row > 8) || (row < 1)) {
    JOptionPane.showMessageDialog(null, "error");
}
if ((col > 8) || (col < 1)) {
    JOptionPane.showMessageDialog(null, "error");
}
```

19.6 ● Other testing methods

Stepping through code

Some debuggers allow the user to step through a program, executing just one instruction at a time. This is sometimes called single-shotting. Each time you execute one instruction you can see which path of execution has been taken. You can also see (or watch) the values of variables. It is rather like an automated structured walkthrough.

In this form of testing, you concentrate on the variables and closely check their values as they are changed by the program to verify that they have been changed correctly.

A debugger is usually used for debugging (locating a bug); here it is used for testing (establishing the existence of a bug).

Testing the test data

In a large system or program it can be difficult to ensure that the test data is adequate. One way to try to test whether it does indeed cause all statements to be executed is to use a *profiler*. A profiler is a software package that monitors the testing by inserting probes into the software under test. When testing takes place, the profiler can expose which pieces of the code are not executed and therefore reveal the weakness in the data.

Another approach to investigating the test data is called *mutation testing*. In this technique, artificial bugs are inserted into the program. An example would be to change a + into a −. The test is run and if the bugs are not revealed, then the test data is obviously inadequate. The test data is modified until the artificial bugs are exposed.

Team techniques

Many organizations set up separate teams to carry out testing and such a team is sometimes called a *quality assurance* (QA) team. There are, of course, fruitful grounds for possible conflict between the development group and the QA team.

One way of actually exploiting conflict is to set up an *adversary* team to carry out testing. Such a team is made up of what we might normally think of as being anti-social people – hackers, misfits, psychotics. Their malice can be harnessed to the effective discovery of bugs.

Another approach is to set up *bounty hunters*, whose motivation for finding errors is financial reward.

Other techniques for collaborative working are explained in Chapter 20 on groups.

Beta testing

In beta testing, a preliminary version of a software product is released to a selected market, the customer or client, knowing that it has bugs. Users are asked to report on faults so that the product can be improved for its proper release date. Beta testing gets its name from the second letter of the Greek alphabet. Its name therefore conveys the idea that it is the second major act of testing, following on after testing within the developing organization. Once Beta testing is complete and the bugs are fixed, the software is released.

Automated testing

Unfortunately this is not some automatic way of generating test data. There is no magical way of doing that. But it is good practice to automate testing so that tests can be reapplied at the touch of a button. This is extra work in the beginning but often saves time overall.

Regression testing

An individual test proceeds like this:

1. apply a test
2. if a bug is revealed, fix it

3. apply the test again

4. and so on until the test succeeds.

However, when you fix a bug you might introduce a new bug. Worse, this new bug may not manifest itself with the current test. The only safe way to proceed is to apply all the previous tests again. This is termed regression testing. Clearly this is usually a formidable task. It can be made much easier if all the testing is carried out automatically, rather than manually. In large developments, it is common to incorporate revised components and reapply all the tests once a day.

Formal verification

Formal methods employ the precision and power of mathematics in attempting to verify that a program meets its specification. They place emphasis on the precision of the specification, which must first be rewritten in a formal mathematical notation. One such specification language is called Z. Once the formal specification for a program has been written, there are two alternative approaches:

1. write the program and then verify that it conforms to the specification. This requires considerable time and skill.

2. derive the program from the specification by means of a series of transformations, each of which preserve the correctness of the product. This is currently the favored approach.

Formal verification is very appealing because of its potential for rigorously verifying a program's correctness beyond all possible doubt. However, it must be remembered that these methods are carried out by fallible human beings, who make mistakes. So they are not a cure-all.

Formal verification is still in its infancy and is not widely used in industry and commerce, except in a few safety-critical applications. Further discussion of this approach is beyond the scope of this book.

19.7 ● Unit testing

When we discussed black box and white box testing above, the programs were very small. However, most software consists of a number of components, each the size of a small program. How do we test each component? One answer is to create an environment to test each component in isolation (Figure 19.2). This is termed *unit* testing. A *driver* component makes method calls on the component under test. Any methods that the component uses are simulated as *stubs*. These stubs are rudimentary replacements for missing methods. A stub does one of the following:

■ carries out an easily written simulation of the mission of the component

■ displays a message indicating that the component has been executed

■ nothing.

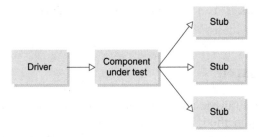

Figure 19.2 Unit testing

Thus the component under test is surrounded by scaffolding. This is a large undertaking. In many developments, the collections of drivers and stubs is often as big as the software itself.

19.8 ● System (integration) testing

Thus far we have only considered unit testing – testing an individual software component, a method or a class. We have implicitly assumed that such a component is fairly small. This is the first step in the verification of software systems, which typically consist of tens or hundreds of individual components. The task of testing complete systems is called *system* or *integration* testing.

Suppose that we have designed and code all the components for a system. How can we test these components and how can we test the complete system?

Here are three different approaches to system testing:

1. big bang – bring all the components together, without prior testing, and test the complete system

2. improved big bang – test each component individually (unit testing), bring them all together and test the complete system

3. incremental – build the system piece by piece, testing the partial system at each stage.

The first approach – big bang or *monolithic* testing – is a recipe for disaster. There is no easy way of knowing which component is the cause of a fault, and there is an enormous debugging task. The second approach is slightly better because when the components are brought together, we have some confidence in them individually. Now any faults are likely to be caused by the interactions between the components. Here again, there is a major problem of locating faults.

An alternative is to use some form of *incremental* testing. In this approach, first one component of the system is tested, then a second component is linked with the first and the system tested. Any fault is likely to be localized either in the newly incorporated component or in the interface between the two. We continue like this, adding just one component at a time. At each stage, any fault that presents itself is likely to be caused by the new component, or by its interface to the system. Thus fault finding is made considerably easier. Various approaches are explained in Chapter 24 on incremental development.

19.9 ● Discussion

We have seen that exhaustive testing is infeasible. Therefore complete testing is impossible and, whatever testing methods are used, they can never ensure that the software is free from bugs. Thus testing is a poor technique but until formal verification becomes widely applicable it is a vital technique.

However much we test our programs, using all our skill and intuition, we can never be sure that we have eradicated all the faults. The situation is well summed up by one of computing's gurus, Dijkstra, in his famous remark, "Testing can only show the presence of bugs, never their absence." This has been (anonymously) rephrased as, "Just because you have never seen a mermaid doesn't mean that they don't exist." It can be reassuring to adopt the view that a test that reveals no bugs is a successful test. But rather we should look upon such a test as unsuccessful!

It is difficult to get accurate data on the number of bugs present in production software because, unsurprisingly, organizations do not want to reveal this kind of information. The indications are that there are typically between 2 and 50 bugs per 1,000 lines of source code in commercial production software. A figure like this is more properly called a *fault density*. It measures the number of known faults per 1,000 lines of code (LOC). A figure of 2 is considered to be most creditable. Ways of measuring this quantity are explained in Chapter 29 on metrics and quality assurance.

The trouble is, of course, that bugs always surface at the worst possible time, for example, when you are demonstrating the completed software to the client. This phenomenon has long been known to students of reliability, who quote Murphy's laws:

1.   "If a system can fail, it will,"
2.   "and at the worst possible moment."

Another, more objective, observation is that some bugs create serious faults, while others lie dormant and do not give any trouble.

Chapter 31 on assessing methods looks at the evidence that is available to compare verification techniques, including testing. The surprising indications are that simply inspecting code is more effective than carrying out testing.

The worrying conclusion to any discussion of verification is that all software (of any significant size) contains faults.

Summary

Testing is one set of techniques for verifying software.

Exhaustive testing is a practical impossibility.

In black box (or functional) testing, sample data based on the specification is used. This is termed equivalence partitioning.

In white box (or structural) testing, the internal structure of the software is used to select test data. This means that every path through the program is tested.

Unit testing tests each component in isolation. Drivers and stubs are used to substitute for missing components. Integration testing tests components as they are brought together.

● Exercises

19.1 Consider a program that has 16 **if-then** statements in it. Then there are 2^{16} possible paths through it. If each test takes 50 microseconds and each action takes 50 microseconds (a gross underestimate), how much computer time is needed to test all program paths?

19.2 Devise black box and white box test data to test the following program. The program specification is:

The program inputs a series of integers from the keyboard using a text field. The program finds the largest of the numbers. The numbers are terminated when a button labeled Start Again is pressed.

Try not to look at the text of the program, given below, until you have completed the design of the black box data.

The program involves the following class:

```
class Biggest {
    private int largest;

    public Biggest() {
        largest = 0;
    }

    public void nextNumber(int n) {
        if (n > largest)
            largest = n;
    }

    public void display(TextField textField) {
        textField.setText("largest so far is" + largest);
    }

    public void startAgain() {
        largest = 0;
    }
}
```

19.3 Devise black box and white box test data to test the following program. The program specification is:

The program is to determine insurance premiums for a holiday, based upon the age and gender (male or female) of the client.

For a female of age >= 18 and <= 30 the premium is $5. A female aged >= 31 pays $3.50. A male of age >= 18 and <= 35 pays $6. A male aged >= 36 pays $5.50. People aged 50 or more pay half premium. Any other ages or genders are an error, which is signaled as a premium of zero.

The Java code for this program is:

```
public float calcPremium(float age, String gender) {
    float premium;

    if (gender.equals("female"))
        if ((age >= 18) && (age <= 30))
            premium = 5.0f;
        else
            if (age >= 31)
                premium = 3.50f;
            else
                premium = 0.0f;
    else
        if (gender.equals("male"))
            if ((age >= 18) && (age <= 35))
                premium = 6.0f;
            else
                if (age >= 36)
                    premium = 5.5f;
                else
                    premium = 0.0f;
        else
            premium = 0.0f;

    if (age >= 50)
        premium = premium * 0.5f;

    return premium;
}
```

19.4 Suggest features for software tools that could assist in using each of the following techniques:

■ black box testing

■ white box testing.

19.5 Substantial testing of a system uncovers not a single error. What conclusions would you draw?

Answers to self-test questions

19.1 A row number is in three partitions:

1. within the range 1–8
2. less than 1
3. greater than 8.

If we choose one representative value in each partition (say 3, –3 and 11 respectively) and a similar set of values for the column numbers (say 5, –2 and 34), the test data will be:

Test number	Row	Column	Outcome
1	3	5	OK
2	–3	5	invalid
3	11	5	invalid
4	3	–2	invalid
5	–3	–2	invalid
6	11	–2	invalid
7	3	34	invalid
8	–3	34	invalid
9	11	34	invalid

We now remember that data near the boundary of the partitions is important and therefore add to the test data for each partition so that it becomes:

1. within the range 1–8 (say 3)
2. less than 1 (say –3)
3. greater than 8 (say 11)
4. boundary value 1
5. boundary value 8
6. boundary value 0
7. boundary value 9.

which now gives many more combinations to use as test data.

→

19.2 There are four paths through the program, which can be exercised by the following test data:

Test number				Outcome
1	3	2	1	3
2	3	2	5	5
3	2	3	1	3
4	2	3	5	5

19.3 There are three paths through the program extract, including the path where neither of the conditions in the `if` statements are true. But each of the error messages can be triggered by two conditions. Suitable test data is therefore:

Test number	Row	Column	Outcome
1	5	6	OK
2	0	4	invalid
3	9	4	invalid
4	5	9	invalid
5	5	0	invalid

● Further Reading

This book surveys studies of the types of fault that occur and explains the different testing methods, in a very readable way: Marc Roper, *Software Testing*, McGraw-Hill, 1994.

A readable practical review of testing techniques: Cem Kaner, *Testing Computer Software*, John Wiley, 1999.

The following book describes lessons in debugging and testing learned at Microsoft. The author, Steve Maguire, is a strong advocate of stepping through code using the debugger as a good way of finding bugs. The examples given are in C: Steve Maguire, *Writing Solid Code*, Microsoft Press, 1993.

CHAPTER 20 | Groups

This chapter explains:

- how to use structured walkthroughs
- how to use inspections
- how to carry out pair programming.

20.1 ● Introduction

This chapter is about collaborative ways of working – both informal and semi-formal. We look at structured walkthroughs, inspections and pair programming. These aim to improve software productivity and quality, and perhaps also enhance the enjoyment of programming.

20.2 ● The individual and the error

Programmers are often seen as loners. Given a clear specification, a programmer often carries out the complete process of program design, coding and testing entirely on their own. Programmers are seen as low-profile technicians in contrast to the articulate extrovert systems analysts. Thus a program is sometimes seen as a personal work of art, the creation of an individual programmer. These attitudes deny that "two heads are better than one", that through discussion with others we can produce better work.

The common experience that someone else can spot errors better than the author lead to the invention of the *structured walkthrough*. Credit for its invention belongs to G. Weinberg, in his book *The Psychology of Computer Programming*. Weinberg suggested that programmers see their programs as an extension of themselves. He suggested that we get very involved with our own creations and tend to regard them as manifestations of our own thoughts. We are unable to see mistakes in our own programs, since to do so would be to find a fault in ourselves, and this, apparently, is unacceptable to us.

The term for this is *cognitive dissonance*. The solution is to seek help with fault finding. In doing this we relinquish our private relationship with our work. Programming becomes *ego-less programming*. This is a completely informal technique, carried out by colleagues in a friendly manner. It is not a formalized method carried out at fixed times and made into a rigid procedure of the organization. Indeed, to formalize ego-less programming would be to destroy its ethos and therefore its effectiveness. If you get a friend or a colleague to inspect your program, it is extraordinary to witness how quickly someone else can see a fault that has been defeating you for hours. Studies also show that different people tend to uncover different types of fault. This further suggests the use of team techniques.

20.3 ● Structured walkthroughs

This is simply the term for an organized meeting at which a program (or some other product) is examined by a group of colleagues. The major aim of the meeting is to try to find bugs which might otherwise go undetected for some time. (There are other goals, which are explained later.) The word "structured" simply means "well organized". The term "walkthrough" means the activity of the programmer explaining step by step the working of his/her program. The reasoning behind structured walkthroughs is just this: that by letting other people look at your program, errors will be found much more quickly.

To walkthrough a program you need only:

■ the specification

■ the text of the program on paper.

In carrying out a walkthrough, a good approach is to study it one method at a time. Some of the checks are fairly straightforward:

■ variables initialized

■ loops correctly initialized and terminated

■ method calls have the correct parameters.

Another check depends on the logic of the method. Pretend to execute the method as if you were a computer, avoiding following any calls into other methods. Check that:

■ the logic of the method achieves its desired purpose.

During inspection you can also check that:

■ variable and method names are meaningful

■ indentation is clear and consistent.

The prime goal of a walkthrough is to find bugs, but checking for a weakness in style may point to a bug.

The evidence from controlled experiments suggests that walkthroughs are a very effective way of finding errors. In fact walkthroughs are at least as good a way of identifying bugs as actually running the program (doing testing).

Although structured walkthroughs were initially used to find bugs in program code, the technique is valuable for reviewing the products at every stage of development – the requirements specification, a software specification, architectural design, component design, the code, the test data, the results of testing, the documentation.

There are several key points in organizing walkthroughs successfully:

- gauge the size and membership of the group carefully so that there are plenty of ideas, but so that everyone is fully involved
- expect participants to study the material *prior* to the meeting
- concentrate attention on the *product* rather than the person, to avoid criticizing the author
- limit the length of the meeting, so that everyone knows that it is business-like
- control the meeting with the aid of agreed rules and an assertive chairperson
- restrict the activity to *identifying* problems, not solving them
- briefly document the faults (not the cures) for later reference.

The benefits of structured walkthroughs can be:

1. *software quality is improved* because

   - more bugs are eliminated
   - the software is easier to maintain, because it is clearer

2. *programmer effort is reduced* because

   - specifications are clarified before implementation
   - errors are detected early, and so costly rework is avoided
   - the time spent at the meeting (and in preparation for it) is more than repaid in time saved

3. *meeting deadlines is improved* because

   - visibility of the project is better (so potential catastrophes are prevented)
   - major errors are avoided early

4. *programmer expertise is enhanced* because

   - everyone learns from everyone else

5. *programmer morale is improved* because

   - people gain satisfaction from better work
   - people get to find out what is going on
   - people enjoy the discussions with colleagues.

Of course walkthroughs do mean that the individual has to be relaxed about presenting their work to colleagues.

20.4 ● Inspections

These are similar to structured walkthroughs – a group of people meet to review a piece of work. But they are different from walkthroughs in several respects. Checklists are used to ensure that no relevant considerations are ignored. Errors that are discovered are classified according to type and carefully recorded on forms. Statistics on errors are computed, for example in terms of errors per 1,000 lines of code. Thus inspections are not just well organized, they are completely formal. In addition management is informed of the results of inspections, though usually they do not attend the meeting. Thus inspections are potentially more threatening to the programmer than walkthroughs.

There are other, minor, differences between inspections and walkthroughs. Normally there are only four members in an inspection team:

■ the moderator, who co-ordinates activities

■ the person who designed the program component being inspected

■ the programmer

■ the tester – a person who acts as someone who will be responsible for testing the component.

The essence of inspections is that the study of products is carried out under close management supervision. Thus inspections are overtly a mechanism for increased control over programmers' work, similar to the way that quality control is carried out on a factory floor. Some programmers might feel threatened in this situation and become defensive, perhaps trying to hide their mistakes. Perhaps this makes the discovery of errors more painful, and programming a less enjoyable activity.

From an organizational point of view, keeping records of faults discovered during inspections provides information to predict the quality of the software being written. Also, by highlighting common mistakes it can be used to improve programmers self-awareness and thereby improve their skills.

20.5 ● Pair programming

Here two people sit down together, looking at the same computer screen, and carry out programming, including writing and applying tests.

The people have different roles. One has the use of the keyboard and mouse. They are thinking and working on the implementation of the current piece of code (usually a particular method). They are thinking on a small scale and locally. The other person does two things:

■ observe, looking for errors

■ think more strategically.

The strategic thinking considers the role of the method within the class, and whether this method is appropriate within the context of the whole system. The person thinks about such questions as: Which other components use it? Can the system be simplified so that this method is just not needed? Can the method be generalized so that it is more widely useful? Is this method in the right place, or should it be relocated into some other class?

The pair periodically switch roles, so that overall they are working as equals. Pairs don't stay together, but change from day to day. It simply depends on who is available, but the people are drawn from the same project team, so they have a shared understanding of the project. And no one forces people to pair up if they do not get along.

When a pair starts work, it may be that one person will have more experience or expertise. Later, the gap narrows, so that they are genuinely collaborating on an equal basis, one person's strengths compensating for the other's weaknesses.

The central feature of pair programming is that two people are communicating intensely, sharing ideas, learning from each other, supporting each other, articulating ideas verbally and solving problems. It is creative, sociable, enjoyable and effective. It is claimed that pair programming improves productivity, code quality and job satisfaction. Even though, at first sight, twice the effort is spent on development, the time is more than reclaimed in more effective working.

Of course, pair programming means that pairs of people are working closely – almost intimately – together. This depends on an organizational culture that is collaborative and supportive.

20.6 ● Discussion

Perhaps the ultimate method for collaborative working aimed at reducing bugs is open source development. This is such an important technique that we devoted a whole separate chapter to the topic.

How effective are the techniques of walkthroughs, inspections and pair programming? The answer is that they are surprisingly effective as compared with using testing. We review the evidence in Chapter 31 on assessing methods.

Summary

A structured walkthrough is a meeting at which a document is examined by a group of people in order to find errors. Structured walkthroughs are based on the premise that ideas that are shared will be the better for it. The careful organization of a walkthrough is important. Walkthroughs can lead to improved software quality – reliability and maintainability – because of the scrutiny of project material by a group. Effort can be reduced and deadlines more easily met.

Inspections are a more formal approach to a group review meeting.

In pair programming, two people sit at the computer, working closely together on design, coding and testing.

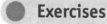

Exercises

20.1 Assess the effectiveness of structured walkthroughs.

20.2 Evaluate pair programming.

20.3 Compare and contrast the structured walkthrough technique with pair programming.

20.4 Argue a case for either walkthroughs or pair programming and suggest how it might be introduced into an organization.

20.5 Try to introduce ego-less programming into your college, university or organization in the following way. When you have written your next program and have a clean-compiled listing, ask one of your colleagues to look through it for you. Explain that you would appreciate comments of any kind on the program's clarity, correctness, etc. Explain that you are trying to identify problems sooner rather than later. Offer to do the same in return.

20.6 Suggest features for software tools that could assist in using each of the following techniques:

- walkthroughs
- inspections.

Further reading

The classic book which introduced the idea of ego-less programming, the precursor to walkthroughs and inspections. It deals at length and in a most interesting way with the informal, social aspects of working in a team. It is most enjoyable to read. G. Weinberg, *The Psychology of Computer Programming*, Van Nostrand Reinhold, 1971.

The original reference describing the technique of inspections: M.E. Fagan, Design and code inspections to reduce errors in program development, *IBM Systems Journal*, **15** (3) (July 1976), pp. 182–211.

Full of practical advice and case studies, jointly authored by one of the industry gurus, all you ever wanted to know about inspections is explained in: Tom Gilb and Dorothy Graham, *Software Inspection*, Addison-Wesley, 1993.

A collection of useful papers on how to do inspections and what the benefits are: David A. Wheeler, Bill Brykczynski and Reginald N. Meeson, *Software Inspection: An Industry Best Practice*, IEEE Computer Society Press, 1996.

There is a website simply for pair programming, with links to sites that report on evaluations, at: http://www.pairprogramming.com/

This is a useful book on pair programming: Laurie Williams and Robert Kessler, *Pair Programming Illuminated*, Addison-Wesley, 2002.

PART

E

PROCESS MODELS

The waterfall model

This chapter explains:

■ how to use the waterfall model for software development

■ the principles behind the waterfall model.

21.1 ● Introduction

The waterfall model is an established approach that dominated software development for a number of years and is widely used. It has the virtue of simplicity.

21.2 ● Principles of the model

In the waterfall model, software development is split up into a number of independent steps (Figure 21.1). These steps are carried out in sequence one after the other. Each stage produces a product which is the input into the next stage. It is important to realize that each stage is pursued until its conclusion before the next stage is begun. Thus, for example, all the coding is completed before testing starts.

Like all process models, the waterfall model says nothing about what methods are used at any of its stages, nor does it stipulate what notations are used for the products at each stage. (This whole book is about the different methods and notations that are available.) It merely provides a framework for a development.

Different people and authors have slightly different ideas about what exactly the steps should be. For example, some people include a feasibility study as the first step. However, the essentials of the approach are the same.

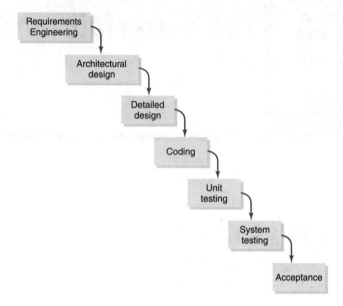

Figure 21.1 The waterfall model

The principles of the waterfall model are:

■ it is a series of steps (like a factory production line)
■ each step is well defined
■ each step creates a definite product (in some cases a piece of paper)
■ each product forms the basis for the next step
■ the correctness of each step can be checked (verification or validation).

The waterfall model gets its name because each stage produces a product, like a stream of water which passes on to the next stage. So the complete development process is like a series of small waterfalls – see Figure 21.1. Just as water cannot flow up a waterfall, information does not flow backwards in the waterfall model. Once a step is complete, there is no going back.

SELF-TEST QUESTION

21.1 Draw up a process model for preparing a meal, including buying the ingredients and washing up afterwards. Don't forget to identify the product at each stage.

The inputs and outputs for each step of the waterfall model are shown in this table.

Stage	Input	Output
requirements engineering	none	requirements specification
architectural design	requirements specification	architectural design
detailed design	architectural design	module specifications
coding	module specifications	coding
unit testing	coding	tested modules
system testing	tested modules	tested system
acceptance	tested system	satisfied client

SELF-TEST QUESTION

21.2 Someone enhances the waterfall model by including a user interface design stage immediately after the requirements engineering stage. What are its inputs and outputs?

21.3 ● Feedback between stages

One of the drawbacks of a strict waterfall model is that the water cannot flow upwards – if a problem is found at a particular stage in development, there is no way of redoing an earlier stage in order to rectify the problem. For example, testing usually finds errors in the (preceding) coding stage, but in the strict waterfall approach, the coding cannot be corrected. When preparing a meal, if you find that some ingredient is missing when you get to the stage of cooking the vegetables, you need to go back to the shopping stage.

To overcome this obvious drawback, a variation of the waterfall model provides for feedback between adjoining stages, so that a problem uncovered at one stage can cause remedial action to be taken at the previous stage. Thus the waterfall model with feedback between stages is as shown in Figure 21.2.

You will see, however, that this approach only provides for feedback to the immediately preceding step. But, in reality, any step may necessitate changes in any of the preceding stages. For example:

- during system testing, an architectural design fault is revealed
- during user acceptance, a problem with the specification becomes evident.

So the reality of using the waterfall model is that development does not proceed in one direction, step by step. Instead, there is commonly frequent feedback to earlier stages, requiring rework (which can seriously disrupt the timescale of a project). To be more realistic, Figure 21.2 should show arrows leading backwards from every activity to every preceding activity. This, of course, undermines the model and any planning.

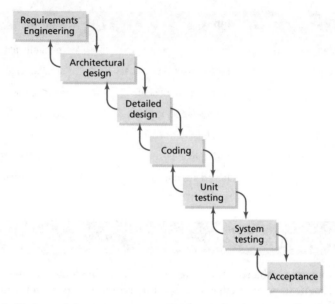

Figure 21.2 Modified waterfall model with feedback

The instigators of the waterfall model clearly and wrongly perceived software development to be simple and straightforward, with development proceeding smoothly onwards from stage to stage without disruption. But, as we have seen, there are fundamental problems with using the waterfall model as a basis for a project plan. Nonetheless, it is common to use this process model.

21.4 ● Discussion

The strengths of the waterfall model are:

■ it divides a complex task into smaller, more manageable tasks
■ each task produces a well-defined deliverable.

Thus the process is well-defined. Anyone can see exactly what has been completed and what remains to be done.

Perhaps the most serious problem with the waterfall model is that the client only gets to see the product at the very end of the development – and if it is not what they want, it is too late! The problem is the huge gap between requirements analysis at an early stage in a project and acceptance testing near the end. There is no opportunity to validate the user requirements at an early stage in development. This is a major problem with the waterfall model.

But there are also less obvious, but equally important drawbacks. If a problem is discovered at any stage which reveals a mistake at an earlier stage, nothing can be done about it.

Summary

The essence and the strengths of the waterfall model are that:

- it divides a complex task into smaller, more manageable tasks
- each task produces a well-defined deliverable.
- each stage is carried out in sequence – there is no going back.

The goal of this approach is to maintain control during development.

Exercises

21.1 Draw up a waterfall process model for a large civil engineering project, such as building a road bridge across the channel between England and France. Identify similarities and differences between this project and a large software development project.

21.2 Validation and verification are clearly important. Identify where validation is carried out and where verification is carried out in the waterfall model.

21.3 Create an outline plan for developing each of the systems in Appendix A using the waterfall model.

21.4 Evaluate the waterfall model using the following criteria:

- capability to accommodate risk
- capability to meet user requirements
- capability to respond to changed requirements
- visibility of the progress of the project.

21.5 Identify the main goals and the main techniques of each of the following process models:

- waterfall
- spiral
- prototyping
- incremental
- open source
- XP
- UP

21.6 "The waterfall model is useless." Discuss.

Answers to self-test questions

21.1 1. buy ingredients (product is ingredients)

2. prepare vegetables (prepared vegetables)

3. cook meat (cooked meat)

4. cook vegetables (cooked vegetables)

5. serve meal (meal on table)

6. wash up (clean utensils).

21.2 The input is the requirements specification.
The output is the specification of the user interface.

CHAPTER
22
The spiral model

This chapter:

■ explains the principles behind the spiral model

■ explains some of the practical aspects of using this model.

22.1 ● Introduction

The main feature of the spiral model is the recognition that there is often enormous uncertainty at many stages during a software development project. It therefore incorporates periodic risk assessment. These assessments are followed by identifying alternative actions, selection of the best action and re-planning.

22.2 ● The spiral model

This model is shown in Figure 22.1. Progress is shown as a line that spirals out from near the centre of the diagram. Each cycle of the project passes through four steps, shown as the four quarters of the diagram. The project spirals outwards from the center of the diagram to convey the increasing expenditure of time, effort – and progress.

As the diagram shows, each cycle consists of four steps:

1. analyze risks and plan
2. analyze requirements
3. construct
4. evaluate.

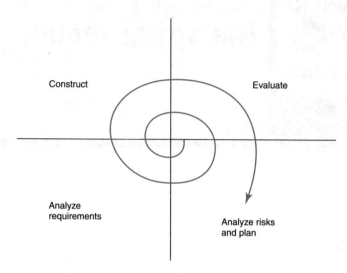

Figure 22.1 The spiral model

The distinctive feature of the spiral model is that it makes explicit the idea of risk. We have seen (Chapter 1) that during software development there can be difficult problems to be overcome. The spiral model explicitly recognizes that there are uncertainties associated with software development and that they should be dealt with as carefully as possible. Examples of risks that are commonly experienced are:

■ the client changes some of the requirements

■ during a long development, the users' requirements are neglected

■ someone leaves the development team

■ one of the component tasks of the development goes beyond its deadline

■ the software performs too slowly

■ the software occupies too much main memory

■ a new software development tool or technology becomes available

■ a user requirement was misunderstood

■ the target hardware configuration changes

■ an intransigent bug

■ a competitor launches a rival package onto the market.

Ideally, any process model should make provision for these and any other pitfalls. However, the spiral model makes explicit and repeated provision for dealing with areas of uncertainty like these and thereby minimizes the risk to the software project. Thus the most important phase of each cycle is the risk analysis stage. Actions can then be taken to control the project, rescue the project, or, as happens sometimes, abandon the project.

Many decisions are taken during software development, and for every decision there is a risk that something will go wrong or a mistake will be made. The later a problem is detected, the more effort is needed to fix it. The spiral model approach is therefore to try to discover errors frequently – at each cycle. This means they are uncovered early. Then something can be done about them immediately.

In detail, the four steps of each cycle are as follows.

Stage 1 – risk analysis and planning

This stage is the essential ingredient of the spiral model. It consists of:

1. establishing the objectives of the product of this stage (e.g. performance, functionality, ease of change)

2. identifying the constraints that affect this stage (e.g. cost, deadlines, interfaces with other software components)

3. identifying risks

4. identifying the alternative ways of implementing this stage (buying it, reusing something else, developing it one way, developing it another way)

5. evaluating the alternative implementation schemes against the criteria set by the objectives and the constraints

6. deciding how to overcome the risk

7. establishing deadlines for the next stage of the project and deciding how many people will be involved.

It is at this stage in each phase of the project that considerable flexibility can be exercised. In effect, the whole of the progress of the project is reviewed and options for continuing are investigated. Use is made of whatever method is appropriate at that stage of the project.

For example, if meeting user requirements is identified as a potential problem, then the decision might be taken to carry out some prototyping to clarify the users needs. (But the use of prototyping, or any other specific technique, is not part of the spiral model.)

Stage 2 – analysis of requirements

This consists of establishing the requirements for the next stage of the project.

Stage 3 – construction

Next the development of a product is carried out. This stage may involve design, implementation, validation and verification, depending on the nature of the product. Examples of the product of this stage are a specification, an architectural design, a prototype or a software component.

Stage 4 – evaluation

Finally, an evaluation is used to establish whether the project is on track and whether all the participants are happy with the plans. This leads on to the next cycle of the project.

Note that the number of cycles is not prescribed by the spiral model – as many cycles as necessary are used. Further, the number of cycles is not known at the outset of a project, but is decided as the project proceeds on the basis of the evaluations that are carried out at the end of each cycle.

22.3 ● Case study

To illustrate how the spiral model works, we will use the example of the ATM software described in Appendix A. Consider part of the project – the creation of a driver for the card reader. We treat this as one spiral model cycle.

At the outset of this cycle, stage 1, the objective is confirmed as the production of a driver to interface with the card reader, providing high-level facilities for the application. There is a deadline (to fit in with the timescales of the project) and a budgeted cost.

Risks are as follows:

- the driver is delivered late, so that the overall project is delayed
- the driver is unreliable
- the specification of the behavior of the card reader is inaccurate
- the card reader does not work properly
- the card reader is not available in time for testing
- the driver is over-budget
- the driver does not meet the specification for interfacing with the application
- there is a shortage of person power to carry out the development.

Possible implementation plans are:

- commission another developer
- write the driver in-house
- modify the primitive driver provided by the card reader supplier.

The decision as to which minimal-risk approach to use depends on factors that are peculiar to the organization, such as the availability of appropriate people. Writing the driver in-house may reduce some of the risks, because the development is under direct control. If the decision is made to develop in-house, appropriate methods for design, coding and testing are selected. (These depend on factors outside the scope of the spiral model.) Finally the deadlines are decided and people allocated.

At stage 2, the detailed requirements are drawn up. This includes the specification for the interface with the application, the specification of the card reader and the nature of validation and verification.

At stage 3, the driver is designed, coded and tested.

At stage 4, the degree of success of the driver is assessed against its requirements. This leads to any necessary remedial action in the first stage of the next cycle.

22.4 ● Discussion

Along with other process models, the spiral model does not say how each step (for example design) is carried out. But it is common to use another process model, prototyping, during one or more cycles in order to resolve uncertainty. This might be either to clarify requirements or to establish the technical feasibility of some course of action.

The spiral model attempts to solve some of the problems of the waterfall model, while incorporating its best features – planning, phases, intermediate products. The spiral model therefore offers greater flexibility than the waterfall model.

SELF-TEST QUESTION

22.1 Identify one advantage and one disadvantage of the spiral model.

Summary

The spiral model consists of a series of cycles. Each cycle consists of a series of steps. At every cycle, any risks to the successful progress of the project are assessed. Then an appropriate method is selected in order to minimize that risk. Thus the spiral model is essentially a cautious and robust approach to development.

The spiral model consists of a repeated cycle of small steps designed to assess and deal with risks at every cycle. Thus the spiral model is termed an *iterative* approach.

● Exercises

22.1 You are preparing a meal for special guests. What risks can you anticipate? How could you use the ideas of the spiral model to cope with problems as they unexpectedly arise? (Suggestions for possible disruptions are: power failure, late guests, missing ingredients and burnt food. But make plans for other contingencies.)

22.2 Using the spiral model, plan how to carry out the development of the user interface part of the ATM system (Appendix A).

22.3 Assess the spiral model for software development. To do this, formulate a list of criteria and then use them.

Answer to self-test question

22.1 Advantage: flexibility in the face of risks.

Disadvantage: absence of an early fixed plan.

● Further reading

For the definitive explanation of the spiral model see: Barry W. Boehm, A spiral model of software development and enhancement, *IEEE Computer*, **21** (5) (May 1988), pp. 61–72.

CHAPTER 23
Prototyping

This chapter:

- explains how to carry out prototyping
- explains the principles behind prototyping
- distinguishes between evolutionary and throwaway prototyping.

23.1 ● Introduction

Prototyping is a process model that offers a solution to the problem of ensuring that the customer gets what they want. In prototyping, the customer is presented at a very early stage with a working version of the system. (It may not be a complete system, but it is at least part of the system and it works.) They can check that it does what they want, or specify modifications. The developer amends the system and demonstrates it again and again until it does what the customer wants. Thus the main purpose of prototyping is ensuring that the user's needs are satisfied. (We shall see that there are, however, sometimes other goals of prototyping.)

23.2 ● Definition

When a new car is being developed, one or more prototypes will be individually built. These prototypes are tested intensively before a production line is set up. It is possible to follow a similar approach with software development. Prototyping is the practice of building an early version of a system which does not necessarily reflect all the features of the final system, but rather those which are of interest.

The purpose is to aid the analysis and design stages of a project by enabling users to see very early what the system will do, that is, to facilitate validation. Users seldom have a clear, concise understanding of their needs. The conventional specification is a narrative description of a system that may be technical and time-consuming to read. The larger the development team, including user representatives, the more difficult communication becomes. Prototyping is one technique that attempts to address these problems and provide possible solutions. The benefits of developing and demonstrating a prototype early in the software process are:

- misunderstandings between software developers and users may be identified
- missing facilities may be revealed
- difficult-to-use or confusing facilities may be identified and refined
- software developers may find incomplete and/or inconsistent requirements.

There are sometimes other objectives:

- to create an acceptable user interface
- a working, albeit limited, system is available quickly to demonstrate the feasibility and usefulness of the application to management
- user training – a prototype system can be used for training users before the final system has been delivered
- to establish that some new technology will provide the facilities needed (e.g. does Java provide sufficient security for electronic transfer of funds?).

An example of using prototyping for user interface design is given in Chapter 5.

23.3 ● Throwaway or evolutionary?

There are two types of prototype:

1. *throwaway* – the various versions of the system are constructed and then thrown away. (The final system is implemented in some different way.)
2. *evolutionary* – an initial implementation evolves towards the final version. (The prototype becomes the final system.)

For example, a throwaway prototype might be written very quickly in Visual Basic to demonstrate the essential functions that a system will carry out. But then the software might be rewritten using careful and systematic development methods.

Alternatively, an evolutionary prototype might be implemented in C# to demonstrate to the user the main features of the system. Having checked that the system does what is required, new features and facilities are added to the prototype, gradually transforming it into its complete form.

In throwaway prototyping, the priority is to understand requirements that are unclear and therefore requirements that are straightforward may never need to be prototyped. In evolutionary prototyping, the first priority is to incorporate well-understood requirements into the prototype then to move on to those requirements that are unclear.

Therefore, in summary:

- the product of a throwaway prototype is a specification
- the product of an evolutionary prototype is a system.

23.4 ● Throwaway prototyping

The starting point for throwaway prototyping is an outline specification for the software. A throwaway prototype implements only those requirements that are poorly understood. It is discarded after the desired information is learned. After the prototype is complete, the developer writes a full specification, incorporating what was learned, and then constructs a full-scale system based on that specification. Thus the purpose of throwaway prototyping is the formulation of a validated specification.

Throwaway prototyping is sometimes called rapid prototyping and as the name suggests, a rapid prototype should cost very little and take very little time to develop. The emphasis is on using whatever methods are available to produce a system that can be demonstrated to the user. Typically the only noticeable difference between the prototype and the desired system is its performance, or in the volumes of data that it handles. Rapid prototyping seems to contradict the idea of using systematic, careful methods during development; a prototype is produced in as quick (and perhaps as dirty) a manner as possible.

To be effective, throwaway prototyping is carried out within a systematic framework. An overview of throwaway prototype development is shown in Figure 23.1.

The stages of throwaway prototyping are:

1. *draw up an outline specification* – the first step in throwaway prototyping is the creation of an initial, often partial, specification. This specification contains areas of uncertainty.

2. *establish objectives* – what is the prototype to be used for? What aspects of the proposed system should it reflect? What can be learned from the prototype? The objective may be to develop a system to prototype the user interface, to validate functional requirements, to explore uncertain new technologies or to demonstrate the feasibility of the application to management. The same prototype cannot meet all objectives. The areas that are most often prototyped are the user interface, and uncertain or vague functions.

3. *select functions* – the next stage is to decide what to put into and what to leave out of the prototype. This is determined by the objectives of the system. If the purpose of prototyping is to clarify users' requirements, then the uncertain areas are the candidates for prototyping. The development of a working model allows the developers to make sure that the solution they are proposing will satisfy the requirements and perform effectively. Depending on the objectives, it may be decided to prototype all system functions but at reduced level. Alternatively a subset of system functions may be included in the prototype.

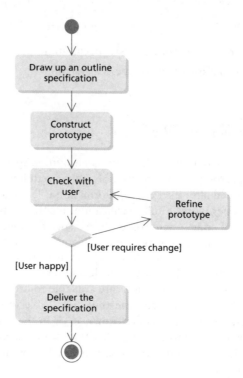

Figure 23.1 Throwaway prototyping

4. *construct prototype* – speed and cost of construction of the prototype is crucial. Fast, low-cost construction is normally achieved by ignoring the normal quality require-ments for the final product (a "quick and dirty" approach), unless this is in conflict with the objectives.

5. *evaluate (check with the user)* – the users use the prototype. This is more effective than watching a demonstration of the software. During evaluation, inconsistencies and shortcomings in the developer's perception of the customer requirements are uncovered. The prototype acts as an effective communication medium between the developer and customer.

6. *iterate (refine)* – the prototype is rapidly modified, evaluation is carried out and the process repeated until the prototype meets the objectives (usually an agreed specification).

7. *deliver the specification* – the product of the prototyping process is a specifica-tion that meets the users' requirements. Since the working prototype has been validated through interaction with the client, it is reasonable to expect that the resultant specification document will be correct. When the requirements are clearly established, the prototype is thrown away. At this stage, a different soft-ware process model, such as the waterfall model, is employed to develop the software.

Users should resist the temptation to turn a throwaway prototype into a delivered system that is put into use. The reasons for this are:

1. important system characteristics, such as performance, security and reliability, will probably have been ignored during prototype development

2. during the prototype development, the prototype will have been changed to reflect user needs. It is likely that these changes will have been made in an uncontrolled way and not properly documented other than in the prototype code

3. the changes made during prototype development will probably have degraded the architectural structure of the software. Therefore the software may be difficult and expensive to maintain.

23.5 ● Evolutionary prototyping

This type of prototyping is based on the idea of developing an initial implementation, exposing it to user comment and refining it through repeated stages until an adequate system has been developed.

To be effective, evolutionary prototyping is carried out within a systematic framework. Evolutionary prototype development is shown in Figure 23.2. Note the similarities and differences between this figure and Figure 23.1.

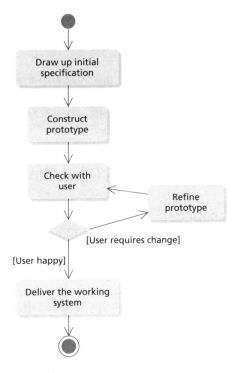

Figure 23.2 Evolutionary prototyping

The stages are:

1. *requirements definition (initial specification)* – a stage of thorough analysis is used to create an initial specification for the software.
2. *prototype construction* – a prototype is built in a quality manner, including design, documentation, and thorough verification.
3. *evaluation (check with the user)* – during evaluation, problems in the developer's perception of the customer requirements are uncovered. The prototypes are the communication medium that enables the developer and customer to communicate with each other.
4. *iteration (refine the prototype)* – evaluation is carried out repeatedly until the prototype meets the objectives. The specification is updated with every iteration.

The product is a fully working system.

SELF-TEST QUESTION

23.1 What are the differences between throwaway and evolutionary prototyping?

23.6 ● Rapid prototyping techniques

A throwaway prototype needs to be created quickly so that users can comment on it at an early stage. A prototype also needs to be altered quickly to incorporate the users' views as the prototype changes to meet their requirements. What we really need is some magical tool that would enable us to create prototypes at high speed. But there are no magical tools. If there were, we would use them for everything. Instead we use whatever tools and methods that are suitable.

Here are some techniques for fast prototyping.

Use a high-level language

High-level languages include many facilities which normally have to be built from more primitive constructs in other languages. Smalltalk is a language that can be used to prototype adventurous GUIs with very little programmer effort. A drawback of Smalltalk is that it can be a massive consumer of processor time and memory, so that after prototyping it may be necessary to rewrite the system in some other language. So Smalltalk may only be usable for throwaway prototyping.

Visual Basic has features for rapid software development, including the capacity to create a GUI using drag-and-drop from a palette.

Reuse components

The time needed to develop a prototype can be reduced if many parts of the system can be reused rather than designed and implemented. Prototypes can be constructed quickly if there is a library of reusable components and some mechanism to combine the components into systems. The reusable components may also be used in the final system, thus reducing its development cost. An example of this approach to prototyping is found in the Unix operating system (Chapter 18 on Scripting). The success of Smalltalk as a prototyping language is as much due to its reusable component libraries as to the inbuilt language facilities.

Use a stand-alone machine

It is often possible to construct a system that appears realistic, but is in fact massively incomplete. For example, if a network solution is to be developed, a prototype running on a stand-alone computer is created. This simulates the complete system for the purpose of validation. But the developer is freed from considerations of networking, large data volumes and possible performance problems that would need to be considered in the production version of the system.

Ignore error handling

In many systems as much as one-half of the software is concerned with error handling. This includes:

- validation of user data input from keyboards
- handling input-output device errors
- exception handling software
- fault tolerant software.

Omit features

It may be that some features can simply be omitted in a prototype. Examples are logging software, security and authentication features. These components of a production-quality system can be significantly costly in development effort and so their omission makes construction of a prototype quicker.

Ignore functionality

This type of prototype is aimed simply at establishing an acceptable user interface. For example, suppose we were setting out to develop a new word processor (Appendix A). We could, very quickly, create a mock-up of what would appear on the screen, while the actual functions of the word processor are simply not implemented. This type of prototype is often used during the design of the user interface (see Chapter 5).

23.7 ● Discussion

Advantages

What are the advantages of prototyping? During requirements specification, the developer can show the user a suggested working system at a very early stage. Users are not always certain what they want a system to do. It is difficult for users to understand properly and be able to state detailed functional requirements unambiguously before they have an opportunity to experiment interactively with the options. A prototype gives the user a very clear picture of what the system will look like and what it will do. By examining options in the various versions of the prototype, the users are stimulated to discover requirements that they might not have thought of until after full implementation using any other method. The user is able to tell the developer their views about the system, and modifications can be made. The value lies in better communication between user and analyst and validation is carried out early in the life of the project. Thus prototyping can eliminate many of the requirement errors in the very early stages of a project. The greatest savings in time and effort stem from avoiding the work in changing a system that does not do what the user really wanted.

Prototyping promotes a participatory approach to development, and when users are involved, they often gain confidence in a system. They see first hand the problems and errors, but they also see the mistakes being resolved quickly.

The advantages of prototyping can be:

- enables developers to cope with lack of clarity in requirements
- gives the user the opportunity to change their mind before commitment to the final system
- user requirements are easier to determine
- systems are developed faster
- development effort is reduced because the resultant system is the right system
- maintenance effort is reduced because the system meets the users' needs
- end user involvement is facilitated
- user-developer communication is enhanced
- users are not frustrated while they wait for the final system, because they can see a working system
- increased chance that a system will be more user friendly
- systems are easier for end users to learn and use because users know what to expect
- enables a system to be gradually introduced into an organization
- facilitates user training while development is going on
- increased customer satisfaction with the delivered software.

The question about prototyping is whether the cost of constructing the prototypes is offset by the savings.

Pitfalls

For users, the problems of prototyping are:

■ because prototyping is carried out in an artificial environment, users may miss some of the shortcomings

■ undue user expectations – the ability of the developers to create a prototype quickly may raise undue expectations that the final system will soon be complete. They see a partial system and may not understand that it is not the finished system

■ inconsistencies between a prototype and the final system – if the prototype is a throwaway, the end product may not be exactly like the prototype. In other words, what the user sees may not be what the user gets

■ users who are never satisfied because they are given too much opportunity to change the development of the system.

For software engineers, the problems can be:

■ incomplete analysis – because prototypes are produced quickly, developers may be tempted to plunge into prototyping before sufficient requirements analysis has taken place. This may result in a system that has a good user interface but is not properly functional. This is how the reputation of prototypes which are quick but dirty came about.

■ iteration is not easily accepted by some designers, because it necessitates discarding their own work

■ omission of non-functional requirements, since a prototype focuses only on functionality.

The project management problems of using prototyping may be:

■ estimating, planning and managing a prototyping project can be difficult because it can be hard to predict how many iterations of prototyping will take place

■ procedures for change and configuration management may be unsuitable for controlling the rapid change inherent in prototyping

■ many project management structures are set up assuming a process model, like the waterfall model, that generates regular deliverables to assess progress. However, prototypes usually evolve so quickly that it is not cost effective to keep pace with the documentation.

Maintenance of a system constructed using evolutionary prototyping can be difficult and costly because continual change tends to corrupt the structure of the prototype.
Prototyping may not always be an appropriate technique, for example, in:

■ embedded software

■ real-time control software

■ scientific and engineering numerical computational software.

SELF-TEST QUESTION

23.2 Identify one advantage and one disadvantage of prototyping.

Summary

The central goal of prototyping is to satisfy users' requirements. The key feature of the prototyping process model is the repeated demonstration of prototypes to users.

There are two approaches to prototyping – evolutionary and throwaway:

■ in evolutionary prototyping an initial prototype evolves as requirements are clarified so that it becomes the final system

■ throwaway prototyping uses rapid techniques to construct prototypes that are thrown away once users' requirements have been established.

It is important to establish the goal of using prototyping as part of a particular project. Although the goal is usually clarifying requirements, prototyping can also be used to design the user interface, demonstrate feasibility, verify that new technology will work or provide a training system.

● Exercises

23.1 Draw up a prototyping model for preparing a meal, including buying the ingredients and washing up afterwards. Don't forget to identify the product at each stage.

23.2 Draw up a prototyping model for a large civil engineering project, such as building a road bridge across the channel between England and France. Identify similarities and differences between this project and a large software development project.

23.3 Validation and verification are clearly important during software development. Identify where validation and verification are carried out in prototyping.

23.4 Compare and contrast throwaway with evolutionary prototyping.

23.5 Review the advantages of prototyping.

23.6 Review the techniques that are available for constructing a prototype easily and quickly.

23.7 Assess whether and how prototyping might be used in the development of each of the systems described in Appendix A.

23.8 Compare and contrast the process models waterfall, spiral, extreme programming and prototyping using the following criteria:

- capability to accommodate risk
- capability to respond to changed requirements
- capability to meet user requirements.

23.9 How is prototyping different from hacking?

Answers to self-test questions

23.1

	Throwaway	Evolutionary
product	specification	system
starting point	unclear requirements	outline specification
construction	quick and dirty	quality

23.2 Advantage: early validation of user requirements.

Disadvantage: need for suitable tool.

Incremental development

This chapter:

- explains the need for incremental development
- explains how to carry out top-down development
- explains how to carry out bottom-up development
- explains how to carry out middle-out development
- explains how to carry out use case based development.

24.1 ● Introduction

This chapter looks at approaches to developing software bit by bit. The appeal of these approaches is reduced risk and a product that appears (at least in part) earlier. The risks that can be accommodated include changed requirements and delays to deadlines. Piecemeal product delivery is a great morale booster and helps ensure that requirements are being met.

Some of these approaches address the whole of software development, while others concentrate on system integration and testing.

There are several approaches to incremental implementation:

- top-down
- bottom-up
- middle-out
- use case based.

24.2 ● Big-bang implementation

Here is a possible scenario: a client and a developer establish a requirements specification and a deadline for some software. The two part company until some time later, near the deadline. Then they have this conversation:

Client: "How is it going?"
Developer: "Very well. It is 95% complete."
Client: "What can you show me."
Developer: "Well, er, nothing."

This is somewhat frustrating for the client. Some time has passed but there is nothing visible. There may well be some design documents, such as UML diagrams, but they are unintelligible to the client. The client has to continue to trust that the developer will deliver the goods. Incremental development avoids this unfortunate conversation.

There is another problem scenario. Anyone who has ever written a sizeable program knows that if you code the whole thing, compile it and run it, there is a gigantic problem of testing and debugging. Similarly with software, if all the components are put together simultaneously, it is almost impossible to locate the bugs. Instead some piece-meal strategy is essential.

Why is it that system testing is so time-consuming? After all, if all the individual components work correctly, why don't they all work when they are combined? The answer is, of course, that it is precisely in their interaction that errors will be exposed. For example, there may be a discrepancy in understanding the exact task of a method or the nature of the parameters to be supplied.

Thus we have seen that there are problems with big bang approaches.

24.3 ● Test beds

We have established the need to construct software in an incremental fashion and we will look at four approaches. We will look at each of these in turn, after we have examined the problem of test beds. When a bridge or a building is being constructed, scaffolding is used. It has two purposes – to enable access to the structure and to support the structure. For example, an arched stone bridge needs considerable support as it is being built. Similarly, software needs support structures as it is being integrated.

An early and essential task is to construct a *test harness* or *test bed* for individual components. This is specially constructed software whose sole function is to invoke a component under test in a way that is consistent with its eventual role in the complete system. A test bed consists of drivers to call the methods of the components, and stubs to substitute for methods not yet integrated into the testing.

Once unit testing has been completed, further support software is required as the system is integrated. Rather than bring all the components together at once, which is a big bang approach, it is probably better to assemble them one by one. But then we need stubs to stand in for the missing components.

Considerable time can be spent on the construction of test harnesses. Worse still, they are usually thrown away when testing is complete. This is like a carpenter who specially makes a new set of tools to build a new house, and then destroys the tools when the house is complete. (The analogy is intended to demonstrate the waste of effort that is involved.)

Finding out exactly where a fault is located is easier using incremental implementation. This is because components are incorporated one at a time. Thus there is a high probability that any fault lies in the single new component or in its interface with the existing components

24.4 ● Top-down implementation

This starts with the architectural design for the software. Top-down development is an incremental approach that starts with the top components of the software. Now object-oriented systems do not usually possess a top – object-oriented software does not naturally possess a hierarchical structure. But while most object-oriented systems are non-hierarchical, some are. Chapter 12 on software patterns describes an architecture in which the software consists of layers. However, arguably, the user interface is the top-most component of object-oriented software. It is the layer of software that calls up the functionality provided by the remainder of the software. So top-down development starts with the implementation of the user interface. Stubs are used to stand in for called but as yet unwritten lower-level components. Test data is constructed, the system is assembled and tested. An immediate outcome is that we can very quickly have something that works. Not only that but it is the most visible part of the system. We also can have something that can be demonstrated to the client as performing an imitation of the total system.

Implementation proceeds by selecting lower-level components (formerly stubs) for coding and incorporation into the system. In general, at any stage in the development there are (see Figure 24.1):

- higher-level components which have already been tested
- the single component which is under test
- stubs.

The strengths of top-down implementation are:

- drivers are not required (the system acts as its own drivers), so time is saved
- there is an early visible (but non-functional) product
- some components of the system are repeatedly tested.

The weaknesses of top-down implementation are:

- stubs are needed at nearly every stage
- not all systems are hierarchical.

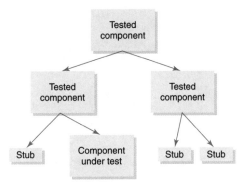

Figure 24.1 Top-down implementation

24.5 ● Bottom-up implementation

This type of implementation starts with an architectural design for the software. Bottom-up implementation starts with the lowest-level components of the system. These are the components that everything else depends on, but that don't use anything themselves. In an OOD design these are the shared, reusable classes that form a common library for the application to use. In many systems this is the software that accesses the database.

The bottom-up implementation starts with the lowest-level components of the system. These are the components that everything else uses, but that don't use anything themselves. The first task is to construct a test bed for each component. Figure 24.2 shows two components at the lowest level of a system and their test beds.

When the lowest level components have been tested in this manner, components are combined into subsystems that are tested in a similar manner, again using a test bed (Figure 24.3). The procedure continues until the complete system is finally assembled and tested as a whole.

Bottom-up implementation suffers from the following drawbacks:

■ drivers are required during almost all the development

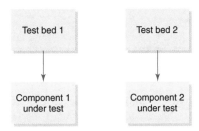

Figure 24.2 Bottom-up testing of the lowest-level components

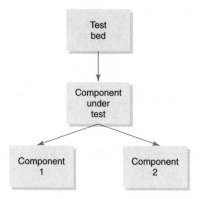

Figure 24.3 Bottom-up implementation

- there is no visible, working system until a very late stage, system testing, is complete. True there are tested components and subsystems, but there is normally nothing that can be demonstrated to the client as even providing a limited vision of what the system will eventually do.
- not all systems have a bottom.

24.6 ● Middle-out implementation

Middle-out development starts with an architectural design for the software. It then chooses some central component as the starting point for testing. A driver and stubs are written and the component is tested. Then some adjoining component is added to the system and testing carried out. The system emerges from its centre.

This approach could be useful in developing a large software system that involves a number of developers. In such a development, the work needs to be divided among a number of people who work concurrently. Hopefully the architecture can be cleanly divided into weakly coupled subsystems, which are initially developed independently. These subsystems need to be surrounded by drivers and stubs, developing in a middle-out fashion.

This approach suffers from all the combined drawbacks of bottom-up and top-down development.

SELF-TEST QUESTION

24.1 Suggest a drawback of middle-out development

24.7 ● Use case driven implementation

A use case is a single independent function that a system provides for a user. For example, the word processor (Appendix A) provides tens of functions to carry out the tasks of editing, formatting and displaying text. Each of these is a use case. This approach takes one use case at a time and implements it.

In the word processor example, we might first choose to implement the **save file** function. This is a good choice because, once it is implemented, this feature is useful in providing a mechanism for testing the other use cases. Implementing this function means single-mindedly concentrating on it to the exclusion of all the other functions. Only the methods necessary to achieving this end are implemented. Drivers are not needed and a minimal number of stubs are required.

The use case approach is different to the top-down approach explained above. Top-down starts with the user interface and implements each of the various functions in a breadth-first fashion. It creates a forest of trees that grow simultaneously. In contrast, the use case approach is a depth-first approach. It creates individual trees one after the other.

The stages of the use case approach are:

1. choose an initial use case to implement
2. implement the use case
3. test the use case
4. demonstrate the use case to the client.

These stages are repeated until the user is satisfied with the product.

The strengths of this approach are:

■ the system acts as its own drivers
■ there are immediate and repeated, visible products.

SELF-TEST QUESTION

24.2 Suggest a second use case for implementation.

24.8 ● Discussion

We have assumed in the above explanation that architectural design is complete prior to incremental implementation. This is one approach, but an alternative is to allow the architectural structure to emerge from the implementation. This means that the structure will probably be subject to frequent refactoring (see Chapter 13). This takes some courage and it might be too risky an approach for a large project.

Summary

The aim of incremental development is easier bug detection. The mechanism is incorporation of components one by one. Incremental methods include:

- top-down
- bottom-up
- middle-out
- use case based.

Use case based development provides early and frequent functionality. This in turn means:

- improved confidence by the client and the developer
- the opportunity for the user to change their requirements
- the opportunity for the user to decide what should be implemented next.

Use case based development also reduces the work of creating test drivers and stubs.

Exercises

24.1 Draw up an incremental process model for preparing a meal, including buying the ingredients and washing up afterwards. Don't forget to identify the product at each stage.

24.2 Draw up an incremental process model for writing a student assignment. The assignment is to write an essay reviewing the process models that are explained in this book. The non-incremental approach is:

Step 1 read and digest all the relevant chapters

Step 2 write the review.

24.3 Draw up an incremental process model for a large civil engineering project, such as building a road bridge across the channel between England and France. Identify similarities and differences between this project and a large software development project.

24.4 Create an outline plan for developing each of the systems in Appendix A, using an incremental approach.

24.5 Compare and contrast the following approaches to development:

- top-down
- bottom-up

- middle-out
- use case based.

24.6 Evaluate the incremental process model the following criteria:

- capability to accommodate risk
- capability to respond to changed requirements
- capability to meet user requirements
- visibility of the development to developers and clients.

24.7 Identify the main goals and the main techniques of each of the following process models:

- waterfall
- spiral
- prototyping
- incremental
- open source
- XP
- UP.

Answers to self-test questions

24.1 The need to create many drivers and stubs.

24.2 The **open file** use case.

 ## Further reading

For a discussion of evolutionary development see: Felix Redmill, *Software Projects: Evolutionary vs. Big-Bang Delivery*, John Wiley, 1997.

Kent Beck suggests an incremental approach to development that is based entirely on writing a series of tests: *Test Driven Development*, Addison-Wesley, 2003.

CHAPTER 25

Open source software development

This chapter explains:

- the principles behind open source development
- the schism in the open source movement
- how to carry out open source development.

25.1 ● Introduction

Open source is a development approach in which the source code of the software is entirely free to access. The term "open source" is used to refer to both the product and the development approach. Any individual is able to view the code, modify it or duplicate it. Access to the source code facilitates the distributed and cooperative approach to software development that is fundamental to an open source style of development.

Some examples of larger open source products are: Mozilla web browser; Apache web server; GNU/Linux and GNU/HURD operating systems; MySQL database software; Perl programming language; MyOffice and OpenOffice office suites. The range of products illustrates that open source software development can produce a diverse range of products.

25.2 ● The principles of open source development

The open source development approach is an extension of the hacker community's attitude to the building of software. The term hacker has been associated with negative aspects of computing. However, hackers are now recognized as a community of highly skilled programmers who relish the act of writing code and participate for enjoyment or to enhance their programming reputation. It is fundamental to the hacker ethic that information and knowledge should be freely shared without restriction because this stimulates collaborative thinking, leading to superior ideas overall.

The same principle is applied in open source development. Rather than the code being confined to a small core of developers, as in proprietary methods, a greater audience facilitates a greater influx of ideas and a greater degree of innovation. It is also believed that because the source code is examined by a larger audience than proprietary software, any imperfections stand a greater chance of being identified and consequently rectified. The sharing of code therefore leads to more reliable code.

Hackers comprise a large portion of the open source development community. Head figures within open source organizations are very often notorious hackers, whose reputation for highly proficient programming strengthens their influence on the open source community.

Because of the openness of the program code, the community has devised its own license agreement for use on products developed as open source. The GNU General Public License (GPL) is a software license which protects its "openness", actually making it illegal for anyone to make the code proprietary or "closed". The GPL restricts private modification to source code without publication and disallows the incorporation of any GPL-covered software into a proprietary program. Some larger open source development projects have devised their own open source licenses, which differ in varying degrees from the GPL. However, the majority of projects still deploy the GPL, particularly most of the founding open source projects and smaller development communities that are not affiliated with proprietary companies.

However, the openness and concept of code sharing does not always mean that open source products are free to buy. Open source is "free as in freedom, not as in free beer". Open source companies do offer their program code for free, most commonly to download from their website. However, they often also sell their software as a complete package, shrink wrapped, sometimes including user manuals and additional help services.

SELF-TEST QUESTION

25.1 What is the primary goal of open source development?

25.2 Can you write and sell software with a GPL license?

25.3 ● The schism within open source development

Whilst there is a common belief in collaboration and openness within the development community, a schism does exist in terms of the motivation and underlying philosophy of open source. The main split is between the Free Software Foundation (FSF) and the Open Source Movement (OSM).

The FSF was founded by Richard Stallman in 1985. This software development community promotes free software projects and places emphasis on the social benefits of working collaboratively. The FSF refer to their software as "freeware", emphasizing the absence of restrictions associated with this type of development. It is intended to be a totally embracing ethic, increasing access to the practice of software development and also the resultant products.

The philosophy of the FSF is that individual freedom should never be compromised and that all individual action should also benefit the wider community. Therefore, whilst individual programmers are encouraged and admired, they are also expected to feed their findings and their skills back into the community of programmers to which they ultimately belong. This is done through the sharing of code and the distribution of good programming practice.

The FSF is absolutely resolute in not allowing any proprietary software to be incorporated into their software and were integral in the creation of the GPL. All their products are covered under the GPL, and they are largely unaffiliated with larger software development companies.

The Open Source Movement is spearheaded by Eric S. Raymond. Their emphasis is on the benefits of open source as a development approach, rather than the moral benefits that can be brought by using this approach. They stress that open source can produce higher-quality software than proprietary software.

The OSM are more willing to collaborate with larger software companies, sometimes including developers of proprietary products. They wish to appeal to the business sector because this enables greater distribution of their product. However, unlike the FSF, greater use of their products is motivated primarily because of the quality, rather than because of the freeness of the software. Forming contracts with larger companies is one way of exposing OSM products to a larger potential market. However, it also means that the product must compete with other commercial package products.

25.4 ● Techniques of open source development

Despite the schism within open source in terms of ethics and philosophy, the development practices principally remain the same between the two.

Within the open source development community, there is often no formal mechanism for gathering initial user requirements. The process often consists of a software requirement that is instigated by a sole developer, with requests for collaboration, targeting the hacker community. The Internet facilitates communication between developers and also the distribution of source code, via the Web, File Transfer Sites and e-mail.

The head developer specifies most requirements. Additional user requirements are either implemented by individual developers themselves via personal modification of the source code, or through a communal process known as "code forking". Code forking occurs when the developer base has alternative requirements or conflicting ideas on how to implement a requirement. The code is seen to "fork" because it is split and each copy of the code is developed in parallel. After this split occurs, the code is irreconcilable and therefore two different products exist, both growing from the same base code. Each fork competes for developer attention, so that the most popular or the most reliable version survives.

The code writing on an open source project is sustained through voluntary contributions. Developers are motivated by the enjoyment of programming, the belief in the sharing of software or their own requirement for the software product. Code is commonly implemented via reuse and most open source projects begin immediately by rewriting the code of existing products, with enhancements and alterations made where necessary. When there is no original from which to copy, a core developer base begins writing the code before offering it to the wider community for critique.

The design of the code is communicated via web-based tools. Sometimes UML diagrams or other cross-reference displays, using hyperlinks to depict the overall structure of the are deployed. However, generally, there is a lack of design documentation within open source products.

An explicit project manager or management group is generally in place on open source projects. They decide on the usefulness and appropriateness of contributions that are made by the wider developer community. They also usually add the patch to the code and therefore act as chief implementer on the project.

Once contributions have been implemented, beta versions of open source products are released. Releases are made frequently, so that the effectiveness of contributions can be tested immediately. Feedback on the latest version is received and contributions again incorporated into the code in a continuous cycle, which continues until the community is satisfied with the eventual outcome. Contributions then slow down or cease.

Development communities and product websites act as sources of support for users of open source software. The websites contain installation tutorials and user forum groups providing technical support. The development community mostly provides these voluntarily.

As an alternative means of support, commercially supported versions of open source software are available to buy. This software is an exact replica of the source code, but is provided with supporting manuals and services. These do not exist for all products and therefore many smaller open source products are only used by technically adept users. However, most of the larger open source projects now have their own commercial subsidiaries.

SELF-TEST QUESTIONS

25.3 What is the main technique of open source development?

25.4 What is the main tool of open source development?

25.5 ● Case study: the GNU/Linux operating system

GNU/Linux is an open source operating system, loosely based upon Unix. It contains over 10 million lines of code and has been developed using over 3,000 major contributors of code throughout 90 countries.

Linus Torvalds, who still oversees the project today, instigated the project in 1991. Torvalds originally began the project because none of the current operating systems served his own requirements. They were either unreliable, too expensive or devoid of the functionality he required. He also feared that another open source operating system, GNU/HURD, was far off completion. He could not wait. Torvalds began to write the kernel for his operating system. He was also motivated by the enjoyment of writing code and claims that he wrote it "just for fun"!

Torvalds targeted developer forums and websites, posting an early release of the kernel and requesting feedback and contributions. Increased contributions and collaborations between GNU/Linux and GNU groups meant that distribution of beta versions was frequent and continuous. The GNU/Linux operating system is licensed under the GPL, ensuring that the source code remains open.

After years of continuous development, GNU/Linux is now a renowned open source operating system, competing on the world market with other commercial and proprietary software companies. What began as a personal project is now widely used and technically reputable. The GNU/Linux software code is still available in its original non-supported format. However, a number of commercial organizations also exist to provide appropriate support for various user markets. GNU/Linux remains in continuous development, often responding to technological advancements.

25.6 ● Discussion

Open source development's most attractive asset is the enormous enthusiasm and passion that resonates throughout the developer community and their building of software. Developers have an unrelenting belief in what they do; voice their pride in their hacker roots; find nothing more fulfilling than the art of programming.

Forking ensures that developer requirements are established and implemented in a democratic process. This means that the requirements of the majority of the development community are satisfied. Similarly, any specific personal modification can be made by individuals, providing that they have the technical ability to implement them.

However, it is worth noting that this process largely ignores non-developer user requirements. The general user does not have the power to register their vote via code implementation; neither can they personally modify their own code.

The reuse of code is an important development approach. However, in the case of open source projects that attempt to rewrite entire systems and applications, a reuse approach can only be facilitated by source code that is not covered by a proprietary license. Liability issues may hinder entire projects because developers may not have legal access to any code that they would like to rewrite. However, the overall expertise of the hacker community usually means that volunteers are willing to take on the alternative and more difficult task of writing entire systems from scratch.

Releasing frequent versions of the software brings benefits of continuous feedback. Whilst the beta code may not contain all the functionality that is required, it means that the developer base can immediately evaluate the code and get a feel for the software. Crucially, the potentially vast audience of testers can immediately begin to track and fix bugs, so that changes can be made incrementally, continuously and at a relatively fast pace.

Inappropriate patches, once incorporated into code can irreparably damage a project. Having an explicit manager on all open source projects means that all contributions are monitored and approved. This ensures that the freedom to contribute is upheld, but lessens the risk of any sabotage attempts.

Open source program code is extremely reliable because bugs are found and fixed by a huge viewing audience with highly proficient programming abilities. Proprietary software corporations are being forced to acknowledge open source development as a valid approach and are beginning to experiment with its techniques. The high viewing audience that can track and fix bugs is seen as an efficient way of "cleaning up" software that is proving to be unreliable. Consequently, some companies have now opened up previously closed code. This suggests that the open source development approach can influence other mainstream techniques.

Contributors to open source projects have a passion for programming, so that writing code is seen as more of a hobby than a chore or a job. They gain enormous satisfaction in seeing their patches integrated into a program. However, because open source projects generally rely upon voluntary contributions, there is always the risk that the community will cease to contribute to the project. This would result in a stagnation of a development project and an unfinished product.

Similarly, the lack of documentation also potentially limits maintenance to the original developer base and lessens the ability of someone else being able to take on the project. If the initial developer base tires of a project, it is not easy for another developer to take on the project without documentation as a means of communicating the design of the program.

The usefulness of informal support mechanisms is questionable, particularly for the general user. Website tutorials are often aimed at a technically adept audience. In addition, since support services are voluntary, there is no guarantee that someone will be available when required and users may have to wait until someone responds to their enquiry.

Summary

Open source development is a collaborative approach relying upon voluntary contributions of program code. It has its roots in a hacker ethic that promotes individual skill, but also upholds the importance of community.

The approach produces extremely reliable software because open source code means bugs are exposed to a vast audience. More bugs are likely to be found and fixed. The regular release of the software also means that program code is continually tested before the final product version is released.

Non-commercial open source is generally deficient in supporting the general user. However, the commercial sector, acknowledging the superiority of the program code, is addressing this problem, providing support services for open source products and adopting open source development techniques.

Exercises

25.1 Can you think of any situations or products for which the open source procedure might be most appropriate?

25.2 Can you think of examples of situations in which open source development of products might be unwise?

25.3 Assess whether open source would be suitable for each of the developments given in Appendix A.

25.4 Compare and contrast the approaches of the Free Software Foundation and the Open Source Movement.

25.5 Is open source development just hacking?

Answers to self-test questions

25.1 Reliable software.

25.2 Yes.

25.3 Code sharing.

25.4 The internet.

 Further reading

This book provides a rare insight into the history of hacking, from its origins at MIT in the 1950s to the rise of open source software: S. Levy, *Hackers: Heroes of the Computer Revolution*, Anchor Books, 2002.

The following title is a comprehensive collection of essays covering topics from licensing issues to the engineering of such major open source products as Mozilla and Perl: *Open Sources: Voices from the Open Source Revolution*, C. DiBona, S. Ockman and M. Stone, O'Reilly, 1st edn, 1999.

This is a very accessible book which depicts the development of the GNU/Linux Operating System, including interviews with major contributors in the open source field: G. Moody, *Rebel Code: Inside Linux and the Open Source Revolution*, Perseus Publishing, 2001.

This is a response to Fred Brooks's seminal proprietary software development text *The Mythical Man Month* (1974). Raymond argues why the open source approach to software development will provide a higher-quality product: E.S. Raymond, *The*

Cathedral and the Bazaar: Musings on Linux and Open Source by an Accidental Revolutionary, O'Reilly, rev. edn, 2001.

Primarily focusing on the life and moral crusade of Stallman, this text also describes the development of GNU project and other projects of the *Free Software Foundation*: S. Williams, *Free as in Freedom: Richard Stallman's Crusade for Free Software*, O'Reilly, 2002.

SourceForge.com is a website that coordinates open source development projects. If you want to contribute to projects, this is the place. The URL is http://www.sourceforge.net

A social scientist's view of open source development, showing how it challenges conventional wisdom: Steven Weber, *The Success of Open Source*, Harvard University Press, 2004.

26

Agile methods and extreme programming

This chapter explains:

- the principles behind agile methods
- the practice of agile methods
- the principles behind extreme programming
- how to carry out extreme programming.

26.1 ● Introduction

Agile methods is a term that embraces a number of techniques that share common principles. These principles are articulated in what is called the agile Manifesto. The principles emerged from an analysis that older methods (referred to as *heavyweight*) were simply too big and unwieldy; that there was a need to use more *lightweight* approaches to development. These new methods explicitly recognize that software development is primarily about individual skill and communication between people (between developers and with the clients). One of the best-known of the methods is named extreme programming (XP), but others are DSDM, SCRUM, Crystal and FDD.

26.2 ● The agile manifesto

The manifesto begins with a statement of four core values:

1. individuals and interactions over process and tools
2. working software over comprehensive documentation
3. customer collaboration over contract negotiation
4. responding to change over following a plan.

These are qualified by the statement that while there is value in the items on the right, the items on the left are valued more. Thus agile methods do not throw out the baby with the bath water; they simply give precedence to certain choices.

The first value recognizes that individual creativity and group collaboration are more effective than following a prescriptive methodology. The second value recognizes that software is code, not the accompanying documentation. The third value recognizes that a good relationship between the clients and the developers is more important than arguing about contracts. The fourth value prioritizes users' changing needs rather than adhering to some meaningless inflexible plan.

Twelve supporting "statements" give guidance on achieving the four core values:

1. our highest priority is to satisfy the customer through early and frequent delivery of software

2. deliver working software frequently, from a couple of weeks to a couple of months, with a preference for the shorter timescale

3. working software is the primary measure of progress

4. welcome changing requirements, even late in development

5. business people and developers work together daily throughout the project

6. build projects around motivated individuals. Give them the environment and support they need, and trust them to get the job done.

7. the most efficient and effective method of conveying information to and within a development team is face-to-face conversation

8. the best architectures, requirements and designs emerge from self-organizing teams

9. continuous attention to technical excellence and good design enhance agility

10. agile processes promote sustainable development. The sponsors, developers, and users should be able to maintain a constant pace indefinitely

11. simplicity – the art of maximizing the amount of work not done – is essential

12. at regular intervals, the team reflects on how to become more effective, then tunes and adjusts its behavior accordingly.

We shall see how these can be put into practice shortly, when we look at extreme programming.

Tools for agile methods

Many people believe that appropriate software tools are vital to successful software projects. Agile methods take an independent attitude to tools and use whatever tools are useful, particularly the simplest tools available. This might mean a computer aided software engineering (CASE) tool but it also includes non-computer tools. Here are examples.

Sketches can be made on paper, using color as appropriate for all sorts of diagrams, informal and more formal (such as UML diagrams). A scanner or digital camera can record the results for computer storage.

A whiteboard and colored pens are useful for drawing diagrams, such as use case diagrams, class diagrams, user interface mock-ups and also informal sketches. It is easy to change the diagram, and it can be viewed collaboratively and discussed by a group of people. A digital camera is a convenient way of capturing the information on a whiteboard.

Index cards and a large table are useful for designing the class structure of software, using CRC (Class–Responsibility–Collaborator) modeling (see Chapter 11). The cards can easily be moved around, changed or removed. Again a digital camera can record the end product.

Sticky notes can be used with a whiteboard or a large sheet of paper to create diagrams during design.

Simple tools such as those mentioned are cheap, portable, quick to use, flexible, assist collaborative working and can be used for communication with the user. On the other hand, simple tools can be limited, are not amenable to computer-assisted checking and do not support distributed working.

26.3 ● Extreme programming

This is perhaps the best-known of the agile methods. Its name conveys something dangerous and foolhardy, but this is far from true. The name instead denotes a radical perspective which is a contrast to heavyweight methods. Centrally, extreme programming (XP) recognizes that requirements continually change and the method embraces the changes, rather than considering them to be disruptive.

Before we look at the values of XP and its full set of techniques, we will explore its principal approaches.

In XP, the client (or a representative) is always present as a member of the development team. This person writes use cases, termed stories in XP. (We met these in Chapter 4 on requirements engineering.) A use case is a small individual function that is required of the software. It is written in English (or another natural language) in non-technical language and typically occupies three sentences. It is a statement of a requirement, not a statement of implementation – what to implement, not how to implement. Thus a use case is a useful fragment of a requirements specification. For each use case, the developers make an estimate of how much effort will be needed for implementation. Because use cases are small, this will typically be a few weeks of person time. A longer estimate means that the use case is too large and needs to be broken down into smaller use cases. Once a use case has been priced, and a decision has been taken to implement it, then the client provides more detailed information about the requirement.

The client specifies acceptance tests for each use case. These are a set of black box (functional) tests to ascertain whether the use case has been implemented correctly. XP uses the term acceptance test, rather than functional test, to emphasize their role in guaranteeing a system that is acceptable to the client. Acceptance tests are automated, so that they can be run repeatedly easily and objectively. A use case has not been successfully implemented until all its acceptance tests have been passed. The client is responsible for checking that tests have ultimately been successful.

Acceptance tests drive the project. They are written before implementation of the use case is begun. They are repeatedly applied before and while the use case is being developed. Initially, of course, the tests fail, but as development proceeds they will be passed one by one, and eventually the implementation is complete. This approach is termed *test-driven development*.

SELF-TEST QUESTION

26.1 Write an acceptance test for a boiling kettle.

The client has a third role. In XP, development takes place incrementally. At any time, only a subset of use cases are selected for implementation. Because the use cases are small, it is possible to estimate with some confidence how long they will take. But usually it is not possible to implement all the use cases at once. It is the client who decides which are implemented next, and which are postponed until later. Usually, the client selects those use cases that meet the most immediate business need.

At the outset of each phase of development (termed a release in XP), the project team (including the client) meet to decide what to do next. It is the client who decides what shall be undertaken next. The information available is:

- the list of use cases, together with estimates of their development times
- the number of developers available.

Ideally a client would like everything done as soon as possible. But the client who is a member of an XP team knows that software cannot be delivered to an acceptable standard in less time than the estimate.

SELF-TEST QUESTION

26.2 What roles does the client take in XP?

XP values

Extreme programming is based on four clearly articulated values:

1. communication
2. simplicity
3. feedback
4. courage.

Maximizing communication between the members of the development team and between the clients and the team is clearly vital in any project. But instead of regarding communication as a problem, XP exploits it, both as a principle and in practice.

Software that has a simple structure (and does the required job) is better than a complex structure. However, XP realizes that achieving simplicity is not easy.

Feedback is about obtaining frequent reliable information about the state of the software as it is being developed, so that any problems can be accommodated. It also describes a relationship between the developers and the client in which the client is immediately aware of the consequences of their requests.

Finally, the most surprising value is courage, which is not a concept that you expect to see in the context of software development. What it means is that the developers must have the courage to throw away code, or even re-design large parts of the architecture, if the need arises. This is dramatically different from the common approach, which attempts to patch up software when it demonstrates faults, minor or serious.

Techniques

Extreme programming uses a combination of 12 techniques (called, in the terminology of XP, practices). The 12 techniques are:

1. *replan frequently* – quickly determine the scope of the next release by resolving business priorities and technical estimates. As reality overtakes the plan, update the plan.

2. *small releases* – put a simple system into production quickly, and then release new versions on a very short cycle

3. *metaphor* – guide all development with a simple shared story of how the whole system works

4. *maintain a simple design* – the system should be designed as simply as possible at any given moment. Extra complexity is removed as soon as it is discovered.

5. *testing* – programmers continually write unit tests, which must run flawlessly for development to continue. Customers write tests demonstrating that features are finished.

6. *refactoring* – programmers restructure the system without changing its behavior to remove duplication, improve communication, simplify or add flexibility.

7. *pair programming* – all production code is written with two programmers at one machine.

8. *collective ownership* – anyone can change any code anywhere in the system at any time.

9. *continuous integration* – integrate and build the system many times a day, and every time a task is completed

10. *avoid overwork* – work no more than 40 hours a week as a rule. Never work overtime a second week in a row.

11. *involve the client* – include a real, live user on the team, available full-time to answer questions

12. *coding standards* – programmers write all code in accordance with rules, emphasizing communication through the code.

SELF-TEST QUESTION

26.3 Which of the techniques suggest that XP is an incremental approach?

Frequent replanning means that the client should decide which function is most important and should therefore be implemented next. The team estimates how long the next stage of the project will take and gains agreement (or not) for it to proceed. This way everyone takes responsibility for the planning.

Pair programming (see Chapter 28 on teams) is a novel idea, which sounds expensive, but in reality saves time and improves quality by harnessing collaboration.

A maximum 40-hour week emphasizes that no good is achieved by continually working too hard. In a conventional project, it is common to resort to overtime to remedy delays. But this is usually a sign that something has gone wrong and the project is at the start of the slippery slope that leads to a disaster. XP avoids the need for desperate measures in two principal ways. First, continual testing prevents unpleasant surprises. Second, frequent releases means that any planning mistakes are quickly evident.

The provision of an on-site customer is quite radical. It stresses that meeting the user requirements is so important that it needs continual special treatment – the permanent involvement of a client representative – which, though time-consuming, saves time overall because reworking is avoided.

The use of coding standards illustrates that some aspects of XP are quite rigorous. Also the code is the paramount product of a project. Emphasis is placed on clear code, rather than auxiliary documentation, such as UML diagrams.

It is important to realize that these techniques complement each other, so that it is sometimes ineffective to use one without another. It is possible, but undesirable to use one of the XP techniques on its own. This is because they complement each other – a weakness in one practice is compensated by strength in another. For example, it would seem expensive in time continually to refactor the design, but the practice of keeping to a simple design ensures that refactoring is easy.

Summary

Agile methods are a range of lightweight techniques that subscribe to the agile manifesto.

XP is one agile method with its own values and techniques. The values are communication, simplicity, feedback and courage. The twelve techniques include pair programming, test-driven development and continual refactoring.

XP makes the coding, rather than any other documentation, the center of the product.

Exercises

26.1 Assess extreme programming.

26.2 Compare and contrast heavyweight methods (in general) with lightweight methods (in general).

26.3 Assess how extreme programming could be used in developing each of the systems described in Appendix A.

26.4 Compare and contrast extreme programming with open source development.

26.5 Assess how well the values and methods of extreme programming match up with those of the agile manifesto.

26.6 "Extreme programming is just hacking". Discuss.

Answers to self-test questions

26.1 The whistle sounds.

26.2 Providing use cases, supplying acceptance tests, verifying that acceptance test have succeeded, deciding what will be implemented next.

26.3 The use of small releases and continuous integration strongly suggest an incremental approach.

 Further reading

Kent Beck, *Extreme Programming Explained*, Addison-Wesley, 2000.

http://www.extremeprogramming.org/index.html

Alistair Cockburn, *Agile Software Development*, Addison-Wesley, 2002.

CHAPTER 27

The unified process

This chapter explains:

- the aims of the unified process
- the techniques involved in the unified process
- how to use the unified process.

27.1 ● Introduction

The unified process (UP) is a process model for developing software. In common with other available process models, it provides an overall plan for a software development project. It also incorporates some recommendations for the techniques to be used as part of the process. The UP provides a general purpose strategy that can be tailored for an individual project – large or small, straightforward or risky.

The UP is sometimes known as the rational unified process or RUP after the company that first promoted it. The word "Rational" was the company name and, of course, it also implies rationality. The "Unified" part of its name derives from the same source as the unified modeling language (UML). The founders of UML, Booch, Rumbaugh and Jacobson, were formerly rivals, but later collaborated (and were then termed the three amigos) to devise UML and the UP. UML is the notation; the UP is the process.

The UP is the most recent process model to be widely used. As we shall see, the UP incorporates many of the ideas we have met in other chapters in this book.

27.2 ● Overview

UP primarily aims to:

- meet user needs
- accommodate risks.

Meeting the user's needs requires no explanation. The second aim of the UP recognizes that there are always risks associated with a development. Examples are changes in user requirements and deadline overruns for components of the software. These can seriously disrupt a project or even cause it to be abandoned.

To meet its aims, the UP makes use of a number of techniques including use cases, iteration and emphasis on the architecture of the software.

A use case describes (in natural language) a small self-contained function that the system provides for the user. A collection of use cases specify the requirements for a system. (Use cases were discussed in Chapter 4 on requirements engineering.)

The UP mechanism for coping with risk is to proceed iteratively. This means that an initial plan is constructed. Then some small amount of development is carried out. Next, the outcome is assessed. In the light of the evaluation, a new plan is devised (or, in the worst case, the project is abandoned).

The UP also emphasizes getting the architecture of the software right. By architecture is meant the grand-scale structure of the software. For example, in a web-based solution, what components run on the server and what components run on the client? What type of database is to be used?

In summary the method makes heavy use of:

■   use cases

■   iteration

■   software architecture.

The UP consists of four phases: inception, elaboration, construction and transition. We will now explore what they involve.

27.3 ● Phases of the UP

The UP consists of four phases: inception, elaboration, construction and transition, as shown in Figure 27.1. We shall see later that within each phase are a number of iterations. The four phases are, in outline:

Phase 1, inception

This consists of a feasibility study to establish whether the proposed system is worthwhile. (We discussed how to carry out feasibility studies in Chapter 3.) An outline of the major requirements is established. A decision is made to commit to the project, or not.

Phase 2, elaboration

During this phase:

■   the list of requirements is completed

■   the general architecture of the system is devised

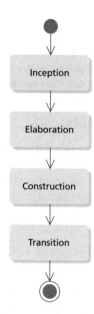

Figure 27.1 The phases of the unified process

- the major risks are identified and assessed
- a plan for the development is drawn up and agreed.

Phase 3, construction

This is the actual system development.

Phase 4, transition

This phase means putting the system into use. This may involve such measures as training or running the new system in parallel with a former system. Other methods call this phase implementation.

Usually the construction phase consumes the most effort, followed by the elaboration phase. Both inception and transition usually take up much less effort.

27.4 ● Techniques

The UP uses several practical techniques designed to ensure successful projects. They are:

Iteration

The UP proceeds in an iterative fashion in order to accommodate ongoing risks. We discuss this in a separate section below.

Use cases

Meeting user's needs is accomplished by employing use cases to record user's functional requirements. Use cases also drive the project – the developers are always aware of the use cases. Use cases are discussed in Chapter 4 on requirements engineering.

Focus on providing executable code

Many projects create pages of documentation – such as specifications, UML diagrams and test schedules – at the expense of working code. The problem is that users do not understand these products and cannot understand how they contribute to the product. The UP emphasizes the overwhelming need to create and show the client demonstrable products.

Establishing a working architecture early on

The architecture is the grand-scale structure of the software. The UP emphasizes the need to devise a good structure early in the development process. Many current applications are internet based and this means that there is usually client software and server software. But there are many options. One option is the balance of work between the client and server. Other options are whether to use applets, servlets, RPC, CGI, ASP, web services, etc. The choice of technologies will be determined by performance, inter-operability, scalability, security, expertise and cost. The decision determines the architecture for the software.

Using components

Using such encapsulated components as Java beans, .Net components or simply classes means that local changes do not disrupt the remainder of the software.

Establishing an effective team

In an effective team, developers communicate effectively and are committed to the project. The UP recommends setting up a single project team, devoted to the project, rather than using a number of functional teams. (These differences are discussed in Chapter 28 on teams.)

Incorporating quality throughout

The main quality goals are to ensure that the software meets its user's needs and works properly. The UP aims to ensure quality by carrying out validation and verification at every cycle.

27.5 ● Iteration

Iteration is a major feature of the UP and it is the mechanism for controlling risks. The UP recognizes that problems (risks) will arise as a project proceeds. Examples are:

- changes to requirements – because they were recorded incorrectly in the first place and because users change and clarify their ideas
- the architecture of the software needs modification
- implementation errors are discovered requiring correction
- difficulty integrating with a legacy system.

If a software project takes large steps, then any problems are hidden for a long time – and their effects can be devastating. If a project employs small steps, each concluding with an evaluation, then progress is more visible and the effects of any changes can be accommodated more easily. Thus the UP accommodates change by taking small steps, repeatedly assessing the cost of changes and making explicit decisions about whether to make changes.

We have seen that the UP consists of four phases. Each of the four phases of the UP consists of one or more iterations. Smaller projects usually require fewer iterations and bigger projects more iterations. Typically the inception phase might employ one iteration, the elaboration phase two, the construction phase three and the transition two. The number of iterations is carefully planned – as is the goal of each iteration. At the end of every iteration, an assessment is carried out.

Each iteration consists of analysis, design, coding and testing. Earlier iterations emphasize analysis and design, while later iterations emphasize coding and testing. Each iteration produces working software that is part of the target system.

27.6 ● Case study

The ATM (Appendix A) is a medium-sized project, network based with many clients and a server. At the outset of a project of this kind, the project manager can identify a number of obvious risks. These threats are anything that might adversely affect the project success, deadline or cost. These might include:

- the specialized devices (e.g. the card reader) do not work according to the specification
- the communications protocol between ATM and server does not function properly
- requirements change
- there is difficulty interfacing with the database on the server.

It is also likely that unforeseen eventualities will occur, for example, late delivery of some of the specialized ATM hardware. However, small iterations mean that damage to the project is controlled and limited.

The inception phase

The goal of this phase is to understand the scope of the project, build a business case and obtain stakeholder agreement.

Understanding the scope involves interviewing the client and recording their requirements. The functional requirements are recorded as use cases and we saw in Chapter 4 on requirements how to accomplish this activity for the ATM system.

Building a business case means carrying out a calculation of the financial costs and benefits, which was outlined (for the ATM) in Chapter 3 on the feasibility study. This calculation reveals that the system is hugely cost effective.

Obtaining stakeholder agreement means checking with the identified groups that they are happy and committed to the project. In the case of the ATM, the stakeholders may include the client, the bank workers, the bank's customers, the senior management of the bank, the bank IT department and relevant public authorities. Let us assume that these various groups are happy for the project to go ahead.

The elaboration phase

This involves completing the statement of requirements, devising the general architecture of the system, identifying and assessing the major risks and drawing up and agreeing a plan for the development.

For the ATM, the user functions can be established and documented as use cases.

For the ATM, a decision about the division of labor between ATM software and server software needs to be made. The protocol for the communication between ATMs and server needs establishing. Then the architecture is checked by constructing a working skeletal system.

Now that the requirements are well established and the architecture is trustworthy, there is greater certainty in the project. However, an assessment is made of any risks to the project and plans made accordingly.

Now, a detailed plan for the remainder of the project can be drawn up.

The construction phase

This phase constitutes the actual construction of the software.

This consists of four iterations. The first is an implementation of the user interface (with no functionality). This establishes that the design of the user interface is acceptable. It also confirms that it will provide the desired functionality.

The second iteration is a program to interface with the database on the server, in order to ascertain that a satisfactory connection can be made, providing the functionality required by the ATM application.

The next iteration is a full implementation of the system, but using only a single ATM. This establishes that the system is technically feasible for a single user.

Finally a multi-user system is constructed.

This account of the four iterations assumes that all goes well. In practice, the assessment at the end of an iteration might reveal that there is a problem. This would need to be solved by such measures as rescheduling the project or using an alternate technology.

The transition phase

This phase means putting the system into use. It involves installing the ATM hardware, the software and communication lines. It means arranging for the ATMs to be serviced, supplied with cash and printer paper. It means installing the server software.

Rather than install a whole number of ATMs at once, it makes sense to install just one in some convenient location to act as a beta test. This first iteration, once successfully concluded, is followed by the installation of multiple ATMs.

27.7 ● Discussion

The UP is not a single process model. It is a framework from which a project manager can select a process model suitable for a particular project. So the model can be applied to large and small projects, involving a few developers or many.

Summary

The UP is a process model that primarily aims to:

- meet user requirements
- accommodate risks.

The process consists of four phases:

1. inception
2. elaboration
3. construction
4. transition.

Each phase consists of one or more iterations. Each iteration consists of analysis, design, coding and testing. The purpose of iteration is to accommodate risks.

The UP employs a number of techniques:

- iteration
- use cases
- focus on providing executable code
- establishing a working architecture early on
- using components
- establishing an effective team
- incorporating quality throughout.

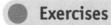 **Exercises**

27.1 Assess the UP.

27.2 Compare and contrast the UP with the waterfall model, extreme programming and the spiral model.

27.3 Create an outline plan for developing each of the systems in Appendix A, using the UP.

27.4 Evaluate the UP using the following criteria:

- capability to accommodate risk
- capability to meet user requirements
- capability to respond to changed requirements
- visibility of the progress of the project.

27.5 Identify the main goals and the main techniques of each of the following process models:

- waterfall
- spiral
- prototyping
- incremental
- open source
- XP
- UP.

Further reading

The following book clearly explains the RUP. It also compares it with waterfall, agile methods and heavyweight approaches: Per Kroll and Philippe Kruchten, *The Rational Unified Process Made Easy*, Addison-Wesley, 2003.

Another straightforward read: Philippe Kruchten, *The Rational Unified Process, an Introduction*, Addison-Wesley, 3rd edn, 2004.

PROJECT MANAGEMENT

28 Teams

This chapter explains:

- the principles behind team working
- how functional teams and project teams operate
- how the chief programmer team operates.

28.1 ● Introduction

Software developers seldom work alone. More commonly, several developers share an office, working on different projects or collaborating on larger projects. The process of establishing requirements usually involves significant face-to-face meetings. So software development is essentially a social activity.

This chapter is about structures that are formally set up to organize a team or group of software developers.

We begin by analyzing some of the problems of group work. We go on to explain techniques for software team organization – functional teams, project teams, chief programmer teams and OO teams.

28.2 ● The principles of teams

Two major aspects of team activity are:

1. the communication between the people in the team
2. deciding who does what work.

These issues are now discussed in turn.

The communication problem

When two or more people are working on a piece of software, they obviously have to liaise with each other. At the very least they have to communicate component specifications – component names, component functions, parameter types, and so on. Often such interfaces are complex, perhaps involving detailed file layouts. Always there are queries, because of the difficulty of specifying interfaces precisely. During the lifetime of a project someone always leaves, is ill or goes on holiday. Someone has to sort out the work in their absence. New people join the team and have to be helped to understand what the software is for, what has been done and why the structure is as it is. They may need to learn about the standards and procedures being used on the project, or even learn a new programming language. This induction of a new person takes up the time of those who remain.

All this adds up to a great deal of time spent in communication that would not be necessary if only a single person were developing the software. Adding two people to a team of four does not increase the communication overhead by half – it more than doubles it. Clearly, as more and more people are added to a team, the time taken in liaising can completely swamp a project.

Compare the activity of picking potatoes. Imagine a large field with a relatively small number of people. They can each get on with the job without getting in each other's way. If we increase the number of people, the work will get done proportionately quickly, at least until there are so many people that they are tripping each other up. The graph of potatoes picked against people employed looks like Figure 28.1.

If we now turn to the task of having a baby, we realize that increasing the number of people will do nothing to the timescale – it remains nine months. The graph is shown in Figure 28.2.

Software development comes somewhere between these two extremes. Initially, if we increase the number of people, the job will get done faster (like the potato picking). But, eventually, the communication overheads will become overwhelming, and the project will actually slow down. The graph looks like Figure 28.3.

One of the gurus of computing, Frederick P. Brooks, has described this problem as follows: if a project is late, then adding further people will only make it even later.

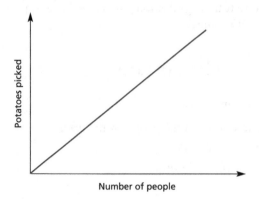

Figure 28.1 Picking potatoes

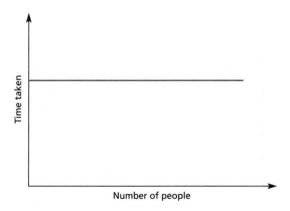

Figure 28.2 Having a baby

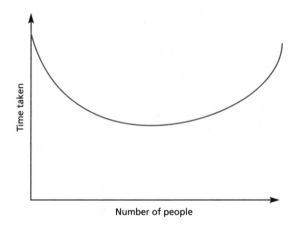

Figure 28.3 Typical software development

To make matters worse, human beings are not well known for precise communication with each other. It is therefore likely that there will be faults in a system constructed by a team.

The division of labor

The second major question in team organization is deciding how to break down the large task into smaller tasks so that several people can carry them out. Developers carry out a whole variety of tasks, some of which, like design, are challenging and others, like keying corrections or filing listings, are less demanding. One way of dividing the work of software development amongst a set of people is to expect everyone to do a mix of tasks. Another approach is to separate out tasks that require different degrees of skill so that, for example, one person does all the design and another all the keying in of test data. This principle of the division of labor has long been recognized.

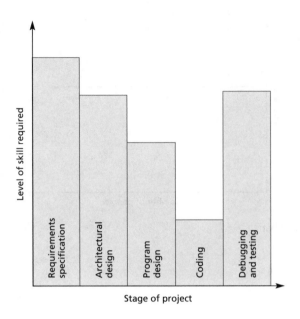

Figure 28.4 Skill requirements at each stage of a project

Figure 28.4 illustrates a (controversial) conjecture about the differing skills involved during the development of software.

Creating specialist roles has several advantages. First, it means that each person becomes an expert, highly skilled and productive at the particular task. Another feature of this type of organization is that instead of paying several highly skilled people uniformly high wages, management can pay people who have different skills different salaries. Overall the wages of the people with unequal skills will be lower than those of the skilled people. Thus the wages bill is reduced. To give a crude example, it would be cheaper to employ a programmer at $50,000 and a designer at $100,000, rather than employ two designer/programmers each at $180,000. It is no coincidence that Charles Babbage, one of the founding fathers of computing, was well aware of this effect.

SELF-TEST QUESTION

28.1 Identify the different roles of the workers in the kitchen of a restaurant.

In summary, specialization offers:

1. greater productivity, since the team member does just one type of work and becomes very skilled at it

2. the chance to pay the different team members according to the separate skills involved in their work, rather than pay everyone at the same rate for the most highly skilled work.

As we shall see, some techniques exploit this principle of the division of labor.

How are teams usually organized? There are two common methods of organizing teams involved in software development – functional teams and project teams.

28.3 ● The functional team

In the *functional team* organization, all the members of the team carry out the same type of work, so that there is a team of programmers, a team of analysts, a team of testers, and so on. At any one time, the members of a team are working on different projects; the work of a single project is carried out by people from different teams.

A major problem of functional teams is that the people who are working on a single project are not a cohesive team. They may even be physically separated in different offices. Close and easy communication is inhibited.

Another problem of the functional team is that the person responsible for a project is not the manager or leader of the people working on his or her project. Thus he or she may not have as much control over them as they would like.

28.4 ● The project team

In a *project team*, everyone in the team is engaged on developing the same system. The team therefore usually consists of people who carry out all the work of the development – requirements analysis, programming, testing and so on. Initially, a team of this kind consists of only a single person. As requirements engineering gets under way, the team grows to two or three people. When the project is fully under way, during coding and testing, it expands to its maximum. Towards the end of the project, members leave the team until finally it is disbanded. The project manager is usually a member of the team, and in control of the team.

The drawback of a project team is that its membership waxes and wanes as the demands of the project change. Initially only one or two people may carry out analysis and architectural design. During implementation the numbers grow to full strength. Then, towards the end, when the system is being put into operation, the numbers diminish.

28.5 ● The chief programmer team

The *chief programmer team* is a project-based organization in which specialization is implemented in an extreme form. The principles behind the chief programmer team organization are:

- to divide the work amongst skilled specialists.
- to structure the team in a well-defined way so that each individual's role is clear and communication is minimized.

A chief programmer team is like a surgical team in which the chief surgeon is assisted by an assistant surgeon, an anesthetist, and one or two nurses. Each team member is a highly trained specialist. In the chief programmer team the job titles are chief programmer, back-up programmer, librarian and other specialist programmers as and when necessary.

The roles of the team members are as follows

Chief programmer

This is a highly skilled software engineer who produces the crucial parts of the system. It is usually the designer of the software who determines and specifies the architectural components of the software.

The chief programmer specifies all the other components in the system and oversees the integration or system testing of the complete system.

The chief programmer's role is intended to be almost entirely a technical one. To this end, administrative affairs like reporting to management and monitoring budgets and timescales are dealt with by a project manager. This frees the chief programmer from non-technical matters. The project manager is not really part of the team and will usually deal with the administrative aspects of several teams.

Back-up programmer

This is a programmer whose skill is comparable to that of the chief programmer. The job is to help the chief programmer with his or her tasks and act as the chief programmer when the latter is absent for any reason. Should the chief programmer leave the organization, the back-up programmer can immediately take over.

Librarian

The librarian maintains the documentation associated with the project. He or she may be a secretary with some training in using a computer system.

Other specialist programmers

When needed, other programmers are brought into the team to develop any subsystems specified by the chief programmer. Each of these programmers is an expert in a particular software area, such as user interfacing, databases or graphics.

The structure of the team is hierarchical, with the chief programmer at the top. In contrast to a network of people each of whom communicates with everyone else, the hierarchy restricts information so that it flows along far fewer paths – only up and down the hierarchy. The use of structured programming (Chapter 7) and top-down implementation and testing (Chapter 24), both of which are hierarchical, complement this scheme very neatly.

There can be no doubt that the technique of the chief programmer team represents a creative application of scientific management to team programming.

The benefits of the chief programmer team to the organization are thus:

(a) improved programmer productivity because

- less time is spent in communication
- each programmer is carrying out specialized work at which they are highly skilled

(b) improved software quality because

- the team is organized around a highly skilled programmer
- the interfaces between software components are clearer
- fewer bugs arise from communication problems because there are fewer programmers

(c) meeting deadlines more reliably because

- there is greater visibility of the project through the high technical involvement of the chief programmer.

Other benefits that are cited concern career paths. Someone who is a good programmer but does not want to go into management can become a chief programmer – largely a technical role.

A number of problems arise for the management of a large project. First, since any team is only manageable with up to about nine people, what do we do if a project is sufficiently large that it needs more than this number? One suggestion (but it is only that) is to start the project with a chief programmer team to carry out the high-level software design and the top-level implementation. When this is complete the original team is broken up and its members become chief programmers within the set of teams that carry out developments of the subsystems. A remnant of the original team carries out system integration and validation.

Another problem of chief programmer team organization is this: the team is supposed to be made up of good experienced programmers, so how do inexperienced programmers gain expertise? Here the suggestion is that they train by doing maintenance on existing programs.

28.6 ● The object-oriented team

Object-oriented development tries to achieve two objectives:

- reuse of existing components from either the standard library or the in-house library
- the creation of new reuseable components for the in-house library.

Thus, organizations using the object-oriented paradigm have found it desirable to divide their personnel into teams of application programmers on the one hand, and teams of class or component programmers on the other. The motivation here is that the benefits of the object-oriented paradigm are only be realized if a concerted effort is made to identify reusable software components and to organize such components within an accessible library. A domain-specific class library becomes viewed as one of the major assets of the organization. Indeed, some large companies have reported that they have been able to reduce the amount of new code written on large projects by a factor of 50% through the use of such libraries.

In such a scenario, application programmers are thought of as *consumers*; they implement application-specific classes, but are always seeking to reuse existing library components whenever possible. They seek better reusable components from the class programmers and also have a responsibility to identify useful abstractions that can be migrated from the application to the library.

Class programmers (or component developers) are thought of as *producers*; they produce reusable components of general use to the organization. Their job is to polish, generalize, reorganize and augment library classes. Their task should not be underestimated – producing reusable components is more difficult than writing components for a specific project.

In a moderate-size project the developers are divided up along class versus application lines. The architecture team contains the key designers and programmers; their responsibility is to oversee the project as a whole and also to take responsibility for critical modules of the system. They are supported by teams of subsystem developers who are responsible for the development of "large grain" subsystems. The class developers are responsible for the development of a reusable component library. This kind of approach has given rise to a plethora of new job titles and functions, for example, application directors, class managers, reuse evaluators.

The key to the success of such an approach is communication between team members, particularly between the architecture/subsystem teams and the component developers. It is highly desirable to develop a culture in which team members are rewarded for producing components that have a broad applicability or design frameworks that can be reused.

28.7 ● Discussion

The chief programmer team is hierarchical and tree-structured. Its organizational structure tends to produce software that has a matching structure. This may be completely appropriate for certain types of software. Indeed, much software is hierarchical in structure. Generalizing, it can be hypothesized that teams tend to produce software whose structure matches their own structure. Suppose, for example, that some software is designed by a committee, acting democratically. What would the structure of the software look like? Perhaps it would be complex, with many interactions (reflecting the many interactions between its designers) or perhaps it would display haphazard structure, without the single clear vision provided by a charismatic leader. But for certain types of software – for example, expert systems – these structures might be completely appropriate. Thus it may be that different forms of organization are appropriate for different types of software project.

Summary

There are two major issues associated with organizing a team that has been set up to develop a piece of software. One is preventing the overhead of communication between team members from overwhelming the project. The second is deciding how the work should be divided amongst the members of the team.

A project team develops a single project while a functional team does specialized work for a number of projects.

The idea of the chief programmer team is to use a few specialized people, each performing a well-defined task within a hierarchical organization with minimal communication paths. Thus the number of people in the team is reduced and the communication overhead controlled.

An objected-oriented team tries to develop reusable software for the current and future projects.

 Exercises

28.1 Investigate the importance of the time taken in communicating within a team. Assume initially that there are four people in a team. Each is capable of developing 3,000 lines of code per year left to themselves. However, 250 lines per year are sacrificed for each communication path to or from an individual. Assume that the team is organized so that everyone needs to discuss problems with everyone else.

    Calculate the productivity (lines of code per year) of each member of the team and investigate how it changes as the team expands to five and then to six members.

28.2 Carry out the same calculations assuming that a chief programmer team is in operation. (In this case each member of the team communicates only with the chief programmer.)

28.3 Compare and contrast the conventional project team organization with that of a chief programmer team.

28.4 Assess the chief programmer team organization.

28.5 Compare and contrast the functional team with the project team organization.

28.6 Assess the OO team organization suggested in this chapter.

Answer to self-test question

28.1 Head chef, assistant chef, salad chef, pudding chef, kitchen porter.

Further reading

The following book is largely concerned with describing the management of software development. Parts of the book describe how to organize teams of programmers: J.D. Aron, *The Program Development Process, Part II, The Programming Team*, Addison-Wesley, 1983.

This classic book contains fascinating sections about the problems of developing large-scale software, using a team of people. There is a section on chief programmer teams: F.P. Brooks, *The Mythical Man-Month*, Addison-Wesley, 1995.

CHAPTER 29

Software metrics and quality assurance

This chapter:

- explains the nature of metrics
- explains the concept of a complexity metric
- reviews reliability metrics and how to estimate bugs
- explains the meaning of the terms quality and quality assurance
- explains how to prepare a quality assurance plan for a project.

29.1 ● Introduction

The issue of quality and quality assurance has become generally important throughout the industrialized world. It has become particularly important for software because of the increasing reliance of business on software and because of the notorious reputation that software enjoys. As a minimum, software is of good *quality* if it:

- meets its users needs
- is reliable (i.e. it does not fail)
- is easy to maintain (i.e. to correct or change).

There are, of course, other factors involved in quality which we will review shortly.

Quality assurance means the measures that are taken to ensure that software is of good quality.

A vital aspect of quality is measurement. In software engineering, measures are termed metrics. A *metric* is a measure, such as cost or size, that can be applied to software. Metrics can be obtained and applied throughout the software development process. Metrics address issues like:

- how big will the software be?
- how complex is this component?
- how reliable is this software?

- how much will this software cost?
- how much effort will be needed to alter this software to meet changed needs.

In this chapter we review various ways of applying metrics to software. The purposes of metrics in software engineering include:

- predicting qualities of software that is about to be developed
- making judgments on the quality of a piece of software that has been developed
- monitoring and improving the software development process
- comparing and assessing different development approaches.

In this chapter we first review metrics, then look at the application of quality assurance.

29.2 ● Basic metrics

The simplest measure of software is its size. Two possible metrics are the size in bytes and the size in number of statements. The size in statements is often termed LOCs (lines of code), sometimes SLOCs (source lines of code). The size in bytes obviously affects the main memory and disk space requirements and affects performance. The size measured in statements relates to development effort and maintenance costs. But a longer program does not necessarily take longer to develop than a shorter program, because the complexity of the software also has an effect. A metric such as LOCs takes no account of complexity. (We shall see shortly how complexity can be measured.)

There are different ways of interpreting even a simple metric like LOCs, since it is possible to exclude, or include, comments, data declaration statements, and so on. Arguably, blank lines are not included in the count.

The second major metric is person months, a measure of developer effort. Since people's time is the major factor in software development, person months usually determine cost. If an organization measures the development time for components, the information can be used to predict the time of future developments. It can also be used to gauge the effectiveness of new techniques that are used.

The third basic metric is the number of bugs. As a component is being developed, a log can be kept of the bugs that are found. In week 1 there might be 27, in week 2 there might be 13, and so on. As we shall see later, this helps predict how many bugs remain at the end of the development. These figures can also be used to assess how good new techniques are.

Collecting and documenting quality information can be seen as threatening to developers but a supportive culture can help.

29.3 ● Complexity metrics

In the early days of programming, main memory was small and processors were slow. It was considered normal to try hard to make programs efficient. One effect of this was that programmers often used tricks. Nowadays the situation is rather different – the pressure is on to reduce the development time of programs and ease the burden of maintenance. So the emphasis is on writing programs that are clear and simple, and therefore easy to check, understand and modify.

What are the arguments for simplicity?

- it is quicker to debug simple software
- it is quicker to test simple software
- simple software is more likely to be reliable
- it is quicker to modify simple software.

If we look at the world of design engineering, a good engineer insists on maintaining a complete understanding and control over every aspect of the project. The more difficult the project the more firmly the insistence on simplicity – without it no one can understand what is going on. Software designers and programmers have sometimes been accused of exhibiting the exact opposite characteristic; they deliberately avoid simple solutions and gain satisfaction from the complexities of their designs.

However, many software designers and programmers today strive to make their software as clear and simple as possible. A programmer finishes a program and is satisfied both that it works correctly and that it is clearly written. But how do we know that it is clear? Is a shorter program necessarily simpler than a longer one (that achieves the same end), or is a heavily nested program simpler than an equivalent program without nesting?

Arguably what we perceive as clarity or complexity is an issue for psychology. It is concerned with how the brain works. We cannot establish a measure of complexity – for example, the number of statements in a program – without investigating how such a measure corresponds with programmers' perceptions and experiences. We now describe one attempt to establish a meaningful measure of complexity. One aim of such work is to guide programmers in selecting clear program structures and rejecting unclear structures, either during design or afterwards.

The approach taken is to hypothesize about what factors affect program complexity. For example, we might conjecture that program length, the number of alternative paths through the program and the number of references to data might all affect complexity. We could perhaps invent a formula that allows us to calculate the overall complexity of a program from these constituent factors. The next step is to verify the hypothesis. How well does the formula match up with reality? What correlation is there between the complexity as computed from the formula and, for example, the time it takes to write or to understand the program?

Amongst several attempts to measure complexity is McCabe's cyclomatic complexity. McCabe suggests that complexity does not depend on the number of statements. Instead it depends only on the decision structure of the program – the number of **if**, **while** and similar statements. To calculate the cyclomatic complexity of a program, count the number of conditions and add one. For example, the program fragment:

```
x = y;
if (a == b)
    c = d;
else
    e = f;
p = q
```

has a complexity of 2, because there are two independent paths through the program. Similarly a **while** and a **repeat** each count one towards the complexity count. Compound conditions like:

```
if a > b and c > d then
```

count two because this **if** statement could be rewritten as two, nested **if** statements. Note that a program that consists only of a sequence of statements, has a cyclomatic complexity of 1, however long it is. Thus the smallest value of this metric is 1.

There are two ways of using McCabe's measure. First, if we had two algorithms that solve the same problem, we could use this measure to select the simpler. Second, McCabe suggests that if the cyclomatic complexity of a component is greater than 10, then it is too complex. In such a case, it should either be rewritten or else broken down into several smaller components.

Cyclomatic complexity is a useful attempt to quantify complexity, and it is claimed that it has been successfully applied. It is, however, open to several criticisms as follows.

First, why is the value of 10 adopted as the limit? This figure for the maximum allowed complexity is somewhat arbitrary and unscientific.

Second, the measure makes no allowance for the sheer length of a module, so that a one-page module (with no decisions) is rated as equally complex as a thousand-page module (with no decisions).

Third, the measure depends only on control flow, ignoring, for example, references to data. One program might only act upon a few items of data, while another might involve operations on a variety of complex objects. (Indirect references to data, say via pointers, are an extreme case.)

Finally, there is no evidence to fully correlate McCabe's measure with the complexity of a module as perceived by human beings.

So McCabe's measure is a crude attempt to quantify the complexity of a software component. But it suffers from obvious flaws and there are various suggestions for devising an improved measure. However, McCabe's complexity measure has become famous and influential as a starting point for work on metrics.

SELF-TEST QUESTION

29.1 Suggest a formula for calculating the complexity of a piece of program.

A valid complexity measure can potentially help software developers in the following ways:

- in estimating the effort needed in maintaining a component
- in selecting the simplest design from amongst several candidates
- in signaling when a component is too complex and therefore is in need of restructuring or subdivision.

29.4 ● Faults and reliability – estimating bugs

The terminology adopted in this book is that a human error in developing software causes a fault (a bug) which may then cause a failure of the system (or several different failures). We have seen in Chapter 19 on testing that every significant piece of software contains faults. Therefore if we are buying a piece of software it makes sense to ask the supplier to tell us how many faults there are. If they respond by saying that there are none, then they are either lying or incompetent. Similarly if we have developed a piece of software, it would be professional (if we are honest) to be able to tell users how many (estimated) faults there are and thus give the users some idea of the expected reliability.

A commonly used metric for faults is *fault density*, which is the estimated number of faults per 1,000 lines of code. Faults are detected both during verification and during normal use after the software is put into productive use. Some faults are, of course, corrected and therefore do not count towards the fault density. We must not forget that, in addition to known faults, there are faults that are present but undetected. In commercially written software, there is an enormous variation in fault densities – figures observed are between 2 and 50 faults per KLOC (kilo lines of code). A figure of 2 is rated highly creditable. The fault density metric is useful in assessing the effectiveness of verification methods and as a measure of correctness (see below) in quality assurance.

Experimental studies suggest that most faults cause only rare failures, whereas a small number of faults cause most of the failures. Thus it is more cost-effective to fix the small number of faults which cause most of the trouble – if they can be found.

It would seem to be impossible to gauge how many faults remain in a thoroughly tested system. After all if we knew what faults there are, we could correct them. One technique arises from the earth sciences. How do you find out how many fish there are in a lake? It would be costly (and kill many fish) to drain the lake. An alternative is to insert additional, specially marked fish into the lake. These could be fish of a different breed or slightly radioactive fish. After waiting a sufficient time for the fish to mix thoroughly, we catch a number of fish. We measure the proportion of specially marked fish, and, knowing the original number of special fish, scale up to find the total number of fish. We can do the same thing in software by deliberately putting in artificial faults into the software some time before testing is complete. By measuring the ratio of artificial to real faults detected, we can calculate the number of remaining real faults. Clearly this technique depends on the ability to create faults that are of a similar type to the actual faults.

One major problem with utilizing the fault density metric is that, as we have just seen, some bugs are more significant than others. Thus a more useful metric for users of a system is *mean time to failure* (MTTF). This is the average time for a system to perform without failing. This can be measured simply by logging the times at which failures occur and simply calculating the average time between successive failures. This then gives a prediction for the future failure rate of the system.

29.5 ● Software quality

How do you know when you have produced good-quality software? There are two ways of going about it:

- measuring the attributes of software that has been developed (quality control)
- monitoring and controlling the process of development of the software (quality assurance).

Let us compare developing software with preparing a meal, so that we can visualize these options more clearly. If we prepare a meal (somehow) and then serve it up, we will get ample comments on its quality. The consumers will assess a number of factors such as the taste, color and temperature. But by then it is too late to do anything about the quality. Just about the only action that could be taken is to prepare further meals, rejecting them until the consumers are satisfied. We can now appreciate a commonly used definition of quality:

> *a product which fulfills and continues to meet the purpose for which it was produced is a quality product.*

There is an alternative course of action: it is to ensure that at each stage of preparation and cooking everything is in order. So we:

1. buy the ingredients and make sure that they are all fresh
2. wash the ingredients and check that they are clean
3. chop the ingredients and check that they are chopped to the correct size
4. monitor the cooking time.

At each stage we can correct a fault if something has been done incorrectly. For example, we buy new ingredients if, on inspection, they turn out not to be fresh. We wash the ingredients again if they are not clean enough. Thus the quality of the final meal can be ensured by carrying out checks and remedial action if necessary throughout the preparation. Putting this into the jargon of software development, the quality can be assured provided that the process is assured.

For preparing the meal we also need a good recipe – one that can be carried out accurately and delivers well-defined products at every stage. This corresponds to using good tools and methods during software development.

Here is a commonly used list of desirable software qualities. It corresponds to factors like taste, color, texture and nutritional value in food preparation. The list is designed to encompass the complete range of attributes associated with software, except the cost of construction.

- *correctness* – the extent to which the software meets its specification and meets its users' requirements
- *reliability* – the degree to which the software continues to work without failing
- *performance* – the amount of main memory and processor time that the software uses
- *integrity* – the degree to which the software enforces control over access to information by users
- *usability* – the ease of use of the software
- *maintainability* – the effort required to find and fix a fault
- *flexibility* – the effort required to change the software to meet changed requirements
- *testability* – the effort required to test the software effectively
- *portability* – the effort required to transfer the software to a different hardware and/or software platform
- *reusability* – the extent to which the software (or a component within it) can be reused within some other software
- *interoperability* – the effort required to make the software work in conjunction with some other software
- *security* – the extent to which the software is safe from external sabotage that may damage it and impair its use.

These attributes are related to the set of goals discussed in Chapter 1. As we saw, some of these qualities can be mutually contradictory, for example, if high performance is required, portability will probably suffer. Also, not every attribute is desired in every piece of software. So for each project it is important to identify the salient factors before development starts.

SELF-TEST QUESTION

29.2 Software is to be developed to control a fly-by-wire airplane. What are likely to be the important factors?

This list of quality factors can be used in one or more of the following situations:

1. at the outset of a software development, to clarify the goals
2. during development, to guide the development process towards the goals
3. on completion, to assess the completed piece of software.

The above quality attributes are, of course, only qualitative (rather than quantitative) measures. And as we have seen earlier in this chapter, the purpose of metrics is to quantify desirable or interesting qualities. Thus a complexity measure, such as McCabe's, can be used to measure maintainability. Reliability can be measured as MTTF. However, for many of these attributes, it is extremely difficult to make an accurate judgment and a subjective guess must suffice – with all its uncertainties.

SELF-TEST QUESTION

29.3 List some other quality factors that can be quantified.

29.6 ● Quality assurance

Quality assurance means ensuring that a software system meets its quality goals. The goals differ from one project to another. They must be clear and can be selected from the list of quality factors we saw earlier. To achieve its goals, a project must use effective tools and methods. Also checks must be carried out during the development process at every available opportunity to see that the process is being carried out correctly.

To ensure that effective tools and methods are being used, an organization distills its best practices and documents them in a *quality manual*. This is like a library of all the effective tools, methods and notations. It is like a recipe book in cooking, except that it contains only the very best recipes. This manual describes all the standards and procedures that are available to be used.

A *standard* defines a range, limit, tolerance or norm of some measurable attribute against which compliance can be judged. For example, during white box testing, every source code statement must be executed at least once. In the kitchen, all peeled potatoes must be inspected to ensure there is no skin remaining on them.

A *procedure* prescribes a way of doing something (rules, steps, guidelines, plans). For example, black box testing, white box testing and a walkthrough must be used to verify each component of software. In the kitchen, all green vegetables will be steamed, rather than boiled.

To be effective, quality assurance must be planned in advance – along with the planning of all other aspects of a software project. The project manager:

1. decides which quality factors are important for the particular project (e.g. high reliability and maintainability). In preparing a family meal, perhaps flavor and nutritional value are the paramount goals.

2. selects standards and procedures from the quality manual that are appropriate to meeting the quality goals (e.g. the use of complexity metrics to check maintainability). If the meal does not involve potatoes, then those parts of the quality manual that deal with potatoes can be omitted.

3. assembles these into a *quality assurance plan* for the project. This describes what the procedures and standards are, when they will be done, and who does them.

More and more the organizations that produce software are having to convince their customers that they are using effective methods. More and more commonly they must specify what methods they are using. In addition, the organization must demonstrate that they are using the methods. Thus an organization must not only use sound methods but must be seen to be using them. Therefore a quality plan describes a number of *quality controls*. A quality control is an activity that checks that the project's quality factors are being achieved and produces some documentary evidence. In the kitchen, an example is an inspection carried out after potatoes have been peeled. The documentary evidence is the signature of the chief cook on a checklist recording that this has been done. These documents are then available to anyone – such as the customer – with an interest in checking that the quality of the product is assured. Depending on the quality factors for the project, quality controls might include:

Action	Document	Factor being checked
Collect a complexity metric for each component in the system	Data on complexity	Maintainability
Component test	Test result	Correctness
Walkthrough to examine component for re-usability	Minutes of walkthrough	Reusability

SELF-TEST QUESTION

29.4 What quality factors would the measurement of fault density help achieve?

29.7 ● Process improvement

We have seen how quality can be measured, attained and ensured. A more ambitious goal is to improve quality. One perspective on improving quality is suggested by W. Edwards Deming, an influential management guru, who suggests that processes can be *continuously* improved. In his approach, the work processes are subject to continuous examination by the workers themselves as well as the organization in order to see how things can be done better.

So, for example, suppose that the number of faults discovered during testing is measured. But simply measuring does not achieve anything; measurements may help to ensure repeatability, but this is not the same as improvement. To improve the process, someone looks at how and why the faults were caused and what can be done to improve the processes. So, for example, it might be that a significant number of faults arise because of lack of clarity in module specifications. Therefore, to improve the process it might be decided that module specifications should be subject to walkthroughs before they are used. Alternatively it might be suggested that a more formal notation is to be used for documenting module specifications. After any changes have been made, measurements are continued, and the search goes on for further improvements. Deming suggests that improvements can continue to be made indefinitely.

Deming argues that quality improvements of this type benefit everyone:

- workers, because they can take control and pride in their work
- organizations, because they can make increased profits
- customers, because they get better quality.

29.8 ● The Capability Maturity Model

The Capability Maturity Model (CMM) is a grading system that measures how good an organization is at software development. This scheme specifies five levels, ranging from level 1 (bad) to level 5 (good). An organization's ranking is determined by questionnaires administered by the Software Engineering Institute of Carnegie Mellon University, USA. The levels are:

- *Level 1, initial* – the development process is ad hoc and even, occasionally, chaotic. Few processes are defined and the success of any project depends on effort by individuals. Thus the organization survives through the actions of individual heroes and heroines who help ensure some success in spite of the way that the organization is run.

- *Level 2, repeatable* – basic project management processes are established within the organization to track cost, schedule and functionality. The processes enable the organization to repeat its success obtained with earlier, similar applications.

- *Level 3, defined* – the development process for both management and software engineering activities is documented, standardized and integrated into an organization-wide development process. All projects use an approved and documented version of the standard process. This level includes all the characteristics defined for level 2.

- *Level 4, managed* – detailed measures of the development process and of the software product are collected. Both are quantitative and measured in a controlled fashion. This level includes all the characteristics defined for level 3.

- *Level 5, optimizing* – measurements are continuously used to improve the process. New techniques and tools are used and tested. This level includes all the characteristics defined for level 4.

Any particular development organization will typically use a mix of good and bad practice and so the level achieved is the average for the organization. An organization with a good rating can clearly advertise the fact to get increased business. If an organization, or individual, is buying or commissioning software, it is clearly better to buy from a CMM level 5 software development organization, who will probably supply better software and not necessarily at a more expensive price. Indeed, the evidence is that an organization that uses better methods achieves higher quality software at a lower cost.

Summary

Metrics support software engineering in several ways:

1. they help us decide what to do during the act of design, guiding us to software that is clear, simple and flexible.
2. they provide us with criteria for assessing the quality of software
3. they can help in predicting development effort
4. they help choose between methods
5. they help improve working practices.

Software complexity can be measured using McCabe's cyclomatic complexity measure, which is based upon the number of decisions within the software.

Coupling and cohesion are qualitative terms that describe the character of the interaction between modules and within modules, respectively. These are described in Chapter 6 on modularity.

Correctness can be measured using fault density as a metric. Reliability can be measured using MTTF as a metric.

The quality goals for a project can be clarified using a list of factors.

Quality assurance is the application of a plan involving procedures, standards and quality factors to ensure software quality.

The CMM is a classification scheme to assess an organization's ability to develop quality software.

Exercises

29.1 Write down two different programs to search a table for a desired element. Calculate the cyclomatic complexity of each and hence compare them from the point of view of clarity.

29.2 What factors do you think affect program complexity? What is wrong with McCabe's approach to calculating complexity? Devise a scheme for calculating a satisfactory complexity measure.

29.3 Devise a plan to measure faults and failures revealed during the course of a software development project. How could this data be used?

29.4 Compare the list of software quality factors identified above in the text with the list of software engineering goals given in Chapter 1.

29.5 Suggest appropriate quality factors for each of the software systems described in Appendix A.

29.6 It is common practice for software development organizations to lay down standards for coding. Suggest a number of coding standards for a programming language of your choice. Suggest quality factors that are enhanced by adherence to the standards.

29.7 Suggest a quality assurance plan for each of the software development projects listed in Appendix A. Assume that each project will use the waterfall model as its process model.

Answers to self-test questions

29.1 There are many possible suggestions. One formula that builds on McCabe, but takes some account of references to data is:

complexity = number of decisions + (number of data references – number of statements)

This has the characteristic that if each statement refers to one data item only, the second term is zero.

29.2 Correctness and reliability.

29.3 Cost, size.

29.4 Correctness, reliability.

● Further reading

A most comprehensive and readable book is: N.E. Fenton and S. Lawrence Pfleeger, *Software Metrics: A Rigorous and Practical Approach*, International Thomson Computer Press, 1996.

McCabe's famous original cyclomatic complexity is described in this paper: J.T. McCabe, A complexity measure, *IEEE Transactions on Software Engineering*, SE-2 (4) (December 1976).

A well-known book that presents a whole number of ways of measuring software: M.H. Halstead, *Elements of Software Science*, Elsevier, 1977.

A most readable book on software quality. It explains what measures can be used during each stage of software development: Darrel Ince, *Software Quality Assurance: A Student Introduction*, McGraw-Hill, 1995.

The seminal book on continuous process improvement: W. Edwards Deming, *Out of the crisis: quality, productivity and competitive position*, Cambridge University Press, 1986.

The definitive paper on the CMM is: Mark C. Paulk, Bill Curtis, Mary Beth Chrissis and Charles V. Weber, Capability maturity model, version 1.1, *IEEE Software*, **10** (4) (July 1993), pp. 18–27.

There is also a book on CMM: Mark C. Paulk, Charles V. Webber, Bill Curtis and Mary Beth Chrissis (principal contributors and eds), *The Capability Maturity Model: Guidelines for Improving the Software Process*, Addison-Wesley, 1995.

This chapter:

- identifies the tasks of project management
- explains how to estimate the cost of a software project
- explains how to select tools and methods
- explains how to plan a development
- suggests how to make teams run smoothly.

30.1 ● Introduction

Project management is the activity of trying to ensure that a software development is successful. The meaning of success will differ from one project to another, but it usually includes meeting the deadline, implementing the required features and meeting the budget. Chapter 1 discussed the goals of software engineering (in general) and these often coincide with the goals of particular projects.

SELF-TEST QUESTION

30.1 Identify another typical goal for a software project.

Project management aims to set up an orderly process so that a project runs smoothly from inception to completion. There are a number of different ways of going about this. What is certain is that difficulties and crises will arise during a project. Project management is difficult. Software projects commonly run late, are over budget and fail to meet the users' requirements.

Why is a large-scale software project such a complex task?

- it comprises a number of individually complex and interacting activities
- it is often carried out by large numbers of people working over lengthy time spans
- it aims to develop a complex product that should conform to prescribed, sometimes stringent, requirements and standards.

Any project manager has the legacy of bad publicity to overcome – the widespread perception that projects nearly always run over budget and beyond deadline. There is no doubt that this is due to the near-impossibility of predicting in advance how much effort is required to develop software. Estimates are commonly too low; the result is embarrassing.

The problems are compounded by the knowledge that there are immense differences between individual developers – it is common to see a twenty-fold difference in productivity between individual developers in the same organization. If you estimate the development time for a software component and then assign the job of designing and coding it to an individual, you have no real idea of how long it should take or will take. This is a nightmare situation for any project manager.

The problems are not helped by the available software engineering techniques. What a manager wants is a well-defined method, with clear products delivered at short intervals. With such a weapon, the manager can closely monitor progress and, if necessary, do something about it. Regrettably, no such technique exists. Instead it is common to experience the well-known "90% complete" paralysis. The manager asks the engineer about progress. The engineer replies, "Fine – it's 90% complete." Reassured the manager does nothing. A week later, they ask the same question and receive exactly the same reply. And so on. Given the nature of software development there is no good way in which the manager can verify whether the report is accurate or misleading. The schedule slips out of control.

30.2 ● Project inception

At the outset of a project, management involves the following tasks:

1. establishing the goals of the project. What are the priorities – is it meeting a deadline? Is it high reliability software? Or what?
2. choosing a process model
3. estimation – estimating the effort required (person months), the duration of the project and its cost
4. choosing appropriate techniques and tools that ensure that the software product attains its required quality factors
5. setting up the team, organized in way that they can communicate effectively in carrying out the different parts of the development work
6. planning – scheduling deliverables, milestones, allocating people to the project.

As we have seen, a process model is a model for the framework or plan for a project. Individual tasks, tools and techniques fit within this overall skeleton. Earlier in this book, we described a number of process models – waterfall, incremental, prototyping, open source, agile methods and the unified process. The project manager can choose between these, or create their own.

Similarly the project manager needs to select a package of techniques and tools that fit within the process model. These techniques are what the main part of this book is all about. For example, a decision has to be made about the choice of programming language.

Different organizations of teams were reviewed in Chapter 28.

Project management usually involves monitoring and control: monitoring ascertains what is happening. Then control remedies things that are going wrong. In order to monitor a project, what is happening must be visible and therefore reliable information about the state of the development must be available.

Another important task associated with project management is people management – dealing with people's needs, behavior and foibles. This involves trying to ensure that people are well motivated. At the end of this chapter, we look at ideas for influencing the behavior of a development team.

30.3 ● Cost estimation

The classic way of estimating software costs is to guess a figure, double it and hope for the best. A better way, often used, is to check whether the organization has carried out a similar project and use the actual figures from that project as a basis for the estimate.

Early methods for cost estimation rely on being able to guess the eventual size of the software. The effort is then derived from this figure. The steps are:

1. guess the size of the product (measured in lines of code)
2. divide by a factor (say 40) to give the effort (measured in person months).

However, this simply shifts the difficulty from one intractable problem (estimating cost) to another (estimating lines of code).

The most recent methods recognize that a number of factors affect the required effort:

- size of the product
- difficulty of the project
- expertise of the developers
- effectiveness of tools
- how much software can be reused from elsewhere.

At the outset of a project, it is impossible to estimate the development effort. If someone says, "We want to develop a new word processor," the requirement is so vague that any estimate of effort is meaningless. It is not until requirements analysis is complete that some estimate can be made. Thus in a word processor, for example, it is relatively easy to assess the effort required to write the software for one small function, such as to save text in a file. Even then there are too many uncertainties to make an accurate estimate. It is only as the project continues that the situation becomes clearer and more accurate estimates can be achieved.

Nonetheless, it is often necessary to make an initial estimate of software cost so that a decision can be made about the feasibility of the project. This is sometimes called *investment appraisal* or a *feasibility study* (Chapter 3). An estimate of the software development cost is compared with the financial value of the benefits that will accrue. If the benefits are greater than the costs, the project goes ahead; otherwise it is canceled. This makes sense until you realize that a crucial decision depends upon an estimate that is almost impossible to make.

A well-known approach to cost estimation is the COCOMO (Constructive Cost Model) approach, developed by Barry Bohm. This suffers from the drawback mentioned above – the cost estimate is based on a size estimate. However, the most recent version of this approach, COCOMO 2.0, adopts an approach similar to the next method we will describe.

Probably the best approach to cost estimation is called *function point analysis*. It assumes that the effort required to develop a piece of software depends on what the software does – the number of functions it implements. Function points are another name for use cases that we met in Chapter 4 on requirements.

Let us consider, for example, an information system that allows the user to browse information and update information held in a database. The system holds information about the employees in an organization. A screen is to be implemented that allows information about a single employee to be displayed. This is one of the function points of the system. Because this is a small task and we can visualize the implementation, we predict with some confidence that the effort required will be 1 person month. This includes clarifying the requirements, creating the specification, testing and validation. Obviously there will be other screens available to users, for example, a screen to change the details of an employee. The number of functions is measured by the number of screens available to the user and the development effort is proportionate. Thus for 6 screens, we estimate 6 person months.

But where does the figure of 1 person month per function point come from? The assumption is that we can accurately predict the effort to implement a fairly small function. But this figure is likely to differ from one organization to another, depending perhaps on the general level of expertise within the organization. To obtain the appropriate factor, a calibration needs to be carried out within the particular organization. This means measuring the development effort on an initial series of projects to obtain an average figure. This might be 0.75 person months per function point. Whatever the factor, the assumption of this prediction model is that the effort is proportional to the number of function points, and the number of function points is determined by the number of screens.

There are, however, additional considerations – we have neglected to consider the effort to design and access the database. For each table in the relational database we add 1 to the count of function points and therefore an additional person month to the total effort. As part of the information system, reports are probably required – on-screen and on hard copy. Again, for each report we add 1 to the count of function points.

In summary, the count of function points is the sum of:

■ the number of data input screens

■ the number of data display screens

■ the number of database tables

■ the number of reports

■ the number of interfaces with other software systems.

Perhaps the system is implemented across a network of PCs, linked to a server that maintains the database. This involves extra complexity and therefore effort. A complexity multiplier of, say, 1.6 can be applied to the effort figure to take account of implementation complexity.

Finally, the new software may be able to reuse software either from a library or from earlier projects, thus reducing the development effort. This can be estimated by deducting the proportion of the software that is being implemented by reuse.

Thus the function point approach caters for factors including the size of a project, the expertise of the developers, the power of the software tools, the complexity of the implementation and the degree of reuse. Most of the factors need to be calibrated within the context of a particular organization, with its own staff expertise, tools and methods.

The function point estimate method uses as its foundation a knowledge of the number of functions that the software needs to provide and this is based on the number of input and output activities. These are sometimes not precisely known at the outset of a project, but become clearer during requirements analysis.

Although software cost estimation models such as this attempt to take account of all relevant factors, they are notoriously inaccurate in their predictions. There are a number of reasons. One problem is that assigning the same weighting to all function points is very crude. Another difficulty is that there are widely different productivity rates amongst developers.

SELF TEST QUESTION

30.4 Estimate the effort to develop the above system, assuming 6 screens, 4 database tables, 2 reports, no interfaces to other systems, 1 person month per function point, no software reuse, a difficulty factor of 1.5 because it is a web-based solution.

30.4 ● Selecting tools and methods

You are the manager of a software development project. What tools and methods would you select for use? How can you go about deciding whether a particular tool or method is worth using?

Chapter 31 looks at ways of assessing techniques, but the results of studies are not generally helpful.

Some development methods are inapplicable to particular domains and can therefore be disregarded. For example, prototyping is not usually of any use in developing scientific or mathematical software. Again, data structure design is only really applicable for serial file processing and it would be difficult or impossible to apply it to scientific programming or to process control.

The customer may demand the use of particular methods. For example, a military client may require the use of Ada in conjunction with formal specification.

Any software development organization has expertise in particular tools and methods. It also has its own standards and procedures. These are huge investments. Thus, a project manager within an organization must usually adhere to local methods and standards.

If there is scope to choose the techniques, a next step is to establish a checklist of requirements and criteria. These must reflect the nature of the software to be developed, the customer and the organization developing the software. How important are such factors as cost, reliability, delivery date, ease of maintenance?

When evaluating a technique, a generic checklist of criteria that can be used includes the following questions:

- what are its special features and strengths?
- what are its weaknesses?
- what is its philosophy/perspective?
- is it systematic?
- can the technique be used in this application area?
- what is the extent of tool support?
- what is the training time for the people who will use the method?
- what level of skill is required by the people using the method?
- does the method lead to maintainable software
- does the method ensure that the software will meet performance targets?
- what is its productivity?
- how good is the reliability of the software produced with this technique?
- is good documentation automatically produced?
- is the method enjoyable to use?

If the decision is taken to introduce a new method, training effort and time will be needed. Training costs typically include buying training and the time that developers spend away from productive work. But that is not all. While a new technique is being adopted, the organization is still learning and therefore productivity slumps – at least temporarily.

While the technical merits of development methods are important, it is often practical considerations that determine which development approach is used. Examples are:

- the computer facility only supports specific tools and languages
- the price of software tools associated with a specific method.

30.5 ● The project plan

A project manager must create a plan for a project that specifies:

- the final deadline
- detailed tasks
- intermediate milestones
- the deliverables at each stage
- who is involved and when
- when project reviews are scheduled
- the dependencies between the stages of the project.

This plan must take account of the process model, the total predicted effort, the tools and methods, the team organization and the expected final deadline.

The first and crucial step is to identify the major activities that are necessary. For example, if the waterfall model is adopted, these are requirements analysis, architectural design, coding, unit testing, system testing. An estimate of the person weeks for each of these stages is made. (It should add up to the total estimate for the project.) Next, these major stages are broken down into smaller tasks, and figures for effort assigned. This planning is not easy and is, at best, tentative, because it makes assumptions about the outcomes of important design decisions which have not yet been made. Finally, the relationships and dependencies are specified. For example, coding of a module comes before testing it.

The product of this planning is a detailed plan that shows all the activities that are needed, the effort required for each and the dependencies between the activities.

There are a number of notations, diagrams and tools that can assist in documenting a project plan:

- Pert (Project Evaluation and Review Technique) chart – shows activities and their interrelationships
- Gantt chart – shows resources (people) and what they are doing
- Microsoft Project – a software package designed to assist in project planning and monitoring
- a spreadsheet package – can be used to describe a project plan, maintaining figures about tasks, their likely duration and their actual duration.

A Pert chart (drawn on paper, a whiteboard or using a software tool) shows the stages of development, their interdependencies and the milestones. Each activity is shown as a line, with time proceeding left-to-right. An individual activity, for example, the requirements engineering stage can be shown as:

1. needing an effort of 4 person months
2. starting 1 April
3. ending 31 July.

A Pert chart shows dependencies, for example, that architectural design must be completed before detailed design. Parallel activities, such as designing two components at the same time, can also be shown. A Pert chart like this allows the critical path to be identified easily. This is the path through the chart that determines the overall duration of the project.

During the course of the development, progress of the project is monitored and compared with the Pert diagram. Should any stage take longer or shorter than planned, the diagram is updated to reflect the new situation.

30.6 ● In the heat of the project

At the outset of a project, the requirements for the system are usually vague and ill-defined. In consequence, any planning is at best tentative. As the requirements become clearer, more meaningful and accurate plans can be made. Replanning – reestimating and rescheduling – is needed to adjust previous estimates as more accurate information emerges as the project proceeds.

People will leave the project because of new jobs, maternity leave and illness. Tasks will often overrun their schedule. Additional or changed requirements will be requested. These all require adjustments to the plan.

All of the above present enormous challenges. It is not uncommon to see panic set in as deadlines are missed and the project seems to be off course. The trick is to recognize at the outset that these things are going to happen – and plan for them. And it is vital to remember Brooks's famous advice, "Adding people to a late project will make it later."

If an initial plan is inflexible, it is difficult to adapt when something unexpected happens. Conversely, if the plan is flexible, change can be easily accommodated. This is where cumbersome approaches reveal their limits, while agile methods are deliberately designed to be adaptive. Incremental methods are also good at coping with risk because development takes place in small steps.

Let us consider some likely and realistic scenarios.

First scenario: someone quits the project. If there is someone else available within the organization (a big assumption), they can take over. They will need to learn about the project and their particular role. So, even if things go smoothly, time is lost. But it could be that no one is available to take the vacant position. The choice is then between abandoning the work, switching someone or delaying deadlines. If someone is switched, something else gets abandoned, so the problem is merely passed around. Thus some hard decisions have to be made.

There are approaches that can help in a situation like this. They use a process model that involves small steps. These tasks are typically as small as an hour or a day. If something goes wrong with a small task, it can easily be rectified, but if something goes wrong during a task that takes months, it is hard to fix.

Second scenario: a task takes longer than expected or will take longer than expected. This is similar to the above case, but here the developer is still around. If the activity is on the critical path, the deadline has already been missed. There is a huge temptation either to put additional people on the project or to ask the current people to work extra hours or to ask everyone to work faster. It is dangerous to give into any of these tactics. The likelihood is that, later, another task will overrun, compounding the problem.

Here, again, if the tasks are small, the damage is small.

Third scenario: the client asks for changes. The scale of changes must, of course, be assessed. However, it is unlikely that the effect is to reduce work. More likely, additional work is needed to provide additional functionality. Worse, significant changes are needed to existing design and code. Now it is natural to want to please the client, and it may be that the new work is full of interest and challenge, but the only answer here is to confront the client with the effects on cost and deadlines. The client can then decide whether to pursue the change, and incur the penalties or perhaps substitute the new request for an old.

SELF-TEST QUESTION

30.5 A meal is in preparation. It looks as if it will be late. What do you do?

30.7 ● Managing people

Software is created by living, breathing people. However splendid the tools and techniques, software development relies on human creativity. There have been many attempts to analyze the problems of software projects and suggest informal ways of creating a successful project team. However well organized the team, there are always informal processes at work – both individual and group. A project manager needs an awareness of these processes and needs to know what can be done to avoid weakening a team and what can be done to improve a team.

One extreme school of management sees people as inherently lazy and needing to be controlled. They need to be told clearly what to do, given frequent deadlines and threatened with the consequences of poor performance. The opposite is the belief that people are motivated by rewards such as respect, praise and money.

Any project faces the dilemma of control versus autonomy. Can the team members be trusted to do a good job with the minimum of supervision? Are mechanisms required to ensure that team members are performing? In a factory production plant, such as a car assembly line, the task that each team member performs is rigorously specified and timed to a fraction of a second. The degree of control is total and high levels of productivity and quality are virtually assured. By contrast, an artist who creates a painting has complete autonomy; deadlines and quality are by no means certain. Developing software probably fits somewhere between these extremes, with a need for some autonomy and some control.

So, on the one hand, a heavyweight technique can be used. Processes are well-defined and reporting is frequent and stringent. The waterfall model has these characteristics – it consists of well-defined steps, each of which leads to a well-defined product. Here there is minimal dependence on the individuals skill.

On the other hand, a lightweight technique can be used. Processes are ill-defined and reporting is less frequent. An example is open source development. Here the skills of the individuals are vital.

Another factor is the individual variability between software developers – some are fast and effective, while some are slower and less effective. If we assume that this is crucial, then the logic is to hire only good developers and fire (or avoid hiring) bad ones. On the other hand, we could accept diversity and plan accordingly.

SELF-TEST QUESTION

30.6 You are part of a group, preparing a meal. You know that someone works slowly. What do you do?

There are no clear answers to these dilemmas. But, if we believe that developers must be respected, there are some things that should be avoided and some that are worth trying.

First, some ways in which a management can weaken a team are:

- show distrust of the team
- overemphasize the paperwork, rather than creative thinking
- scatter the team members in different locations
- ask team members to work on a number of different projects (functional team), rather than focusing on the particular project (project team)
- press for earlier delivery at the expense of reducing the quality of the software
- set unrealistic or phony deadlines
- break up an effective team.

Some management approaches for enhancing team activity are:

- emphasize the desirability of the quality of the software product
- plan for a number of successful completed stages (milestones) during the lifetime of the project
- emphasize how good the team is
- preserve a successful team for a subsequent project

- reduce hierarchy in the team, promoting egalitarianism, placing the manager outside the team
- celebrate diversity within the team members.

Summary

- software project management is difficult
- project management involves selecting a process model, a team organization, tools and methods
- one approach to estimating the cost of a software system involves counting function points
- planning involves deciding on milestones and scheduling tasks amongst people
- the informal aspects of team working during software development can be as important as the technical aspects.

Exercises

30.1 Suggest facilities for a software tool that supports the planning and monitoring of software project activities.

30.2 Draw up a plan for the following software development project. Document the plan as a Pert chart, in which each activity is shown as an arc, with a bubble at its starting point (the event which triggers the activity) and a bubble at its completion (the event which concludes the activity). The plan is to adopt the waterfall model. The development must be completed in two years. The following activities are envisaged:

1. requirements analysis – 4 person months
2. architectural design – 3 person months
3. detailed design – 4 components, each at 6 person months per component.
4. coding – 2 person months for each component
5. unit testing – 6 person months for each component
6. system testing – 6 person months.

How many people will be required at each stage of the project to ensure that the deadline is met?

30.3 Suggest features for a software tool to support software cost estimation.

30.4 You are the manager of a software development project. One of the team members fails to meet the deadline for the coding and testing of a component. What do you do?

30.5 You are the project leader for a large and complex software development. Three months before the software is due to be delivered, the customer requests a change that will require massive effort. What do you do?

30.6 For each of the systems in Appendix A:

- suggest a process model
- predict the development cost
- suggest a team organization
- suggest a package of tools and methods.

Answers to self-test questions

30.1 There are various satisfactory answers including reliability

30.2 Yes.

30.3 10,000/100 = 100 person weeks.

This is more than 2 person years, allowing for time spent on activities such as vacations and training.

30.4 The number of function points is 12, which gives $12 \times 1 = 12$ person months. Multiplied by the difficulty factor of 1.5, this gives 18 person months.

30.5 Ascertain whether a reduced meal of adequate quality can be produced in the available time. Otherwise, tell the diners that the meal will be late.

30.6 You could put them under pressure, hoping they will deliver on time. But, perhaps better, you could accommodate their work rate in the planning.

Further reading

A good collection of articles on project management is presented in: Richard H. Thayer (Editor), Winston W. Royce and Edward Yourdon, *Software Engineering Project Management*, IEEE Computer Society, 1997.

This book is a readable and practical discussion of dealing with software costs: T. Capers Jones, *Estimating Software Costs*, McGraw-Hill, 1998.

The seminal book on software cost estimation is still the classic: B.W. Boehm, *Software Engineering Economics*, Prentice Hall, 1981.

This view is updated in: B. Boehm, C. Clark, E. Horowitz, C. Westland, R. Madachy and R. Selby, Cost models for future life cycle processes: COCOMO 2.0, *Annals of Software Engineering*, **1** (1) (November 1995), pp. 57–94.

This account of the development of Windows NT reads like a thriller and has significant lessons for software developers. It charts the trials, tribulations and the joys of developing software: G. Pascal Zachary, *Showstopper: The Breakneck Race to Create Windows NT and the Next Generation at Microsoft*, Free Press, 1994.

Life within Microsoft and the lessons that can be learned are well-presented in this readable book: Steve Maguire, *Debugging the Development Process: Practical Strategies for Staying Focused, Hitting Ship Dates and Building Solid Teams*, Microsoft Press, 1994.

Accounts of failed projects are given in: *Stephen Flowers, Software Failure: Management Failure: Amazing Stories and Cautionary Tales*, John Wiley, 1996, and in Robert Glass, *Software Runaways*, Prentice Hall, 1998.

The classic book that deals at length and in a most interesting way with the informal, social aspects of working in a team. It is a most enjoyable read: G. Weinberg, *The Psychology of Computer Programming*, Van Nostrand Reinhold, 1971.

This is the classic book on the problems of running a large-scale software project. It is worth reading by anyone who is contemplating leading a project. There is a section on chief programmer teams. This is a classic book, revisited in a celebratory second edition with additional essays: Frederick P. Brooks, *The Mythical Man-Month*, Addison-Wesley 2nd edn, 1995.

A most readable book about the informal processes that are at work in software development and how teams can best be organized: Tom DeMarco and Timothy Lister, *Peopleware: Productive Projects and Teams*, Dorset House, 1987.

There is a whole host of management books – both serious and popular – about how to run teams and projects. Many of the ideas are applicable to software projects. This is one example, actually about software development, with lessons learned at IBM. It covers recruitment, motivation, power struggles and much more: Watts S. Humphrey, *Managing Technical People*, Addison-Wesley, 1997.

PART

G

REVIEW

CHAPTER
31

Assessing methods

This chapter:

- discusses the problem of assessing tools and methods
- reviews current techniques
- examines the evidence about verification techniques
- suggests that there is no single best method
- discusses the challenges of introducing new methods.

31.1 ● Introduction

We saw in Chapter 1 that there are usually a number of objectives to be met in the construction of a piece of software. A major goal used to be high performance (speed and size), but with improved hardware cost and performance, this issue has declined in importance. Nowadays factors like software costs, reliability and ease of maintenance are increasingly important. For any particular project, it is, of course, vital to assess carefully what the specific aims are. Having done this, we will usually find that some of them are mutually contradictory, so that we have to decide upon a blend or compromise of objectives.

This book has described a variety of techniques for software construction. All of the techniques attempt in some way to improve the process of software development and to meet the various goals of software development projects. The purpose of this chapter is to see how we can assess methods and choose a collection of methods that are appropriate for a particular project.

31.2 ● How to assess methods

Is it possible to identify a collection of tools and methods that are ideal in all circumstances? The answer is no. Software engineering is at an exciting time. There are a dozen schools of thought competing to demonstrate their supremacy and no single package of tools and methods seems set to succeed. Some methods seem particularly successful in specific areas, for example, the data structure design method in information systems. Other methods, like structured walkthroughs, seem generally useful. In the field of programming languages, declarative languages have become important in expert systems, while highly modular imperative languages are widely used in real-time and command and control systems.

Ideally, metrics (Chapter 29) would enable us to determine the best method or combination of software development methods. Regrettably, this is virtually impossible. The first problem is identifying the criteria for a best method. As we saw in Chapter 1 on problems and prospects, there are usually a number of goals for any software development project. In order to choose between methods it is necessary to establish what blend of criteria is appropriate for the particular project. For example, the set of goals for a particular project might be to optimize:

- development effort,
- reliability, and
- maintainability

and these are in conflict with each other. In general, the most significant conflict is probably between development effort and reliability of the product. For example, a safety-critical system needs to be highly reliable. However, for a one-off program for a user to extract information from a database, the prime goal may be quick delivery. There can be no set of factors that allow universal comparison between methods. Equally, it is unlikely that there will ever be a single best method.

Suppose that we had narrowed down the choice to two applicable methods, called A and B. What we would like to have is hard evidence like this: "Method A gives 25% better productivity than method B." Regrettably, there is no such data available today, because of the enormous difficulty of creating it. Let us examine some of those difficulties. Because of cost, it is virtually impossible to conduct any realistic experiments in which two or more methods are compared. (The cost of developing the same piece of software twice is usually prohibitive.) Usually the only experimental evidence is based on scaled-down experiments. Suppose, for example, that we wanted to compare two design methods, A and B. We could give ten people the specification of a small system and ask them to use method A, and similarly we could ask a second group to use method B. We could measure the average time taken to complete the designs and hence hope to compare the productivities of the methods. We could go on to assign additional problems and employ more people to increase our confidence in the results. Ultimately, we might gain some confidence about the relative productivity of the two methods.

But many criticisms can be aimed at experiments like these. Are the backgrounds of the participants equal? Is the experience of the participants typical? (Often students are used in experiments, because they are cheap and plentifully available. But are students typical of professional software developers?) Have sufficient number of people taken part so that the results are statistically significant? Is the problem that has been chosen typical, or is it a small "toy" problem from which it is unreasonable to extrapolate? Is there any difference between the motivation of the participants in the experiment and that of practitioners in a real situation? These questions are serious challenges to the validity of experiments and the significance of the results. The design of experiments must be examined carefully and the results used with caution.

While the problem of measuring and comparing productivity is fearsome, the story gets worse when we consider software quality. Again, what we desire is a statement like, "Method A gives rise to software that is 50% more reliable than method B."

Whereas with productivity we have a ready-made measure – person months – how do we measure reliability? If we use the number of bugs as a measure, how can we actually count them? Again, do we count all the bugs equally or are some worse than others? Such questions illustrate the difficulties. Similarly, if we want to quantify how well a method creates software that is easy to maintain, then ideally we need an objective measure or metric.

There are, of course, additional criteria for assessing and comparing methods (see Chapter 30 on project management). We might choose from amongst the following checklist:

- training time for the people who will use the method
- level of skill required by the people using the method
- whether the software produced is easy to maintain
- whether the software will meet performance targets
- whether documentation is automatically produced
- whether the method is enjoyable to use
- whether the method can be used in the required area of application.

The outcomes of experiments that assess methods are not encouraging. For example, it is widely accepted in the computer industry that structured programming is the best approach. But one review of the evidence (see the references below) concluded that it was inconclusive (because of problems with the design of experiments). Similarly, there seems to be very limited evidence that object-oriented methods are better than older methods.

Clearly there are many problems to be solved in assessing methods, but equally clearly developers need hard evidence to use in choosing between methods. We can expect that much attention will be given to the evaluation of tools and methods, and it is, in fact, an active area of current research. This research centers on the design of experiments and the invention of useful metrics.

31.3 ● Case study – assessing verification techniques

We now discuss the results of one of the few small-scale experiments that have been conducted to assess methods. This particular study assessed verification techniques, in particular black box testing, white box testing and walkthroughs. Black box and white box testing techniques are explained in Chapter 19. Structured walkthroughs are explained in Chapter 20 on groups.

In the experiment, 59 people were asked to test a 63-line PL/1 program. The people were workers in the computer industry, most of whom were programmers, with an average of 11 years experience in computing. They were told of a suspicion that the program was not perfect and asked to test the program until they felt that they had found all the errors (if any). An error meant a discrepancy between the program and the specification. The people were provided with the program specification, the program listing, a computer to run the program on and as much time as they wanted. Different groups used different verification methods.

While the people were experienced and the program was quite small, their performance was surprisingly bad. The mean number of bugs found was 5.7. The most errors any individual found were 9. The least any person found was 3. The actual number of bugs was 15. There were 4 bugs that no one found. The overwhelming conclusion must be that people are not very effective at carrying out verification, whichever technique they use.

Additional findings from this study were that the people were not careful enough in comparing the actual output from the program with the expected outcome. Bugs that were actually revealed were missed in this way. Also the people spent too long on testing the normal conditions that the program had to encounter, rather than testing special cases and invalid input situations.

The evidence from this and other experiments suggests that inspections are a very effective way of finding errors. In fact inspections are at least as good a way of identifying bugs as actually running the program (doing testing). So, if you had to choose one method for verification, it would have to be inspection. Studies show that black box testing and white box testing are roughly equally effective.

However, evidence suggests that the different verification techniques tend to discover different errors. Therefore the more techniques that are employed the better – provided that there is adequate time and money. So black box testing, white box testing and inspection all have a role to play. If there is sufficient time and effort available, the best strategy is to use all three methods.

The conclusion is that small-scale experiments can give useful insights into the effectiveness of software development techniques.

Incidentally, there is another technique for carrying out verification, which has not been assessed against the above techniques. Formal verification is very appealing because of its potential for rigorously verifying a program's correctness beyond all possible doubt.

However, it must be remembered that formal methods are carried out by fallible human beings who make mistakes.

31.4 ● The current state of methods

The methods, tools and approaches discussed in this book are well-established and widely used. There is a diversity of approaches to software development. This, of course, reflects the infancy of the field. But it is also part of the joy of software engineering; it would be boring if there was simply one process model, one design method, one programming language, one approach to testing, and so on. Today the software developer has a rich set of tools and methods to choose from. The choice will, of course, depend upon the nature of the project.

One of the current debates is between the heavyweight methods and lightweight approaches. Heavyweight methods are heavily prescriptive – they specify in detail the steps to be taken and the documents to be produced. Lightweight methods are more pragmatic – they use methods and tools advisedly, as and when appropriate.

Do not forget, also, that there are many legacy systems, written some time ago that were developed and documented using what are now antiquated methods and tools. These systems need maintaining, and so the methods that were used in their development live on.

31.5 ● A single development method?

There is a variety of methods and tools on offer. At the present time many approaches – and many combinations of methods – are considered feasible. Is there a unique combination that will ensure success? We know that we need a package of methods to:

- establish the feasibility of the system
- elicit and record requirements
- design the user interface
- design the architectural structure
- ensure that requirements are satisfied (validation)
- test and debug
- maintain the system
- organize a team
- plan the development (a process model).

In choosing a set of methods, the individual characteristics and goals and the project must be taken into account. It is likely that a unique combination will be selected. There is no single best package.

It is perhaps strange that, as with designing a motor car, we do not consider using different approaches for different parts of the system. Many software systems consist of qualitatively different parts, for example:

- the human–computer interface
- the database
- the network software
- the business logic

and it seems reasonable that these different components are developed using different, appropriate approaches.

31.6 ● Introducing new methods

Suppose that it has been decided that a new method should be introduced into an organization or into a particular project. The first, alarming, thing to be prepared for is that there will inevitably be a temporary drop in productivity while people spend time becoming familiar with the method. So the initial experiences with any method will be negative; courage and patience are needed before any benefits appear.

Perhaps the most important aspect of any new method is its effect on the people in the organization. In most organizations, there is a hierarchy, with the senior and more skilled, perhaps older, people in senior positions. A new method can pose a threat to these people. First, they may fear that they will find it impossible to learn or adapt to a new method. Second, they may see a new method as a criticism of the methods they have used successfully in the past. Third, a new method will mean that everyone is a novice again, so that their status may be eroded.

It is generally agreed that new methods should be introduced one at a time. If too many new approaches are adopted at once (big-bang), it is difficult to see which of them are being effective. In addition, too many of the existing skills are made redundant, threatening morale.

Summary

The software engineer is faced with a bewildering number of available methods, techniques and tools. Before choosing, the first task is carefully to identify the specific goals of the project. Little hard data is currently available to allow comparison of methods. This is partly because of the difficulty in mounting experiments. Software metrics hold the promise for objective comparison of methods, but at the present time, evaluation of tools and methods is extremely difficult.

This book has presented a menu of techniques, and made some assessment of those techniques, but it is impossible to provide completely comprehensive guidance for selecting items from the menu. The evaluation and comparison of methods is currently the subject of research, debate and fashion.

Exercises

31.1 List each of the goals of software engineering (see Chapter 1). List all the techniques of software engineering. Draw up a table, with the goals as headings across the top of the page and with the tools and techniques down the left-hand-side. Place a tick at the places where a method contributes to a goal.

31.2 Draw up a list of criteria for assessing a software development method. Use it to evaluate:

- functional decomposition
- OOD
- data structure design
- data flow design.

31.3 Different design approaches tend to model some important aspect of the problem domain. For each of the following design methods, identify what is modeled:

- functional decomposition
- OOD
- data structure design
- data flow design.

31.4 For each of the systems given in Appendix A draw up a list of techniques that you would use.

Further reading

Read all about how Microsoft do it. A most comprehensive survey of the software development methods used by Microsoft is given in: Michael A. Cusumano and Richard W. Selby, *Microsoft Secrets*, Free Press, 1995.

It is widely agreed that structured programming is a vital ingredient of software development. For a review of the (inconclusive) evidence about the effectiveness of structured programming, see: I. Vessey and R. Weber, Research on structured programming: an empiricist's evaluation, *IEEE Transactions on Software Engineering*, **10** (4) (1984), pp. 397–407.

For a review of the (limited) evidence on the effectiveness of other software development methods, including object-oriented methods and formal methods, see: N.E. Fenton, How effective are software engineering methods?, *Journal of Systems and Software*, **20** (1993), pp. 93–100.

An example of an experiment, mentioned in the text, comparing the effectiveness of various verification methods: G.J. Myers, A controlled experiment in program testing and code walkthroughs/inspections, *Communications of the ACM*, **21** (9) (1978).

CHAPTER
32 Conclusion

This chapter:

- assesses the role of software tools
- reviews the world of programming languages
- assesses the role of software reuse
- examines the evidence of how software engineers really work
- briefly reviews the issue of control versus skill
- briefly looks at history
- assesses the future of software engineering.

32.1 ● Introduction

This book has described a variety of techniques for software construction. All of the techniques attempt in some way to improve the process of software development and to meet the various goals of software development projects. The purpose of this chapter is to survey this spectrum, see how they fit together and try to look into the future.

32.2 ● Software tools

Tools permeate the whole of software development. Software tools are relevant to every method and every chapter in this book. Just as in production engineering, architecture, electronic design and in design generally, computer aids are being used throughout software development. There is an explosion in the demand for software products that aid or automate parts, or the whole of software development. The whole process of development is now commonly carried out entirely on a computer-based system, without any resort to paper. Not only the development itself, but the planning, allocation of people, monitoring of progress and, documentation are all maintained on computers.

32.3 ● The world of programming languages

In the early twenty-first century, the major programming languages that are used for software engineering are Ada, C++, C#, Visual Basic.Net and Java. Ada was designed for use by the US Department of Defense for use primarily in real-time embedded systems. C++ evolved from the widely used C language, adding object-oriented features to it. Visual Basic started out as a toy and became a widely used tool for serious Windows-based applications. Java emerged as a secure and portable language with net-centric features.

Any language for serious use in software engineering must now have object oriented features. Ada, C++, Visual Basic.Net, C# and Java are objected-oriented languages and this aspect of languages is discussed in Chapter 15.

Historically, programming language design goes in cycles: First, a large and complex language (such as C++) is designed. This provokes the design of a small and concise language (such as Java). This has happened several times: Pascal was the small reaction to extravagant Algol 68. Unix and its companion language C were a reaction to the sophisticated but complex Multics operating system. Finally Java has been the reaction to complicated C++. Large languages are rich in facilities, but (because of complexity) can be hard to learn, master and debug. By contrast, a small language can be elegant and concise, providing the fundamental building blocks needed for the construction of large systems.

Some people argue that the choice of programming language has only a small influence on the success of a software project. They assert that the coding phase of development is much less important than the design stage. They also argue that desirable programming concepts can be implemented (with care) in any programming language – even, perhaps, assembler language. Other people claim that the features of an implementation language can have a profound effect on the success or failure of a project. They argue that the language must match the ideas used during design (e.g. encapsulation). They suggest that if the language embodies the required ideas, then the compiler can carry out checks that would be otherwise impossible. Further, when maintenance comes, the language is assisting in understanding the software.

Fashion plays a role in determining which languages become widely used. Mandatory adoption by a powerful government agency (as in the case of Ada) also obviously affects adoption. The selection of a programming language for a particular project will be influenced by many factors not directly related to the programming language itself. For example, many organizations have a substantial investment in a particular programming language. Over a period of time, hundreds of thousands of lines of code may have been developed and the programming staff will have built up considerable expertise with the language. In such a situation, there is often considerable resistance to change even if a "superior" language is available.

There are other factors which can influence programming language selection. The software developer may be bound by a contract which actually specifies the implementation language. Decisions by the US government to support Cobol and, more recently,

Ada considerably influenced the acceptance of those languages. Support from suppliers of major software components, such as language compilers and database management systems, will influence language selection for many developers. If an apparent bug appears in a compiler, for example, they need to know that they can pick up the telephone and get the supplier to help them. Similarly, the availability of software tools such as language-sensitive editors, debugging systems and project management tools may favor one programming language over another. The provision of integrated software development environments which combine the programming language with a set of development tools, such as debuggers, browsers and version control tools, has an influence on language selection.

There can be little doubt that news of the death of programming and programming languages has been greatly exaggerated. Software will continue to be written in languages like those we know for the foreseeable future. Old languages, like Fortran and Cobol, will not go away because of the millions of lines of legacy software written in these languages which will continue to need maintenance. As ever, new programming languages will continue to emerge.

32.4 ● Software reuse

This is an important approach to constructing software that has been repeatedly addressed in this book. The argument goes like this: software developers are continually reinventing the wheel. Instead of writing software from scratch over and over again, they should emulate people like computer hardware designers. Hardware designers make heavy use of catalogs that describe hundreds of off-the-shelf components. All that the designer has to do is to select components and collect them together to carry out the required purpose.

The proponents of reuse, therefore, envisage comprehensive libraries of reliable and well-documented software components from which developers can select. The controversy starts with the choice of mechanism for representing the components in the library. Two main contenders are on offer:

- libraries of filters like those in Unix
- libraries of classes provided in object-oriented systems, such as Smalltalk, Visual Basic .Net, C++, C# or Java.

Components need to:

- provide a useful service
- provide a simple programming interface
- be freestanding.

Classes from a library can be used in either of two ways:

1. instantiated, to create a new object
2. inherited, to create a slightly different class.

32.5 ● The real world of software engineering

In a book like this, it is expected that a number of systematic methods are presented. But are they really used in practice? Real world practices often differ from the theory. For example, Microsoft generally uses the following methods:

- training on the job, rather than formal study
- minimal documentation other than source code
- C rather than object-oriented C++.

and, in spite of these surprising methods, they are (at least in one sense) highly successful.

If you talk to a professional software developer, the likelihood is that they will say that they use one of the respectable methods described in this book. Nowadays there is tremendous pressure to use a "proper" design method. The truth is, however, different. Let us hypothesize that architectural design is a crucial part of software development (or at least that design is a representative part of software development). A number of studies have been carried out to discover how professional engineers really carry out design. This work started back in the 1960s when people like Peter Naur tried to observe their own thought processes as they carried out a program design. Later studies usually proceed by observing developers as they carry out the task, or else by getting them to speak aloud what they are thinking as they go about development. In this section we review the results of such studies. (It should be pointed out that the observational methods used to obtain these results are not without problems and so some caution must be used in interpreting the results.)

The first revelation is that there is an enormous diversity amongst developers as to the strategies they adopt. There is also an enormous diversity amongst the designs that developers produce to solve the same problem. Different developers use different methods and construct different designs. Some designs are good and some are bad. Moreover the evidence is that there are enormous productivity differences between individual software developers.

The second revelation is perhaps even more surprising – *developers do not use the approved methods.* However, this evidence must be qualified – it seems that professional developers do use a method, but only when they understand all aspects of the situation very thoroughly. If the developer has a mastery of the language, and if the problem seems to be very simple (to them), then the developer may use an approved method.

If, as it seems, software engineers do not use a proper method, what do they do? It appears that what they commonly do is to break the problem down into smaller problems – but not in an approved way. They select fragments of the problem for consideration. They do this by using a whole range of personal strategies. At the end of the day, when they have completed their design, they then legitimize it by documenting it according to one of the credible design notations. So they pretend that it was done properly.

It seems that there are other ways that competent developers carry out design. They reuse parts of old programs, like parts of scrap cars. They remember a program that they may have written some time ago that is in some way similar to the new program. They retrieve the listing and copy those parts that are useful. Another similar approach is to use memories of old programs. Experienced developers build up Aladdin's caves of memories of the designs that they have created. The provision of catalogs of reusable design patterns explicitly exploits this approach.

No review of approaches would be complete without a mention of hacking. As we have seen, this term has two distinct meanings. One meaning describes the act of getting admittance to a secure computer system in order to steal money or secrets or to cause mayhem. The other meaning, used in this book, describes a style of programming. Hacking means plunging into a solution to a problem without any design whatsoever. A hacker takes the program specification and immediately starts to write down programming language instructions. Probably the hacker will not even pause to write them down – they will immediately start to key in instructions to the computer. Hacking makes use of intuition, creativity and individuality. It dates from the early days of programming, when programming was regarded as an individual creative act and when there were no well-established design methods. Nowadays hacking is often frowned upon as being unsystematic and undisciplined. So hacking is either famous or notorious, depending on your point of view. One of the places where hacking still has some credibility is in open source development (Chapter 25).

LISP programmers have long championed a design strategy which lies somewhere between hacking and the disciplined approaches described in this book. Perhaps this is because the application areas in which LISP is used (such as artificial intelligence, AI) demand an exploratory approach in which programs may be written in order to try to demonstrate a theoretical premise. Thus AI tries to solve "ill-formed problems" – it is difficult to determine when (or if) we have solved such problems, because they are only partially understood. Moreover, LISP programmers regularly embark on the design and construction of programs they don't know how to write. This kind of *exploratory programming* clearly requires a great deal of help from the language and its programming environment, and a flexibility in the way in which ideas can be expressed which is not found in such languages as Java and C.

For example, in LISP you can use variables without declaring their type, or define functions which can take arbitrary numbers of arguments. You can define and use functions which call other functions that haven't been written yet. You can edit, test and debug a program incrementally even while the program is running. And, very importantly, LISP blurs the distinction between program and data – which is the reason for LISP's much maligned bracketed syntax. It is this dynamic, rather than static, approach to program construction which enables and supports exploratory programming. Erik Sandewall has described this method of program development as *structured growth*: "An initial program with a pure and simple structure is written, tested, and then allowed to grow by increasing the ambition of its modules. The growth can occur both horizontally, through the addition of more facilities, and vertically through a deepening of existing facilities". Sandewall argues against the view that this could be considered as hacking under another name, on the grounds that "even if some kinds of program changes are dangerous and/or bad, that does not prove that all of them are".

Finally, there is evidence that men and women carry out design differently. Men, it seems, tend to regard the computer as a slave that has to be controlled, dominated and brought under the will of the programmer. In this approach, the computer may have to be wrestled with or struggled with in order that it does the programmer's bidding. In contrast, women approach the computer as a machine that has to be accommodated to, something that has quirks to come to terms with. The female designer proceeds by trying something and, if it is not successful, trying something else. The design emerges from the process of negotiation.

Assuming that most professional software engineers are required by the organization that employs them to use a systematic design method, what do they do? We speculate that a professional developer first creates a design using their own personal method. They then legitimize it by casting it into the shape of one of the approved methods. This involves producing the documentation that accompanies proper use of the method.

In summary there is evidence to suggest that:

- software engineers do not use the approved methods
- the productivity and quality of work differs significantly from one individual software engineer to another.

If we believe this analysis, the best strategy for a software producer is to hire individuals who are good at it and let them get on with it.

32.6 ● Control versus skill

As we have seen, software is hugely expensive, difficult to construct, often late and over budget. Current software engineering tools and techniques are helpful, but not totally effective. Thus software development currently requires enormous skill. It is similar to groups of craftspeople building cars using skills that they have accumulated over years of experience.

However, research into software engineering methods strives to devise new and more effective methods. This research tries to analyze the processes involved in software development and thereby suggest more systematic methods. In software development, the data structure design method (Chapter 10) serves as a dramatic example of the regimentation of the process of design. Scrutiny of the software development process also means that certain tasks can be identified as requiring minimal skill and these can be automated. An example is the use of a program generator that automatically creates source code from UML diagrams. This is more like a car assembly line, where workers perform simple routine tasks. Ultimately, some of their work is so well-defined that it is carried out by robots.

Thus the tendencies in software engineering are:

- more systematic methods
- automation and tool support.

Some people fear that more systematic methods will reduce the scope for individual creativity. In addition, automation tends to mean that fewer people are needed than would otherwise be required. The introduction of new methods has always been linked with the erosion of skills and job losses. In England, the Luddites revolted against employers who replaced their labor by machinery, then reduced wages and the number of jobs. Thus more effective methods often imply:

- reduced skill (deskilling)
- lower wages
- fewer jobs

and at the same time a small, highly skilled elite to carry out the difficult tasks.

The argument for using systematic approaches is that simple tasks should be made simple – there is no point in struggling to design a software component when there is an easy way. So a method can be empowering, creating time to spend on intrinsically difficult tasks.

In conclusion, there is a tension between, on the one hand, the desire of an individual software engineer to exercise their individual creativity and, on the other hand, the wish of organizations to systematize methods and exercise quality control.

32.7 ● Future methods and tools

Reflecting the current diversity, there are a number of suggestions for the future of methods and tools for software development.

Software tools

Some people see software tools as the future. They see such tools as UML editors, compilers, linkers, debuggers, version control software and test frameworks as a means of assisting or automating parts of development. This would improve productivity and software quality. This approach has as its apotheosis the complete automation of software development along with the elimination of creativity and skill.

Amongst others, the proponents of agile methods have reacted against this approach, arguing that tools can constrain and debilitate development. They argue that tools should be used judiciously, as appropriate. Indeed some valuable tools, such as a whiteboard, need not be automated at all.

Requirements engineering

Some people believe that eliciting and clarifying requirements is the single major problem of software engineering. They concentrate on devising methods and notations that not only accurately capture users' requirements but also ensure that the developer meets the requirements.

The challenge here is to address the problem of communication between user and developer. One has a knowledge of the problem domain; the other has a knowledge of the technology. Their common ground is natural language.

Formal methods

Formal (mathematical) methods are beginning to be used and may become popular, particularly for safety-critical systems. There are two related techniques – formal specification and formal verification. These methods offer the promise of completely reliable software – software that has been proved to meet its specification.

These approaches begin by documenting the users requirements in a formal mathematically based language such as Z.

Two factors seem to have inhibited the take-up of these methods: one is the problem of communication with the user, when the specification is expressed in a specialist language such as Z. The second problem is the training of developers in the non-trivial methods used to transform the specification into an implementation.

Declarative programming languages

Logic programming languages, such as Prolog, are used in developing expert systems. Functional programming languages such as LISP and Haskell, offer the promise of directly expressing what a program should do rather than how it should do it. These languages exist and have an excellent pedigree, but there are problems with executing the programs at an acceptable speed. Their acceptance into mainstream software development therefore remains speculative.

UML

After years of rivalry with competing notations, the "three amigos", Ivar Jacobson, Grady Booch and James Rumbaugh, came together with the single diagrammatic notation UML. It is now the prevalent notation for describing software, but it is only a documentation notation, not a method or a technique. The unified process, suggested by the same authors, came along soon afterwards.

There can be no doubt that UML will continue to be important and, indeed, dominate the scene for some time. There are, however, problems with UML. First, it is a graphical notation and therefore there are limitations on the ease with which diagrams can be processed using a software tool. For example, it is desirable to convert diagrams into code and to check for consistency between diagrams. Second, the semantics – the real meaning – of UML has not been defined with the same thoroughness that the semantics of programming languages has been analyzed. This limits any fundamental understanding of the meaning of UML diagrams. Third, while UML is a large and comprehensive notation, there are some things it cannot describe. For example, data flow diagrams are not a part of UML, and the information in a data flow diagram cannot be described in UML. Now it may be that diagrams such as dataflow are redundant, but alternatively it may be that they still have a useful role in design.

Components and reuse

If only complex software could be constructed by simply taking existing components off the shelf and combining them. This is the aim of component-based software engineering. Such components need to be useful, easy to use and interoperable. They also need to be reliable, fast, secure and scalable. They need to work across networks, the internet and with web browsers.

At the time of writing, the major players in the software industry are offering technologies that claim to meet these goals.

32.8 ● History

Let us look at some of the history of software development methods. In the early days of computing, the hardware was the challenge and programming was considered to be easy – an undemanding activity very similar to clerical work. The first programmers were exclusively women because it was considered unsuitable work for men. Fairly soon it was realized that programming demanded a logical approach and abstract thinking. (Regrettably, sexism asserted itself and the women were replaced by men.)

As the problems of software production began to restrict the application of computers, the principle of the division of labor was applied to software development. First, the job of the analyst was separated from that of the programmer. Later, with the invention of high-level languages, operating systems and packages, the work of applications programmers was distinguished from that of systems programmers.

Sometimes looking at the past helps us to visualize the future. Arguably there have been a number of significant milestones in the history of software engineering. The first was high-level languages, such as Fortran and Cobol, that allowed programmers to express solution in problem-oriented rather than machine-oriented notations. Next was structured programming, the idea that some constructs (such as `goto`) are dangerous and that design is important. Then came object-oriented design and programming as a way of modularizing software.

While each of these innovations was significant, none of them has dramatically solved the problem of ensuring that software is reliable and useful. Perhaps the lesson of history is that there is no silver bullet that can be applied to these problems. Arguably this is because software has an inherent complexity which cannot be eliminated.

32.9 ● The future of software engineering

The demise of applications programming has been regularly predicted for many years, and yet the demand for programmers is ever-increasing. What methods are likely to be used in the future? What is likely to happen to the jobs of those involved in software development?

Today, the cost of software generally overwhelms the cost of the hardware it runs on. Software production is labor-intensive and developers are in short supply. A major remedy offered is to provide developers with more powerful tools – usually computer based. Examples are UML editors, high-level languages and software development environments.

In the short-term future, it seems likely that we will continue to see enormous effort spent in developing tools and in ensuring that a set of tools fits together in an integrated manner. At the same time we can expect that end users will carry out their own system development using software packages that require them to know little about the computer. Coupled with the availability of inexpensive applications packages, the applications programmer seems (as ever) doomed.

In the long term, the nature of programming itself could be transformed by a declarative style of programming in which the programmer describes a solution to a problem rather than having to specify explicitly how that solution is to be obtained.

While the applications programmer may vanish, the role of the systems programmers may be enhanced. Their mission will be to develop products of high quality – reliable, powerful and easy to use. The skills involved in their development may be considerable – not least in the requirement to create demonstrably reliable software, perhaps using formal, mathematical approaches. At the other end of the spectrum, the analyst will not become extinct. Their role will be to guide users and an organization in making best use of the available packages.

The general trend seems to be:

- the increasing scrutiny of the software development task

- systematization of software development

- the division of labor amongst specialists

- the automation of tasks using tools

- software reuse.

Summary

Software development methods have changed dramatically in the past and look set to do so in the future. The trend is towards the increased use of packages, program generators and automated tools.

Long-term, traditional procedural programming languages may vanish to be replaced by declarative languages (functional and or logic languages) – at least for application programming.

There is sometimes a tension between the desire to exercise control during project management and the individual programmer's desire for autonomy.

One thing is certain: software engineering will continue to be supremely challenging, creative and enjoyable.

Exercises

32.1 Compare and contrast the following two approaches to software development:

1. placing trust in individual skills
2. relying on systematic methods.

32.2 Compare and contrast the following approaches to software reuse:

- Unix filters
- object-oriented classes.

32.3 "Programming is easy." Discuss.

32.4 "Software engineering is just programming, and programming is just hacking." Discuss.

32.5 "The scrutiny of software development methods, together with the imposition of standards and procedures for quality assurance has taken all the fun out of it." Discuss.

32.6 "The tasks involved in software engineering are going to dramatically change over the next five to ten years. In particular, conventional programming will no longer exist." Discuss.

32.7 Predict the future of software engineering.

 Further reading

Ed Yourdon is one of the gurus of software development. In this book he gives a very readable account of the problems with software development today. The book continues by giving a survey of the possible remedies for the problems. It's altogether a very readable book, free of technicalities and free with opinions. The title reflects the author's opinion that American programmers are under threat from competition from programmers in Asia – who are paid less, but are better! Edward Yourdon, *Decline and Fall of the American Programmer*, PTR Prentice Hall, 1993.

The sequel to *Decline and Fall*, which is much more optimistic about the future of the American programmer, provided that they take the initiative and learn about new technologies, like Java: Edward Yourdon, *Rise and Resurrection of the American Programmer*, PTR Prentice Hall, 1995.

A possible future for software development is described in the following reference. Have the predictions turned out to be correct? A.J. Wassermann, The future of programming, *Communications of the ACM*, **25**(3) (March 1982).

An extensive treatment of the issue of de-skilling is given in: P. Kraft, *Programmers and Managers: The Routinization of Computer Programmers in the United States*, Springer Verlag, 1984.

There have been several exciting accounts of the personal outlook and work methods of programmers. They give insights into how programming is actually done. They also contribute to the folklore of programming. The first, classic book is: G. Weinberg, *The Psychology of Computer Programming*, Van Nostrand Reinhold, 1971.

An example of a book on how programmers actually work. In the book, the author reports on interviews with notable programmers: Susan Lammers, *Programmers at Work*, Microsoft, 1986.

Steven Levy, *Hackers: Heroes of the Computer Revolution*, Anchor Books, 1994.

APPENDICES

APPENDIX
A
Case studies

Case studies are used throughout this book to illustrate the explanations. They are also used as the basis for some of the exercises at the end of chapters. Some cases are specific to particular chapters, while others are used (in different ways) in a number of chapters.

The cases are designed to capture the reader's interest and to be typical of a range of applications. They are also applications that are familiar to most readers.

The cases could also act as projects that can be carried out in parallel with studying the book.

The cases are:

- an ATM
- a word processor
- a computer game
- a library
- a patient monitoring system.

Each application is presented as an outline requirements specification. Note that they are not offered as model specifications. On the contrary they are presented as specifications for review and criticism, in particular as exercises for Chapter 4 on requirements engineering.

A.1 ● The ATM

The ATM has a screen, a card reader, a small printer, a cash dispenser and a keyboard. The keyboard has numeric buttons, an enter key and a clear key. On both the left and right of the screen are three buttons that allow selection of any options displayed on the screen. The ATM is connected to the bank via a telephone line.

The ATM provides facilities to:

- dispense cash
- display the current balance.

The user must first offer up their card to the reader. The display then asks the user to enter their PIN, via the keyboard. If this is successful, the display presents a set of options.

The system must be highly robust, since it is to be used by untrained bank customers in public places.

A.2 ● The word processor

This is an example of general-purpose software that would be used by a large number of diverse people.

The word processor provides facilities for its user to enter text, amend text, save text, print text and retrieve a saved document from a file.

The word processor displays a blank panel which displays text entered from the keyboard.

The user can:

- save the document in a specified file
- retrieve a document from a specified file
- print the document.

A document consists of sentences ending in a period character. A paragraph consists of zero or several sentences ending in a special end-of-paragraph character. A new page break can be inserted anywhere within a document.

A section of text can be selected by clicking just before the start of some text, then dragging the cursor with the button down. Selected text is shown highlighted.

The clip board is a temporary storage that is not visible. Commands are provided to:

- cut selected text and copy it to the clip board, replacing any text already in the clip board
- copy selected text to the clip board, replacing any text already in the clip board
- paste text at the cursor position from the clip board.

A document can be displayed either as raw text or as formatted text suitable for printing.

A.3 ● Computer game

Cyberspace invaders is a variation of a game that was popular in the early days of computer games. This software is appealing because it has a fun user interface. It is also easy to see a connection between the visual appearance and the software structure. The specification is as follows.

A window displays a defender and an alien (Figure A.1). The alien moves sideways. When it hits a wall, it reverses its direction. The alien randomly launches a bomb that moves vertically downwards. If a bomb hits the defender, the user loses and the game

Figure A.1 Cyberspace invaders

is over. The defender moves left or right according to mouse movements. When the mouse is clicked, the defender launches a laser that moves upwards. If a laser hits the alien, the user wins and the game is over.

A button is provided to start a new game.

A.4 ● The library

This application is a typical information system.

Software is required to maintain information about books held in a library. The system is intended for use by the library staff.

The software must run on standard networked PCs. There may be up to 20 PCs on the library network.

For each book, the following information is held in the computer:

■ title
■ author
■ ISBN

- year
- borrower identification (if on loan)
- date of issue (if on loan).

The computer should be able to store information on up to 100,000 books.
The computer system should provide facilities to:

- issue a book to a borrower
- receive a book returned by a borrower
- create information about a newly acquired book
- display a list of the books on loan to a particular borrower.

The facilities should be accessible via a GUI.

The computer must respond within one second to any request.

The system should provide a search facility to find out whether the library possesses a particular book.

With suitable security precautions, the system will initialize the library information so that it contains zero books.

When a book becomes overdue, the system should display appropriate information.

The system should provide secure access by only the library staff.

The software must be delivered by such-and-such a date and cost no more than $100,000. It must be fully documented and easy to maintain.

A.5 ● Patient monitoring system

This is an example of a safety-critical system. Other similar systems include a control system for a power station and a fly-by-wire system for an airplane.

A computer system monitors the vital signs of a patient in a hospital. Sensors attached to a patient continually send information to the computer:

- heart rate
- temperature
- blood pressure.

Some of the readings require conversion to useful units of measurement (e.g. micro volts into degrees centigrade). The computer displays the information on a screen. It also logs the information in a file that can be retrieved and displayed. If any of the vital signs exceed safe limits, the screen flashes a warning and an alarm sounds. The limits have default values, but can also be changed by the operator. If a sensor fails, the screen flashes a warning and the alarm sounds.

Glossary

Within the field of software engineering, different people use terms differently. The following are the meanings of terms as used in this book.

development approach – a particular collection of tools, methods and work styles that are used in carrying out software development

development life cycle – the complete process of software development from inception through to release and maintenance of the product

development process – specific activities that are carried out during software development

maintenance – fixing bugs, responding to changed requirements and upgrading the software for a new platform

method – the term for a procedure, subprogram or subroutine

methodology

1. the study of methods, or
2. a collection of methods, techniques and notations used for software development

portability

1. the degree to which a piece of software runs on different platforms (machine and/or operating system), or
2. the issue of whether software needs to run on different platforms

porting – moving a piece of software to a new platform

process model – idealized plan of software development in general, or an analysis of the approach adopted for a particular software development project

UML summary

The Unified Modeling Language (UML) is a graphical notation for describing object-oriented software. It is not a method for design, but a notation that can help with designing software or help to document software once it is complete.

This appendix gives a summary of those aspects of UML used in this book. UML is a large and potentially complex notation and therefore we have only used a part of the notation. Thus the diagrams described and used in this book are:

- use case diagrams
- class diagrams
- package diagrams
- activity diagrams.

C.1 ● Use case diagrams

These diagrams describe, in outline, the use cases associated with a system. Figure C.1 shows an example of a use case diagram for users of a bank ATM. In this example there is a single type of user, a bank customer. A customer can ask the system to carry out either of two functions – withdraw cash and check balance.

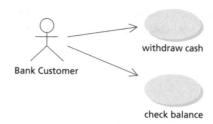

withdraw cash

Bank Customer

check balance

Figure C.1 A use case diagram

C.2 ● Class diagrams

These describe classes and their interrelationships. Classes are shown as rectangles containing the class name. The simplest relationship is where a class uses another. For example, in Figure C.2, class **Game** uses classes **Defender**, **Alien**, **Laser** and **Bomb**. This means that **Game** creates objects from these classes and/or calls methods in objects created from these classes.

A class diagram can also show the inheritance relationships between classes – the subclasses and superclasses. As illustrated in Figure C.3, to show that a class extends another, a line is drawn from the subclass to the superclass, with the arrowhead pointing to the superclass. Thus **Sprite** is the superclass of both **Alien** and **Bomb**.

If a class is an abstract class, the name of the class is written in italics. This can be difficult to see, particularly when hand-written. So the name of an abstract class can be followed by the text **{abstract}** to clarify the meaning.

An interface is described in the same way as a class – as a box. The difference is that the text **<<interface>>** precedes the name. A class that implements an interface has a dashed line with an arrow leading to the interface box (see Figure C.4).

A class can be described in more detail, as illustrated in Figure C.5. There are three compartments in this type of class diagram. The first compartment holds the class

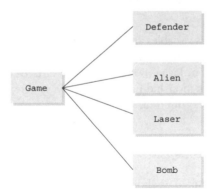

Figure C.2 Class diagram

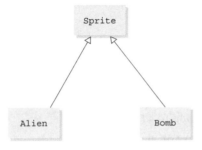

Figure C.3 Class diagram showing inheritance

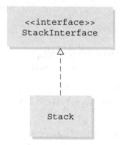

Figure C.4 A class and its interface. The arrow should be hollow

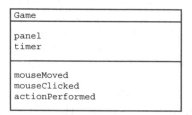

Figure C.5 Class diagram showing the detail of a class

name, the second describes variables and the third describes methods. Any class (static) variables or methods are shown underlined. The visibility of an element can, optionally, be described in a prefix as in Java – **public**, **private**, **protected** or default.

In keeping with information hiding, the diagram is often drawn with the second compartment (the variables) omitted.

C.3 ● Package diagrams

A package can be diagrammed as shown in Figure C.6. It is a rectangle with a tab at the top that holds the package name. Optionally, the classes within a package can be shown within the rectangle. This shows a class **util** that consists of classes **Random**, **ArrayList** and **Stack**.

C.4 ● Activity diagrams

An activity diagram describes a *sequence of activities*. Thus an activity diagram can be used to show the flow of control through software. An activity diagram can show:

■ conditions (corresponding to **if** statements)

■ loops (corresponding to **for** and **while** statements)

■ concurrent activity (corresponding to threads).

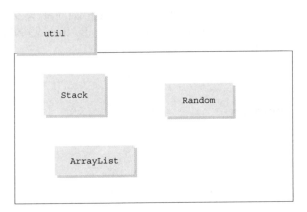

Figure C.6 A package diagram

An activity diagram can also be used to show a human activity, such as carrying out throwaway prototyping, Figure C.7. Actions are written in boxes with curved corners. The sequence of actions is shown by the arrows. A sequence starts with a special "blob" symbol. A sequence ends with a different symbol, as shown.

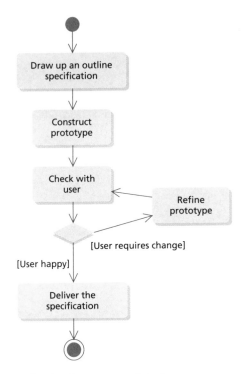

Figure C.7 Activity diagram showing throwaway prototyping

This diagram also uses the diamond-shaped branch symbol. Associated with each output from the branch is a condition (termed a guard). If the condition is true, the route is taken – just as in an `if` statement.

 Further reading

Two very clear and readable books on UML are:

Martin Fowler, *UML Distilled*, Addison-Wesley.

Perdita Stevens, and Rob Pooley, *Using UML*, Addison-Wesley.

Bibliography

References to books and websites are given at the end of each chapter. This bibliography presents some general sources. Dates are not given because new editions of them are produced frequently.

Software engineering

Here are the major books on the subject:

Ian Sommerville, *Software Engineering*, Addison-Wesley.
Carlo Ghezzi, Mehdi Jazayeri and Dino Mandrioli, *Fundamentals of Software Engineering*, Prentice Hall.
Hans van Vliet, *Software Engineering: Principles and Practice*, John Wiley.
Roger S. Pressman, *Software Engineering, a Practitioner's Approach*, McGraw-Hill.

The Software Engineering Institute at Carnegie Mellon University, USA, is a prestigious organization. They publish articles on software engineering topics and were the instigators of the capability maturity model. Their website is at: http://www.sei.cmu.edu/

UML

Here are two short and simple books on UML:

Martin Fowler, *UML Distilled*, Addison-Wesley.

Perdita Stevens and Rob Pooley, *Using UML*, Addison-Wesley.

Programmers – their lives and work

There are several exciting accounts of the personal outlook and work methods of programmers. They give insights into how programming is actually done. They also contribute to the folklore of programming.

An example of a book on how programmers actually work. In the book, she reports on interviews with notable programmers: Susan Lammers, *Programmers at Work*, Microsoft Press, 1986.

Another really exciting book, which charts the lives of the early programmers: Steven Levy, *Hackers: Heroes of the Computer Revolution*, Anchor Books, 1994.

This is a good read if you are interested in how software projects really get done and what life is like at Microsoft: G. Pascal Zachary, *Show-Stopper: The Breakneck Race to Create Windows NT and the Next Generation at Microsoft*, Free Press, 1994.

This book describes the methods used at Microsoft: Michael A. Cusumano and Richard W. Selby, *Microsoft Secrets*, Free Press, 1995.

Index

abstraction 99, 107
acceptance test 251, 332
activity diagrams 414
Ada 177, 189, 215, 233, 254, 393
adaptive maintenance 11
adversary team 275
agile manifesto 330
agile methods 330
Algol 68 393
anti-patterns 151, 161, 162
architecture 338
array list 206
arrays 194
assertions 253
assessing methods 385, 387
ATM case study 32, 45, 62, 154, 157,
    158, 300, 341, 407
audit module 241
automated testing 275
automatic garbage collection 215
automation 398

backward error recovery 244
beta testing 275
bibliography 417
big-bang development 315
black box testing 269, 387
blob anti-pattern 161
Bohm, B. 373
Booch, G. 337
bottom-up implementation 317
boundary values 269, 271, 273

bounty hunter 275
breadth-first 107
Brooks, F.P. 348, 377
bugs, estimating 361

C 176, 214, 225, 254
C++ 214, 225, 254, 393
C# 177, 189, 191, 196, 212,
    223, 233
call by reference 188
call by value 188
Capability Maturity Model, *see* CMM
case studies 407
casting 193
chief programmer teams 351
class 201
class diagram 143, 144, 170, 209,
    228, 413
class programmer 353–4
classes, finding 142
class–responsibility–collaborator cards, *see*
    CRC cards
CMM, 366
Cobol 176, 393
COCOMO 373
cohesion 79
command line interface 54
communication 333, 347
compile-time checking 240
complexity 70, 358
component programmer 353–4
component size 70